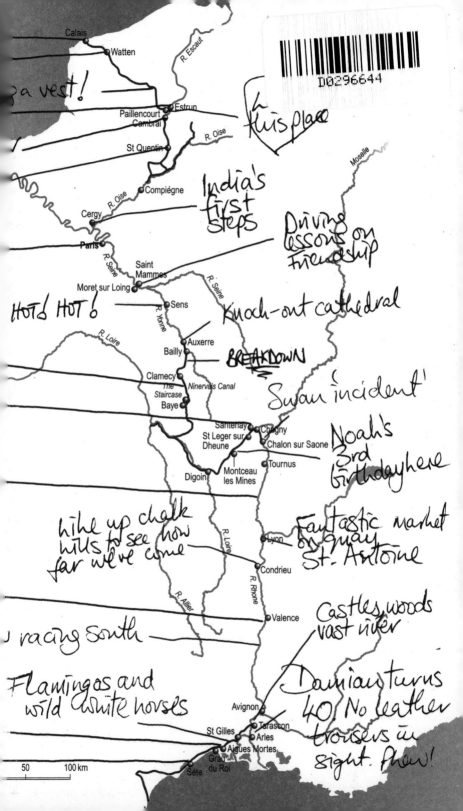

Calais
Watten
a vest!
Paillencourt Estrun
Cambrai
St Quentin
R. Escaut
R. Oise
this place
Moselle

India's first steps

Driving lessons on Friendship

Compiègne
R. Oise
Cergy
Paris
R. Seine
Saint Mammes
Moret sur Loing
Sens
R. Yonne
HOT & HOT 6
Knock-out cathedral

Auxerre
Bailly
BREAKDOWN
Clamecy
The Staircase
Ninervais Canal
Baye

Swan incident!

Santenay Chagny
St Leger sur Dheune
Chalon sur Saone
Tournus
Digoin
Montceau les Mines

Noah's 3rd Birthday here

hike up chalk hills to see how far we've come

R. Loire
R. Loire
R. Allier
Lyon
Condrieu
R. Rhone

Fantastic market on quay St. Antoine

Valence
Castles, woods vast river

racing south

Flamingos and wild white horses

Avignon
St Gilles
Tarascon
Arles
Aigues Mortes
Grau du Roi
Sète

Damian turns 40 No leather trousers in sight. Phew!

50   100 km

FOR RICHER
FOR POORER

Siobhan Horner

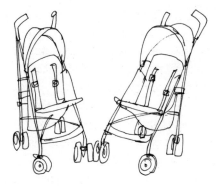

Weidenfeld & Nicolson

LONDON

U-shaped cushioned seating- turns into our bed each night

Dining table folds away each night

All our clothes stored under this seat, as well as our library of books

Luxury super sized space where the kids sleep

Damian's favourite corner to read at night

My favourite chill-out spot at night

The galley (kitchen) A whole 2x1 m²

Noah and India make their den here under the Captain's seat

the 'heads' (bathroom)
2×1m² - privacy
impossible!

Noisiest place
aboard - on
top of the engine
kids play here
every day

the 'fridge-seat'
A comfy spot
above the fridge
to watch the
world go by

IKEA handrail for
kids to grip when
boat wobbles

bathing platform
for diving off into
the Mediterranean Sea!

Attached to
these rails
are also :-
- baby bath
- storage baskets
- umbrella
- metal trolley
for carrying
gas canisters

Shiv's acknowledgements

Thanks to my Dad. And to my Mum. Without them this wouldn't have been in me. Neither the journey nor the book.

To the 3Ls, S, A, M, R and all the other wonderfully warm people at Weidenfeld & Nicolson who urged and encouraged me on and who especially made me believe I could do it.

To all my friends and family who have listened to me over the past two years, who have read snippets, helped with line-edits, dished out honest feedback and made lots of cups of tea. Grawny-G, Caz, Amanda, Raul, Alison and Andy, Roger and the rest – massive thanks! To Neil and Deirdre – thanks for egging me on and for phone calls at just the right time.

And especially, Damo, big thanks and love, for always believing in me, no matter what. The best bits are yet to come.

For the kids. Yes, I know you aren't baby goats.
India, Willow and Noah – though you get older may you never lose the child inside you.

DAMIAN – So ... we both have our own front covers and our own titles, but the actual story has to start at *one* end of the book. Whose should it be?

SHIV – Well, I guess I wrote the first paragraph and introduce the first part of the adventure so to compensate, why don't we start the story at *your* end of the book?

DAMIAN – Aaah, that's nice of you.

SHIV – Yes, I thought so

DAMIAN – The only problem is that it means anyone reading this has got to turn the book upside down in order to go back to the beginning of the story.

SHIV – 'Back to the beginning' – I like that.

DAMIAN – Yes, me too. It feels like a good way to start ...

EPILOGUE

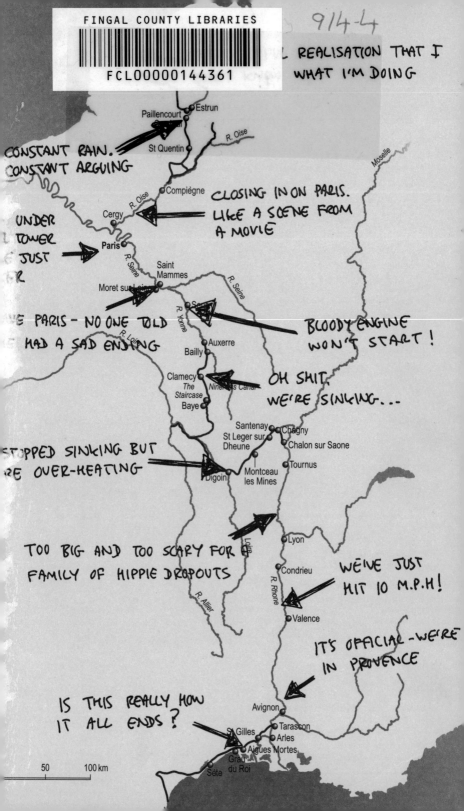

FOR BETTER
FOR WORSE

Damian Horner

Weidenfeld & Nicolson
LONDON

FRIENDSHIP

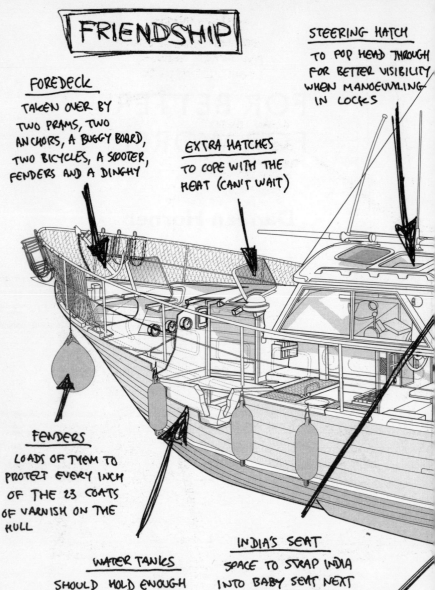

STEERING HATCH
TO POP HEAD THROUGH
FOR BETTER VISIBILITY
WHEN MANOEUVRING
IN LOCKS

FOREDECK
TAKEN OVER BY
TWO PRAMS, TWO
ANCHORS, A BUGGY BOARD,
TWO BICYCLES, A SCOOTER,
FENDERS AND A DINGHY

EXTRA HATCHES
TO COPE WITH THE
HEAT (CAN'T WAIT)

FENDERS
LOADS OF THEM TO
PROTECT EVERY INCH
OF THE 23 COATS
OF VARNISH ON THE
HULL

WATER TANKS
SHOULD HOLD ENOUGH
WATER TO LAST A WEEK
(IF SHIV DOESN'T SPEND
TOO LONG IN THE SHOWER)

INDIA'S SEAT
SPACE TO STRAP INDIA
INTO BABY SEAT NEXT
TO PERSON STEERING

ENGINE
38 YRS OLD AND
NEVER GONE FURTHER
THAN 10 MILES

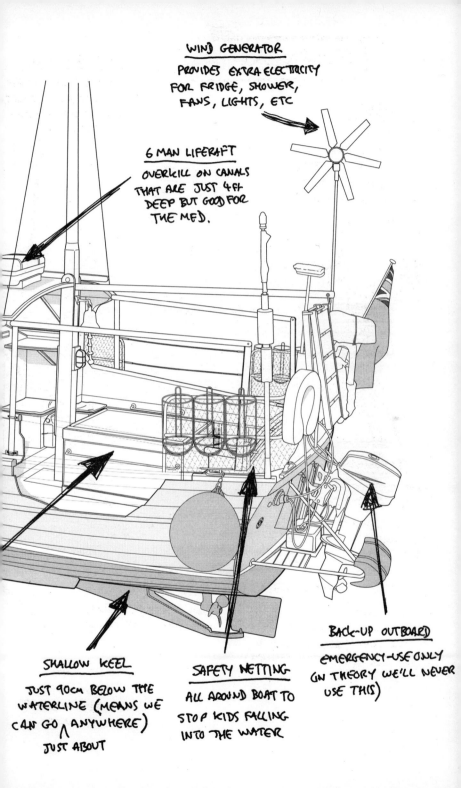

WIND GENERATOR

PROVIDES EXTRA ELECTRICITY
FOR FRIDGE, SHOWER,
FANS, LIGHTS, ETC

6 MAN LIFERAFT

OVERKILL ON CANALS
THAT ARE JUST 4 ft
DEEP BUT GOOD FOR
THE MED.

SHALLOW KEEL

JUST 90cm BELOW THE
WATERLINE (MEANS WE
CAN GO ∧ ANYWHERE)
JUST ABOUT

SAFETY NETTING

ALL AROUND BOAT TO
STOP KIDS FALLING
INTO THE WATER

BACK-UP OUTBOARD

EMERGENCY-USE ONLY
(IN THEORY WE'LL NEVER
USE THIS)

For Better for Worse, For Richer for Poorer
First published in Great Britain in 2009
by Weidenfeld & Nicolson

1 3 5 7 9 10 8 6 4 2

A CIP catalogue record for this book
is available from the British Library.

ISBN-13 978 0 297 85423 4

Typeset by Input Data Services Ltd,
Bridgwater, Somerset

Printed in Great Britain by CPI Mackays, Chatham ME5 8TD

Weidenfeld & Nicolson
The Orion Publishing Group Ltd
Orion House
5 Upper Saint Martin's Lane
London, WC2H 9EA

An Hachette UK Company

www.orionbooks.co.uk

Damian's acknowledgements

Thanks to David Baines for his friendship and for my *Friendship*, to Nick Barley for Arles, to Captain Mir for his stories, Susan Lamb for her faith, Lisa Milton for her support and Tim Lewis and David Tazzyman for their icing on the cake.

I know that I've been difficult to work with on this book so special thanks to the W&N team. Especially Lucinda, James and Rebecca. Not forgetting Lucie, Alan, Mark and the whole of the Sales team.

Thank you to all my family; Mummy, Daddy, Dom, Kate, Dulcie, Tony, Duncan and Clare for keeping me going through 'The Friendship Years' and then 'The Book Years'.

Finally, thanks to Shiv for all the 'For Better' bits.

For Noah, India and now Willow

CHAPTER 1

I feel almost cool again – a reckless woman, free and excited about the unknown. Well, as cool as you can get when you are pushing two kids under three in buggies, lugging a bright yellow potty and an inflatable boat too. At my side is a man muttering, shifting on both feet, checking his watch and trying to look relaxed.

Staring out through the rain-splattered windows of the Dover to Calais ferry, a dark-haired, glamorous foreign student looks me up and down, probably thinking something along the lines of, 'God, I hope I don't end up like that woman when I'm older'. I catch sight of my reflection. My hair is bed-ruffled from carrying India, my baby. There's a vomit stain on my shoulder and bags under my eyes.

I assure myself that I am a youthful 39 ... at the start of an Alice in Wonderland adventure, chasing a white rabbit down a rabbit hole in a magical world. In my story however the white rabbit is my husband, Damian. That twitchy man by my side.

Damian. On the verge of turning 40 and already talking wistfully about Jaguar E-types and other classic sports cars (has he forgotten we have two children?). He's on Day One of our 'new life' and growing a beard in haste, wanting to shed his image of burnt-out advertising hard-man before we set foot in France. He's almost six feet tall and good-looking, although I always thought he'd improve with a little more stubble and a lot less gloss. Now he's walked away from his work life in London, his big salary, his bright and witty colleagues, his sleek suits and polished boots, his secure and comfortable existence. There'll be no room for such comforts where we are going. In Calais we'll board our old wooden boat to head south on canals and rivers that weave through France. We are trading our secure London life for a one-way ticket into the unknown. No work, no house, no plans.

As I nibble my sandwich, perched uncomfortably on what looks like a sack of potatoes but is in fact our rolled-up inflatable dinghy, I worry that I won't be an interesting enough companion on the days that stretch ahead of us. I mean you marry for life, not for lunch. What will I be like after several months on a boat? What will we discover about each other? Will we be able to get through the inevitable 'for worse' bits of the trip?

As I eat my canteen-bought sandwich, I gaze out at the choppy sea and wonder what the hell we're doing. Furtively I look at Shiv with India in her arms and a potty by her side. I know I've been a complete pain in the arse over the last few months (maybe even years) and lately I have been unhappy with big chunks of my life. Not the important stuff like Shiv and the kids but the things that dictate the day-to-day *structure* of my life: my job, commuting, living in a city ... you know, the problems that most men bang on about. When I think about it now though, I can't believe that running off on a boat was the best solution I could come up with. Suddenly I'm overwhelmed by a huge sense of responsibility and realise that somehow I have to make sure Shiv really enjoys this experience. She looks shattered. Maybe I *should* have done what every other bloke does when they have a mid-life crisis and bought a pair of leather trousers and a motorbike.

Here, on a grubby ferry in the middle of the English Channel, reality is starting to bite. This is supposed to be a big adventure but already it feels as if nothing is turning out the way I had imagined it (and not in an exciting way either).

I look back at the sea and remember last week when I was crossing the very same water in our own boat, *Friendship*. The Channel crossing was supposed to be the start of the whole thing; a symbol that marked the jettisoning of our old lives.

The reality was much less dramatic. In the end, after days of debate, Shiv was left, stuck at her mum's house in Peterborough (looking after the kids) while I made the crossing with Dave, the coxswain of the Dover lifeboat team. I didn't know Dave from Adam but in his spare time he works as a pilot, helping incompetent people like me to cross difficult stretches of water.

Although it was a bit of a let-down to leave Shiv and the kids for the Channel crossing, it made absolute sense for two reasons:

1) The Channel is one of most treacherous seas in the world and we didn't want to drown our children on Day One of the trip.

2) I haven't got a clue what I'm doing when it comes to navigation, tidal shifts and cross-track error so the chances of drowning my family would have increased exponentially if I had been left in charge.

When it came to it, I felt a bit empty on the big day. It was like a huge false start. It simply didn't count if Shiv and the kids weren't there too. Even worse, after so much work to get *Friendship* seaworthy, I wasn't the skipper on her first big voyage. I knew I needed Dave, but having him at the helm made me feel emasculated and embarrassed, particularly as he was a man who *really* knew the sea and had risked his life on countless occasions to save others. I mean he was the skipper of a lifeboat, for God's sake – a *proper* bloke. I could just tell that he thought I was some tosser from London taking a jolly old sabbatical. Frankly it didn't help that I had worked in advertising and was called Damian.

Nevertheless, I warmed to him immediately when he said how much he liked *Friendship*. 'She's a tough old sea boat,' he told me, 'she could probably withstand anything.' That was all it took to win me over.

The weather was miserable but the eight-hour crossing was utterly uneventful, boring even. I could hardly believe that this was the leg of the trip that had kept me awake at night (and in meetings) for the last few months. The Channel in a word? Grey.

Grey sea. Grey sky. Grey clouds. Grey ships ... Grey. Grey. Grey.

After a full day in the drizzle we pulled into the yacht marina behind the ferry port in Calais and moored up on a pontoon. The hatches were secured, the doors locked and then we ran back to the ferry terminal to get the next ship home. I think I was in France for all of half an hour.

Just one week later, here I am again in the middle of the English Channel. This time on a ferry, with Shiv looking emotional, Noah, our two-year-old, looking excited and India, our one-year-old, looking for more food. Then there are the three rucksacks, two pushchairs, a changing bag full of nappies, a rolled-up inflatable dinghy and a potty. Oh yes, and how could I forget? We're also accompanied by an enormous canvas cover for *Friendship*'s cockpit that turns out to be impossible to manoeuvre. If you've ever carried a double mattress up a flight of stairs, you'll have some idea of what it is like to lug it on and off a ferry as a foot passenger. You can imagine the arguments as we take over two hours to squeeze off the ship with all our clobber and then stagger the half-mile to the marina where the yachts are moored and where *Friendship* lies waiting for us.

Our first evening aboard, as *Friendship* bobs in the safety of Calais Marina with the kids curled up in their bunks, Damian paces up and down the tiny wooden cabin, head bent to avoid cracking it on the ceiling struts.

Four steps forward and Damian passes, to his left, the galley (kitchen), dining area and sitting room. Four steps back past a seat, shower room and toilet. That's it. There is no more. He pauses at the two wooden steps up to the cockpit, where I sit, watching him and waiting. He tuts, turns, takes four steps away from me and stops short again at the cream-painted wooden doors that open into the kids' bedroom, the forepeak. It's a triangular space in the front of the boat (usually used to store sails and anchors) once converted into a luxurious more-than-double-bed for us, pre-kids. Now it's divided into two with a complex structure of netting and hooks to enable both Noah and India to sleep separately without falling a metre onto the floor.

With paper-thin walls made of painted plywood, their breathing fills our pauses in conversation. We shall live no more than ten feet away from them, and each other, from here on in. There is absolutely nowhere to sulk.

'I just don't feel anything big. I'm so disappointed. It's such a massive life-change. And I feel nothing,' Damian moans, his arm hanging from a ceiling strut, looking like he is on the Tube. He looks forlorn. I am angry.

'How on earth can you be like this?' I hiss viciously so as not to wake the kids. Although I am coiled with tension, I know if I shout we'll end our first night in a fight and I really do not want that.

Today has been so thrilling for me – so far removed from my monotonous existence in Queen's Park. I'm joyous that tomorrow will not be a biscuit-making day: walk to the park, kids in sandpit, cappuccino kick-start, punctuated conversation with mummy friends, walk home, lunch, sleep, ditto for afternoon till bath and bed, dinner with husband, whinge about stress, read, collapse in bed. What makes my heart beat is that I have NO idea what will fill tomorrow.

I stand up, poised at the cabin entrance, not sure what to do now – there's no space for me to pace too. At home I would have left the room to avoid an argument.

We've been together for nine years, married for four of them, but the voices of peers echo in my head as I survey our new living quarters and my disgruntled husband: 'Living on a boat will be miserable' and 'You'll be divorced within months.' Even good friends jittered. 'Incredible for a man to leave his career at its peak', 'Are you mad? Where will you storm off to when you have a row?', 'What? You mean you'll have no television?!', 'You're going with two kids? Are you crazy?' In fact, come to think of it, only our families egged us on.

I make an excuse to take the rubbish out after we've argued about being different to one another, and stomp off down the pontoon. The sky is purple-black, mirroring my feelings towards Damian right now. I can just make out yacht masts pointing skywards. Halyards chat in the light evening breeze. My mood deepens. Maybe we've been too rash. Maybe we should have stayed put. Maybe we were caught up with the idea of having a romantic adventure. Well, it's not an idea any more.

Looking back at *Friendship* from the quay, even in this dying light our new home stands out from the rest, with her solid wooden hull, her bow stretching upwards and varnish gleaming. My family are lying, snoring and pacing inside that ten-metre-long boat. A dim yellow light from the cabin windows draws me back on board to join them.

By the time I've returned to climb over the taut wire safety lines and stoop under the new green canvas awning of the cockpit, Damian appears more relaxed and hands me a glass of red. Acutely aware that holding onto arguments will make boat life hellish, I soften, accept the wine and survey our new living quarters. I knock back the rest of my glass as it sinks in just how small our new home is.

Friendship is actually a converted fishing boat, made for carrying tonnes of cod, herring and mackerel from the north seas – not a warm-blooded family of four from London used to central-heating, fluffy carpets and rooms to disappear into. Tonight, we have to piece together a jigsaw of six-foot-long wooden boards, place cushions on them and then try to disguise this arrangement as a bed with sheets and duvet. Our bodies will have to entwine on this narrow platform for the next few hundred nights or more. I wonder how many nights will pass before it gets to me. I never ever make the bed at home, let alone dismantle one every morning.

I scrub 'adults' dinner' from the menu as I'm too tired to cook for Damian and myself now, and anyway I have no idea where anything is. For their dinner, Noah and India each had to make do with a bag of ferry crisps and a banana. Before departure I had stocked the bilges with food: rice, tinned tomatoes, pasta, sardines. I wasted hours wrapping goody bars for the kids in plastic bags, squeezing cartons of UHT milk into unused parts of the boat and stacking tins of beans in the dark recesses of cupboards. Somehow I felt that if we were surrounded by a full larder then nothing really bad could happen. Perhaps it's something to do with being half-Indian. This obsession with food and where the next meal is coming from is ingrained. I know we're in France, not Tibet, but I've read that there are parts of the canals where one is miles from habitation and supplies. What I forgot to do in England was make a list of where everything is stored (which Damian suggested) so now there's no dinner.

My chaos and forgetfulness is balanced by Damian's love of order. He lives by lists, planning and looking ahead. He knows what is on the calendar in November next year. As long as I've known him, his world has been framed neatly by what he is planning for and what he needs to achieve to get there. Now, for the first time, he is removing the safety net and venturing forth with no plan. We have left England on our boat with no destination and no fixed double bed.

'Please look after us all,' I whisper to God as well as to Damian as I lie rigid in our new bed in our new home with my 'new' husband. For a moment, I wonder whether we'll be crawling back to England in a few weeks' time, making excuses to all our friends. My mind and stomach are doing somersaults but I pretend to sleep.

Shiv seems so calm and relaxed but I'm freaked out by everything. I spend most of the night lying awake in our awful bed, wondering what we should do next. We have no plan and no timetable for this trip so in theory we could stay in Calais Marina for days, weeks even. But that seems ridiculous, we're only 20 miles from England and most people travel further to work each day. So shouldn't we just get on with it and

motor south in search of sunshine and sunflowers? Then again, why rush? Let's make the most of every place we visit ...

I can't cope. I'm not used to having no agenda. For the last five years, Camille, my beautiful and über-efficient PA, has told me what I should be doing and when I should be doing it. Now I'm on my own, I'm feeling disorientated. I need lists, targets and goals. I am a man after all; I can't think for myself.

CHAPTER 2

The next morning, far too early for starting a new life, we wake, backs aching from the stiff wooden boards below us, heads groggy from a restless night's sleep and a cheap bottle of Merlot. We both stare at the ceiling, only two feet above us, unable to quite believe what we are in the midst of doing.

I spring out of bed, confident that standing up will be more comfortable than lying down and it may help to steady my nerves. The thing is, I don't have a clue what I'm doing on board, as even the simplest task, like making a cup of tea, is monumentally different on our boat. Firstly I have to stumble out into the cold of the cockpit to locate the gas locker. Then, having lifted the cushion cover and the wooden lid, I need to grapple in the back of the cupboard for the tap to turn the gas on. By the steering wheel (again out in the cold), I need to flick the correct water switches to pump water into our taps. Next, ducking back down below into the smell of sleep and cosiness, I fill the copper kettle and screw it to the hob with two metal rods so it can't fall off in a storm (highly unlikely in Calais yacht marina but I'm not taking any chances). I locate the UHT milk from under one of the 'floorboards' (or the cabin sole as it's called by real sailors), pour it into our mugs and then freeze while waiting for the tea to brew.

I don't know what to do about the fridge. Where do I put the rest of the milk now it's open? There's no electricity on board.

Not like on land anyhow. You can't just plug things in and they'll work. I don't really understand it but apparently there are two kinds of electricity – 240 and 12 volts. I'm sure they taught us this in school, but that was 23 years ago and it's a little hazy now. Anyhow, what it means is that we can keep the fridge cold only when the engine is running. When we stop for the night and cut the engine, the fridge immediately turns off. We could run it from one of the three huge boat batteries. However, it would drain the battery in a matter of hours. So, as I see it, we can either have cold milk or a boat that moves. Tricky decision. At 6 am on the first morning of our new life, I'd rather have a cup of tea than move forward. I nestle the opened carton of UHT into the fridge and decide to tackle it later.

Clasping hot cups of tea, kids still snoring, and milk slowly curdling in our warm 'fridge', we clamber on deck and recommence arguing, this time about what we should do. I want to savour my tea on deck in the cool morning air. Damian wants to be first into the lock. The lock opens only for half an hour so Damian wins. We have to be quick so we untie all ropes, check the engine (Damian's territory involves oil sticks, water pouring, and a bit of umming and ahhing under the engine cover), and then motor off, praying we don't crash into any other boats. God, suddenly I wish I was in the arms of the Queen's Park Café, safe and secure, with no quick decision-making required.

So this is it, we're off. *Friendship* slips her moorings, then clumsily, we crash and bang our way into the open water between the pontoons (thank God for the big rubber fenders that we've hung over the sides to protect the hull).

It's great to be moving for the first time but I also feel very self-conscious. One of the things about a beautiful old boat with a varnished hull is that people look at it. Obviously, being vain, this is what I like about it, but it has its downsides. The major one being that people think if you own a boat like this, you must be a wily old sea dog. And I'm not.

The truth is, apart from a few jaunts up the River Orwell, I have precious little experience of handling *Friendship* and

Shiv has even less. All of which means when I'm behind the wheel, I'm like a nervous 17–year-old car driver; I'm nominally in control but only just.

In an ordinary boat I might have got away with it but in *Friendship*, too many people are watching. They stop what they are doing for a moment or two, to look at the lovely old boat, and that's when you realise that everything you do is being acutely observed. It's hard enough trying to convince Shiv that I know what I'm doing, let alone every Tom, Dick and Pierre in Calais too. It's only just past sunrise but already there seem to be people everywhere. And being in a major port, I'm convinced that everyone knows how to handle a boat apart from me.

Once ropes are coiled, I settle down in the bow – as far away from Damian as I can manage, in order to sip my tea at my own, slow pace. Ahead of us, spanning the channel of water we are on, is a low bridge and, to its side, on the bank, a man waving hysterically. At me. I wonder why he's doing that. And wave back. Glancing behind me at Damian to point out this loony, I suddenly realise why the man is hopping about and I jump up, shriek, spilling my tea on deck.

'Cut the engine, get to the side,' I yell. Damian has that look of the confused and it dawns on me that he cannot hear me over the pounding roar of the engine. I make cut-throat gestures with my hand, dump the rest of my tea overboard and skirt along the side-deck to the cockpit.

The problem is our wind generator at the back of the boat, which sticks its regal windmill-head high above the bridge height. If we keep motoring forward, in less than 60 seconds we're set to lose £600 worth of kit, a wedding present, and our pride as the stone bridge will smash the generator clean off its perch. Not a good start just minutes into our journey.

A Lara Croft lunge across the cockpit topples over Damian's cup of tea but I save our wind generator by yanking *Friendship*'s wheel over. We slam into the bank, kill the engine and humbly unscrew the offending article, trying not to glance at the 'friendly man'. Row number three ensues – something about 'looking around'.

The next half-hour is a haze as we scream and shout our way towards the first lock. My throat is hoarse, I'm sweating with stress and loathe Damian as he bellows instructions at me to untie, tie, jump, skip and bow simultaneously. While I'm hopping about on deck like Darcy Bussell, he stands serenely at the steering wheel, pretending he is totally in control.

'I'm not Camille, you know!' I yell. 'I can only do one thing at a time.' He ignores this comment, he probably can't hear me.

I'm not sure I can stand him telling me what to do for months on end.

I'm trying to look calm but after the (oh so public) humiliation of the wind generator, I worry whether I'm up to this. We are searching for the lock that will let us into the French canal system but I realise that I have no idea what a lock actually looks like. Obviously I've seen the ones on the little canals in England but all I can see ahead is a wall of wooden pilings and a bridge.

I do what is only natural in the situation – I scream at Shiv and tell her we must have come the wrong way (after all, she's supposed to be the navigator). She is unrepentant and adamant that we've come in the right direction. She's insisting the lock entrance must be here somewhere.

Great start to our trip. The only consolation is that being on a boat, Shiv won't demand that we stop and ask someone the way. At an impasse we sit in the water and wonder what the hell to do. (And of course, several people watching us are wondering the same thing.) The marina has a canal running off it, allowing boats to leave the sea and enter the inland waterways of France – rivers and canals. To enter this waterway, we first need to locate the doorway – a wooden lock gate. With the background clutter of boats, masts, pontoons and all things sea-like, spotting the lock gate is an almost impossible task. Then suddenly a wooden wall in front of us begins to move and a lock reveals itself. It seems a lock-

keeper has spotted the boat and opened it for us. Thank God for a boat that people look at.

After two or three botched attempts, we finally succeed in getting *Friendship* into what feels like a ridiculously narrow lock. Within minutes we nervously edge our way out the other side and I quietly congratulate myself on not killing anyone.

We're now officially on the French canals. We are actually here! It feels bizarre. It's as if we have somehow reached our destination, yet we haven't even started.

When we finally join the Canal de Calais my adrenalin surges. Which way now? I hadn't imagined it'd be this tricky. My only experience of canals is the long, obvious, linear water channels in the Fens. The ones I'm looking at now offer choices. Ducking down below to retrieve the charts, a hideous image flashes through my mind: a red plastic crate of French canal maps sitting on the pavement in Peterborough, still waiting, no doubt, to be loaded into the boot of our hire car. In the fluster and tears of departure I forgot to put them in. I've made a terrible mistake and we've embarked on this epic journey without a single map. I have NO idea where we're going. Worse still, it was my responsibility to get all the books and paperwork for the trip. Down below are a hundred tomes covering everything from offshore sea-survival to Mediterranean fish. But no maps. I'm never, ever going to hear the end of this from Damian.

We have no option but to hover until someone passes and then follow them. After a while, a white fibreglass motorboat duly obliges. There is a couple on deck wearing matching shorts and T-shirts, immaculately ironed and no stains that I can see – they cannot possibly have children. We try not to make it obvious that we're in pursuit and keep a few hundred yards behind; in fact, we argue about just how far behind we should travel. They stop and so we stop too, emotionally exhausted, on the far side of Calais Town. We've moved two kilometres. The town bell peels out loud. It's still only 9 am and the kids are just stirring.

Admitting to the 'Couple-in-the-know' on the fibreglass

motorboat that we haven't a clue where we are, they advise us to buy Navicarte maps in Calais. The rest of the day is spent trying to find one and arguing. It turns out that in Calais, it's easier to find a road map of England.

So far this feels like a holiday from hell. We attempt a reconciliation from the 'map incident' by sitting at a market café surrounded by French dogs, bawling kids and warm croissants. It doesn't really work. We are, I'm sure, both wondering why on earth we signed up for this torture. The thing is, Calais is an odd place to like. Not much survived the Second World War except the magnificent Hôtel de Ville. Its 75-metre-high belfry looks down on us but offers no help with maps. Although the Gauls, Louis XVIII and even Napoleon himself have been in Calais, we feel no weight of history here. It's all a little bland. Perhaps Anne Boleyn felt the same too, as she never left her hotel room – she's reputed to have got pregnant with Elizabeth I whilst on a long weekend break with Henry VIII.

Calais may have a fascinating history but I don't like the place. It's a stop-off point rather than a destination in itself. It's no-man's-land in a war zone. I don't believe that anyone actually lives here – who would want to? I'm convinced that everyone is either a daytripper from England looking for the cheapest Stella Artois they can find or they're workers from outlying areas, making a living by fleecing the English and then returning to the serenity of their own villages each evening. I'm sure Calais has *some* redeeming qualities but I haven't been intrigued enough to look for them. Instead I want to get on with the next leg so I can feel like we are in 'real' France.

At the end of our first day on the canals, we are exhausted and have also exhausted Calais. No map in hand, we struggle on board as the 'Couple-in-the-know' eye up our two kids warily and crack open a bottle of red. They don't invite us to join them. Instead they throw advice safely from their deck and warn us to lock our bikes to the boat overnight. There are unsavoury types lurking. It is Calais after all, gateway to Europe for more than just us.

I get busy with dinner as the kids are starving. Noah is smashing Lego with a fork. India is hitting Noah with Sticklebricks. I turn the tap to fill a pan with water for spaghetti. Nothing gushes out. I try again. Check the water switches by the steering wheel. They are on. This cannot possibly be happening. The tanks cannot possibly be empty. On board we have four water tanks, holding about 400 litres in all. Sounds plenty, doesn't it? Then you work out that a very quick shower uses twenty litres; a kettle for two teas, half a litre; water for spaghetti, two litres. So we can last for just thirteen days if we all have a quick shower once a day but don't drink any tea, cook any food or wash any dishes. If you begin to count brushing teeth, well ...

While Damian struts around outside basking in the glory of a well-tied knot, chatting to the 'Couple-in-the-know', I fume below. It's too much. I storm up on deck, try desperately to remain calm as I question, in a high-pitched voice, why he didn't fill up with water at the main marina in Calais. 'There should be plenty. Are you sure you've turned on the pressure switch?' he asks, presuming feminine incompetence. I tell him what I'd like to do with the pressure switch, then throw my eyes to heaven as he sheepishly admits that he hasn't actually filled up with water since *Friendship* left Walton-on-the-Naze on the east coast of England. That's several days ago. Our water has clearly been frittered away on jovial mugs of tea with Dave, the cross-Channel pilot.

I hurl my bike from the bow onto the pontoon with that superhuman strength only possessed by the furious, jump off *Friendship* and cycle rapidly down the towpath, searching for a water tap while letting off steam. Five miles and a lot of steam later, I return, nodding with a tight smile to the 'Couple-in-the-know'. There isn't a water tap in sight. Clearly, friendly France has got a few surprises for us.

We're far too embarrassed to admit to the 'Couple-in-the-know' that we are canal virgins. Not only have we no maps, we have also run out of water. We manage to glean from them that the magical Navicarte maps highlight every water tap along the canal. So it *is* possible to plan a trip without running out of water. We resolve to beg, borrow or steal one of these maps.

That second night aboard is spent uncomfortably, having had no shower and only goody bars and a tin of tuna for dinner. Hot meals seem to be relegated to history. The kids are delighted to be going to bed without a bath. I'm not. Damian has cycled into town to carry back some bottled water to keep us going, and to keep me quiet. We throw the bed together, angry again and I lie still with my stomach in free fall, wondering whether to get the ferry back home.

The next morning saves our marriage by ushering in a bright blue, holiday sky. Tea is brewed with bottled water, ropes are untied and we set off south along the 'Canal de Calais' without an argument. In fact, we do not talk at all.

The 'Couple-in-the-know' have donated us an out-of-date Navicarte map. I wonder whether they heard us at loggerheads in bed last night. After all, there were only about ten feet and a bit of wood and fibreglass between us. This communal close living is going to be tough. Now I understand why our friends are moving to big houses in the country.

It isn't until we leave Calais completely that I feel the trip has *really* begun, even if we do have to suffer the ignominy of following *Magellan*, the shiny white speedboat of the 'Couple-in-the-know'. I'm watching them now, dressed in matching navy blue shorts and white polo shirts, neat haircuts and shiny boat shoes. They would fit into any smart boat club in the world. I'm not sure the same could be said about us, in our current unwashed state.

However, appearances can be deceptive and I have to admit that I'm feeling a bit more smug about the 'Couple-in-the-know' now. This morning the husband let slip that they had to delay their trip by two weeks because he had forgotten to open their seacock when they left Dover. Basically, this means no water could run around their cooling system so he bug-gered up their engine, necessitating major repairs. Frankly,

forgetting to open the seacock is a schoolboy error and as we meekly trail behind them I console myself with the fact that *even I* wouldn't be that stupid.

The canal in these parts is effectively a straight line through flat fields. There are no pretty villages lining the banks and no points of real interest apart from the odd factory or haulage depot. It doesn't matter though, I absolutely love it. This is what I have dreamed about for so long (well, not exactly this but I'm not going to split hairs now). The point is, we're here. We're doing it.

Shiv is wearing a pair of Gore-Tex hiking shorts that I find strangely sexy, and a sleeveless black T-shirt. I have decided to wear a white vest. Not the type my granddad wore in the Fifties but the kind that made Jude Law look good in *The Talented Mr Ripley*. I have never worn anything like this before and for some reason it feels like a statement. This is all part of trying to be free and relaxed. It's an essential part of my shift from pale and pasty Londoner to chilled and bohemian Mediterranean beach bum. I like to think that if my clients could see me now they would be stunned by the change in me. In truth, though, I suspect this would be less about my similarity to Jude Law and more about the speed with which their former image-maker has turned into a tramp.

As we chug noisily along, the kids still shell-shocked into staring-mode by our new life, Damian reminds us what we would have been doing back home. It's a Monday morning and he would have been in a planning meeting, probably getting bollocked for not bringing in any new business. I'd have been wearing my Weetabix-stained jeans, heaving the double-buggy uphill to Queen's Park Café for my cappuccino fix.

I'm not missing the park though; I'm missing the peace of my walks. *Friendship* is loud and smelly. Too loud. This much is blatantly clear after only a few hours. The engine is situated right in the centre of the cockpit, which is primarily where we live during the day. Imagine an articulated lorry's engine plonked in your sitting room, close to your television. This gives you some idea how hard it is to talk or listen while the engine is running. I think Damian is secretly quite pleased that he can't hear most of my mutterings and it certainly dulls the kids' whining.

After a couple of hours we leave the Canal de Calais and join the River Aa. Shiv and I still haven't figured out how to use the complicated Navicarte charts but at least we have worked out that coming up soon on the right, there is a mooring at Watten. Immediately we see a large stable-type building and a sign for a restaurant so deduce that this must be it. We slow down and look for the entrance to the pontoon area.

The boat-to-boat radio crackles into life. It's the 'Couple-in-the-know' telling us that we have just missed the entrance. 'Hadn't we seen it?' they ask incredulously. I realise that what I had thought was a sewage outlet is in fact the cutting off the river that we should have taken.

'Oh yes, thanks. Yes I saw it but thought it best to go past and make sure we knew what it was like instead of blindly ploughing in.' I, for one, think this sounds pretty convincing and even quite seaman-like. I don't want to reinforce my burgeoning reputation as the most incompetent man on the French canal system and just hope he assumes I'm cautious (which isn't a label I would normally aspire to but I figure it's the lesser of two evils in this situation). We wave our goodbyes to the 'Couple-in-the-know' and turn back to the tiny cutting.

To 'park up', we must navigate Watten's narrow channel of water, with boats moored on one side and shallow water on the other. One false move and we'll grind to a halt in a suck of mud. We cruise slowly towards the moorings. The river cutting narrows rapidly and I can make out the colour of the stones underwater from my position at the bow. It's suddenly very shallow indeed. I break out into a hullabaloo of shouting, wild gesticulating and screeches – then the kids follow suit.

Jesus – our depth readings are dropping like a stone. The whole family seems to be shouting at once and there's barely a foot of water under the boat. One old pram or shopping trolley lying on the riverbed and we are going to be stuck.

Obviously I'm terrified about making a mistake and try to hide my fear under a steely exterior but Shiv knows that when I suddenly go deathly quiet, *that's* when we are in trouble. It's critical that we find a space to tie up as quickly as possible.

It's a bit like cruising around the parents' and toddlers' parking spaces at Tesco on a Saturday morning. High tension, lots of screaming and pulling of hair. Dad ready to pounce at a departing vehicle, looking disgustedly at a double space greedily taken up by one badly parked 4x4. Suddenly aware of people watching us from the moored boats, I recover my composure. I gesture to Damian to turn around before we plough into the mud (perhaps that's why it's called a *Halte Nautique*).

We edge past the other boats and I notice they are all flat-bottomed so no wonder they had no problems with the depth. Nevertheless, we might make it ...

Just then, two things happen which make the situation a hell of a lot worse. First of all, a steady stream of people from the other boats and even the restaurant come to the bank to gape, point, wave and shout advice (this is the last thing I want at the moment). The second thing is a steady churn of mud starting to come up to the surface of the water – our propeller is scraping along the bottom.

I have visions of us running aground in the middle of this sodding stream. Stuck in only a couple of feet of water but just far enough from the bank that we'll all have to jump in and wade ashore. However, this would be the least of our problems because the real issue would be how to pull a five-ton boat off the mud, turn it round and then push it back out into the river.

Just as I screw up my eyes and wait to hit mud, Damian spots a mooring and shouts. I snap open my eyes, size up the space and figure we can't fit. We're a Volvo trying to squeeze into a Mini's space. I close my eyes again, breathe in and pray. The kids are both yelling and Noah's crying to get out on deck to 'be like Mummy'. Damian's hollering at me to jump eight feet through mid-air onto a pontoon with a rope in my hand. I have always hated being shouted at. It's a childhood thing. I just clam up like a rabbit caught in the headlights.

Shiv's flatly refusing to go for Watten's long jump record so I can't think of anything better to do than lurch *Friendship* towards the nearest boat. Hopefully the man who is on board can pull us into the one space that's left. It's not a very pretty mooring technique and you won't read about it in the sailing books but I don't have many options.

The incendiary way that we moor is highlighted acutely by the serenity of a solitary brown arm calmly stretched out from a white cruiser that takes our bow rope, loops it round a pontoon cleat and secures us to dry land.

After 20 minutes of panting and struggling with the other ropes, finally we manage to tie up. I'm convinced that ours has been the loudest arrival that Watten has seen all summer.

A collective sigh of relief tumbles us off *Friendship* and into the brown body of the brown arm. The brown face introduces himself as Jean Yves. His boat, *Bag An Arnaud*, is next to ours. A long, low, plastic canal cruiser.

Tanned, tall and slim, Jean Yves, who is a very young-looking 50-something, epitomises everything about boat life that I have imagined. He is completely at ease in his own skin. We're rubbing shoulders and strakes with a real Frenchman. In contrast to how we feel right now, he exudes self-confidence, inner calm and style. It feels exotic, more Caribbean than European. In comparison we're pasty, uptight, English boaters.

Everyone comes over to greet us at once. As they walk around *Friendship* I note just how odd she looks. Equipment and 'kit' is hanging off every part of her. I'm sure the locals wouldn't be surprised if Ellen McArthur had emerged from the cabin instead of Shiv.

I blame my parents for this excess of paraphernalia. You see, when I was a kid my family moved to Canada for four years. I was at that age when cars were becoming interesting and consequently fell in love with the huge Buicks, Pontiacs and Chevrolets that everyone owned. When people talked about these cars there was one phrase that always fired my imagination – 'fully loaded'. This was reserved for the vehicles that had every conceivable extra, from air-con to electra-glide transmissions. They were the crème de la crème and everyone wanted one.

You need to know this in order to understand how I approached preparing *Friendship* for the canals. To a bystander it might appear that my logic was very simple: the boat is going to be our home for a considerably long time so it should be equipped accordingly. Also, with two young kids on board we have to make sure she is utterly safe.

The truth, however, is much more prosaic. Basically this was my chance to indulge every fantasy about *Friendship* and buy anything I wanted for her. And the best bit of all was that Shiv was happy with my spending spree because she mistakenly assumed it was all about 'our safety and comfort'.

So for months I spent night after night with the bedside light on, circling things to buy in boat equipment catalogues (yes, such things do exist and yes, I am that sad). I went completely overboard so that no-one else would. We ended up with a piece of kit for every eventuality. I bought everything from clip-on mug holders to folding shopping trolleys; lanterns; safety netting; man overboard recovery systems; bolt cutters; picnic tables and even solar showers. There was so much stuff that once it was all fitted on board, *Friendship* actually sank by two inches and we had to repaint the water-line. Yep, this boat was 'fully loaded' all right.

The problem with all this was that our boat stopped looking like a boat. Overnight she seemed to change from a beautiful old fishing vessel into a floating gypsy caravan.

Now that I see the boat tied to the grassy bank of the quiet canal at Watten, I do have to question the ocean-standard life raft, the triple-anchor system and the huge flare pack. To explain myself, I take the coward's way out. I gush that all this kit is because I love my family and nothing is too much for their safety. This seems to go down well, so I decide to ignore the bit about my childhood infatuation with the magical phrase 'fully loaded'.

As I fill the tanks with water from a hosepipe (I'm not taking any chances now), a rotund neighbour tells us that Watten stands on the smallest mountain of the Mont des Flandres. We're impressed that we've 'climbed a mountain' in our boat until we realise that at a height of 72 metres, it's still lower than the Hôtel de Ville in Calais.

In 1072 monks founded an abbey here and Watten grew up around it. The French Revolution saw the sale and destruction of the abbey, although the tower remains as a navigation mark and the monks have now been replaced by boaters who cram into a black wooden auberge serving food and drinks by night.

That evening we can't wait to get to the auberge for a relaxing glass of wine. It's only a few feet from where *Friendship* is tied up so we'll be able put the kids to sleep and watch the boat from our table.

It has been scorching hot and the inside of the boat feels like an oven. The sunshine has burnt onto the wooden hull all day and apart from a couple of small hatches there is no way to let the heat out or the fresh air in. The temperature inside is unbearable but Noah and India hardly notice. They collapse into their beds and are asleep immediately. Both are dressed in nothing more than their nappies but I worry about them. The heat is only going to get worse as we head south.

I'm not used to having to worry about things like room

temperature or what the kids should wear in bed. Normally I would be scraping home at this time and all the thinking would have been done by Shiv. In fact, I'm behaving just like Shiv used to when we first had Noah; she worried constantly that she didn't know what she was doing. I used to think she was being neurotic. Now here I am, unable to relax as we drink our wine because all I can think about is rushing back into the cockpit to check if Noah and India are still breathing.

The next day we pile most of our belongings onto the bank and recreate *Friendship*'s cabin 'al fresco' on the grass. There is a lot more space here than on board. Like everyone else, we lounge in deckchairs with either coffee or wine, dependent on the time of day. There's a 40-foot sailing boat deflowered with her mast lying flat across her length. The inmates are a couple from Newcastle. He strums his guitar sitting on the pontoon, his thick, swollen ankles resting on the grass. She reads nearby, her freckled face almost swallowing her tiny, pinhead eyes. They both smoke their way through the clear, clean days. On board for several months, they already seem jaded with boat life. They sold a house in England for this freedom and have been courted by disaster from day one. We donate some new books to cheer them up and wonder whether we too will have taken up Gauloises within a few months of this life.

It's 'The Smokers' who tell us about some of the sights in the local area. Propelled by our new thirst for adventure, we resolve to set forth and explore by bike. Unfortunately, these aren't the little folding cycles that you see on most boats (the clever, lightweight things that can be carried in one hand and hidden in a small bag). No, these are thumping big mountain bikes complete with lights, horns, dynamos, huge child seats and panniers ('fully loaded'). Great once you are on the towpaths, but they take up the whole of the front deck of *Friendship* and they are a nightmare to lift on and off. These are the kind of mistakes you only realise you've made once you are a long way from the shop, struggling to get your purchase hoisted onto a wobbling pontoon.

We make two major excursions from Watten (although I'm finding that with two kids under the age of three, even a trip to the toilet block is a huge journey). First we go to the Blockhaus at Eperlecques, a place where the Nazis planned to manufacture, launch and fire V-2 rockets towards Britain.

There are no signs for the Blockhaus but after an hour of cycling through pine forests with Noah and India dozing in their baby seats on the back of the bikes, we finally come across it, slap bang in the middle of nowhere (which I suppose is a sensible place for a bomb-making factory).

The site was chosen for its discreetness and also because supplies could be delivered via the canal. Such a sinister use of the same gentle canal system we are meandering along is difficult to comprehend.

In 1943, over 35,000 French, Belgian, Dutch and Russian prisoners worked night and day to build the factory. Workers unloaded the gravel, sand and cement from the barges at Watten onto small trains which ran in and out of the forest of Eperlecques, 24 hours a day. It must have made one hell of a racket. Suddenly life on board with two toddlers feels almost quiet.

The Blockhaus is quite shocking in its size. Imagine two massive out-of-town B&Q stores completely filled from floor to ceiling with reinforced concrete and then plonked on top of one another in the middle of a forest and you get some idea of its scale.

Apart from this huge block of concrete, there isn't actually much to see, but the sheer size of the thing is very dramatic, almost sculptural. The sense of drama is heightened by the fact that loudspeakers are hidden in the trees piping the sounds of aeroplanes flying overhead with accompanying anti-aircraft fire. It's all pretty eerie and I leave feeling that I need to know more about the two world wars. Like most people of my generation, I know sod all about history. In my school, instead of learning anything useful, we studied *The Development of Medicine* for History 'O' level (all very innovative but bugger-all use in life).

When we get back to the boat, I root through our library (a locker filled with books) and flick through our 'history section'. I select *The Second World War for Dummies*. Admittedly this is not a classic but I think it's all I can handle at the moment and at least it will help me answer some of the more difficult questions posed by Noah, particularly as he is now obsessed by the toy V-2 rocket that we bought him in the shop at Eperlecques. It strikes me that it probably isn't the most politically correct of toys for a place like that to sell, especially as now all Noah wants to do is bomb things. Still, I guess they have to make their money somehow.

The next major excursion is one that I undertake alone. It's to the local supermarket. I'm determined that we should embrace France in every way while we are here so I make it my mission to buy every product that I *don't* recognise. It's in this supermarket that I decide we should spend no more than two euros per bottle of wine while we are in France. I have no idea why I choose this arbitrary (and ridiculous) sum but it feels right that we should be living on a really tight budget.

I leave the checkout absolutely laden with stuff we'll probably never want to eat and suddenly remember that I don't have a car parked outside. Instead there is my bike leaning forlornly against a wall. I tie bags to every part of the frame, rest some on the seat, hang others off the handlebars and fill the baby carrier with wine bottles. In my romantic vision of myself, I imagine that I look like the boy struggling up the hill in the old Hovis advertisement but in reality, I probably look like a middle-aged man who has spent too much at the supermarket and has a drink problem. The walk back to the boat takes a long, long time.

At the end of each of our excursion-filled days, Watten becomes our Moulin Rouge. It's a glorious haze of steak-frites, red wine and flowing conversation with each other and fellow boaters. We pad back to *Friendship* through soft grass with a sense of calm over us. Perhaps the souls of the monks do live on after all.

One night Jean Yves treats us to a local apple liqueur, Genieve. We ask him to join us and discover he's a retired French professor. The kind of professor you'd have mooned and crooned over. 'You'll be having baby number three soon,' he quips, raising a glass of Genieve in the air. 'That's what happens when you take on boat life. Moi, I have four children, all big now. One looks after my house in Brittany while I am cruising.'

I dare to ask where Mrs Jean Yves is. There isn't one. He is divorced, roaming Europe for months on end with his dog, philosophising with other boaters. 'There's no such thing as Europe,' he advises us one day as he lends us an electricity lead. 'English, German, French, phahhhh!! When you are on a boat and someone needs help, you help. We are all people, not Europeans.'

After several days here I wonder whether we could get away with spending our new life in Watten. No-one would ever find us here. Maybe we could emulate Donald Crowhurst, the amateur sailor who cheated in a round-the-world race in the 1960s by sailing in a big circle in the Atlantic while sending radio messages home, pretending to be in different parts of the world.

However, after a while we realise we're getting cosy and remind ourselves we have an adventure to live. So we unhook electricity and water, wave goodbye to our new friends, Jean Yves and 'The Smokers' and venture out of the Watten channel with no-one to follow, no route and no schedule. At least we now have a map.

As we set off again, I think to myself that even though I'm probably less than a hundred miles from London, this is a heck of a long way from Queen's Park.

CHAPTER 3

An hour out of Watten, India is pawing at my leg and Noah is crying.

'Indy has probably filled her nappy ...' Shiv shouts helpfully from the steering wheel, '... and haven't you noticed that Noah has got his lifejacket caught in the safety netting?' she adds incredulously. No, I hadn't realised. I'd been too concerned that Shiv was over-revving the engine and she hadn't turned the battery switch onto the full charge position.

I disentangle Noah and take India into the cabin to change her nappy. At least in here I'm on more familiar ground. I still feel proud when I look around me at the restored woodwork, the thick varnish and the antique brass. Appreciatively I note that we aren't the only ones who have come a long way; this is part of a much bigger journey for *Friendship* too.

I was 28 when my father rang me to tell me about a lovely old wooden boat he had found in a yard outside York. 'Lovely' probably isn't the word most people would have used but I seem to have this extraordinary attraction to anything that is old and knackered that could be brought back to its former glory with a bit of love and hard work (apart from women, of course).

The boat was *Friendship*. A 32–foot converted fishing vessel that had been lying abandoned for several years. An outcast among the white, plastic 'gin palaces' that surrounded her.

Friendship was rough. Very rough. The wooden hull was rotting, there was green mould on the inside of the windows, her protective covers had shredded in the wind, the blue paint was peeling off, the insides smelt dank and the metalwork was rusting away. No one in their right mind would touch her with a bargepole. Needless to say I fell in love straight away.

The thing is, she was beautiful and I've always been a sucker for things that are beautiful. Her lines were long and fluid. The wood curved and twisted where on modern boats it's flat and square. The front climbed high into the air to cut through the water while the back was rounded and flared to protect her from following waves.

Everything about her shape was dictated by the way the sea behaves, whereas everything about a modern boat is driven by consumer demand: people at boat shows looking for a status symbol with ever more beds and better headroom.

Within a week I had tracked down the owner and by the end of January, I had bought *Friendship* for the price of an old and rusty Ford Fiesta. In my mind (enthusiastically cheered on by my father who wasn't the one risking any money), I had a bargain. The boat just needed a bit of sanding down and painting before a glorious launching ceremony. Then hey presto, I would have summers full of lazy days on the water, nights aboard tucked up in a cosy bunk and evenings drinking wine and chatting with friends in the cockpit.

It wasn't long before my dreams came crashing down around me. With the same screwed-up logic that led me to buy *Friendship* in the first place, I decided to have her surveyed *after* I had paid the money.

'Burn her,' the surveyor said. 'The wooden hull is made from the cheap mahogany they used in the 1960s to keep costs down. It's vulnerable at the best of times but usually the salt in seawater acts to preserve it. Unfortunately, *Friendship*'s been kept on a river so the hull has rotted through. Not only that; since she's been dumped at the back of the boatyard, she has dried out so the wood has shrunk, leaving gaps between the planks ... she's a wreck. Even if you were mad enough to restore her, what you have to remember is that they don't make boats like this any more. Look at the size of all the fittings, all the woodwork – everything is massive, she's been built for hard work on the North Sea. It would cost you a fortune to rebuild her like that nowadays. Even in the 1960s when they first made her, she would have been a throwback to another era, especially as that was when all the fibreglass boats were coming onto the market. I'm very sorry to tell you that you should forget about this boat, young man. Cut your losses and get out while you can; it's just a question of common sense.'

It was the words 'common sense' that did it for me. I hate those words (probably the result of repeatedly being told by my parents that I didn't have any). In the way that only men can, I managed to convince myself that the surveyor didn't know what he was talking about. After all, he was probably not used to seeing wooden boats, and anyway, all surveyors are pessimistic. It's what they're paid for.

There was also the fact that I had just paid good money for *Friendship* and I didn't want it wasted. So I decided to carry on regardless. After all, how hard could it be to sand off a bit of paint and whack on new stuff? Okay, there was quite a lot of it, but if I did some each weekend she'd be sorted before I knew it.

I had *Friendship* put on a trailer and taken to a cheap boatyard in Essex so that she was closer to my work in London. I also tracked down a wooden boat builder who could help me out on the 'tricky bits' of doing her up. My plan was to have her painted and in the water by that July, six months later.

Friendship didn't go in the water that summer. Or the next one. Or the one after that. Or even the one after that. Five years of spending almost every weekend and every Bank Holiday working on the boat and she'd still not even sniffed the water. Instead I was now stuck in the middle of a full-blown boat restoration and there was no end in sight.

It was at this point that my cursing of the surveyor had

really built up a head of steam. Frankly I couldn't believe that he hadn't been clearer about the scale of the task I had taken on. Why wasn't he more insistent? Couldn't he see that I hadn't a clue what I was doing?

The worst thing was that *Friendship* looked worse now than when I first bought her (if such a thing was possible). All the wood had been removed from her hull. Half the decks had been ripped up. Several feet of rot had been cut out of the cabin roof. The engine still lay lifeless and the insides had been gutted completely. There was hardly anything left of her. You could actually see right through the hull to the other side. It had turned out that almost every single plank needed to be replaced. It was like buying a house and then being told you need to remove all the bricks one by one and insert new ones.

I spent so much time at the boatyard that David Baines, the boat builder, became a good friend. In truth, with his long hair, knackered jeans, rough hands and years of knowledge about wooden boats he became a bit of a hero for me. An antidote to the slick-suited, smooth-talking, shallow world of advertising, in which I spent every other waking hour of my life.

David and I gradually arrived at a simple arrangement that seemed to suit us both: I would send him whatever spare money I had at the end of each month and he'd then work on *Friendship* until the cash ran out. This meant that the major work was done on a stop-start basis while in the meantime I would drive up to Essex every Friday night and do as much as I could before I limped home shattered, every Sunday.

When I wasn't on *Friendship*, I was researching her history. It turned out that she had been launched in 1967 and she was one of just a handful that had been built at a boatyard in Yorkshire called Whitehall's. The boats were part of a plan by the eccentric millionaire, Keith Schellenberg, to revive the fortunes of Whitby.

Schellenberg was an extraordinary character: member of

the 1956 British Olympic bobsleigh team, powerboat and car racer, one-time Yorkshire county rugby captain, water-skier and eventually, the controversial laird of Eigg, a Scottish island that he careered around in his 1927 Rolls-Royce.

He bought the Whitehall shipyard in the 1960s with the aim of turning it into a modern marina, complete with restaurants and even a boutique (it was the Sixties, after all). Part of the scheme was to use the skills of the local fishing-boat builders to create a traditional vessel for the general public. The result was a class of boat called the Scoresby and *Friendship* is probably the most important of them all as she was the first to be built and was taken to London to be shown at the Boat Show.

Apparently, when she was unloaded from the trailer at Earls Court, it was clear she had been very badly scratched during transit. She looked terrible under the bright lights in the exhibition hall and the only solution was to repaint her before the show opened the next morning.

Union rules demanded that any painting which required a brush more than one inch wide had to be done by official Earls Court tradesmen. Schellenberg refused to pay their 'extortionate' rates so made an apprentice from Whitehall's work through the night, repainting the whole boat with a half-inch 'touch-up' brush (the equivalent of cutting the grass at Wimbledon the night before the men's final with a pair of scissors).

Despite the setback, the show was a success and soon after, *Friendship* appeared in a couple of boat magazines and even in the advertising of the time, where it was proudly proclaimed that the Scoresby was 'a real man's boat'.

Even with that kind of promotional support, the Scoresbys failed to sell and only eight more were built. No-one wanted wooden boats now that 'maintenance-free' fibreglass had arrived on the scene. *Friendship* passed through an assortment of different owners over the following years. Each one of them either adored her or abused her. (This always seems to happen with boats – there is *never* a happy medium.)

Eventually I came to own *Friendship*. Or rather she came to own me. But even that felt like it was meant to happen. It turned out that one of the previous owners had replaced her floorboards using oak from tables that had been sold off by the maternity ward in York, the very same maternity ward where I had been born. There was something Zen about knowing I'd been born on the very same wood that I was now killing myself to bring back to life.

By years six and seven, *Friendship* had begun slowly to come together once more. Eventually every bit of paint had been scraped off, every piece of wood had been sanded smooth, every rusted bolt pulled out, each bit of sealant picked away, every plank slowly put back onto the ribs, each piece of the cabin rebuilt and each bit of the decks relaid.

Things would have moved faster had I not made the incredibly naïve decision to varnish the hull instead of paint it. In my mind, it was simply a matter of aesthetics: varnished boats are utterly beautiful, so why not? What I hadn't realised is that whereas paint hides a multitude of sins, varnish exposes every fault. The fact that you can see right through to the grain of the wood means every joint has to be flawless, every screw has to be covered with a wooden plug, and every bit of rot has to be cut out. There can be no filler, no bodging, no secrets. Everything has to be perfect and *that* is why varnished boats are so rare.

Predictably, once I'd fallen in love with the idea of a varnished hull I couldn't let it go, so I ploughed on. And to be fair, there are few things more rewarding (for me at least) than applying that first coat of varnish to clean dry wood and watching it soak in, turning the almost white grain into a deep gold. The trouble is, one coat isn't enough. In fact, I had to put 23 coats of varnish on *Friendship* (yes, 23). Each one could only be applied after the last had been sanded flat and that couldn't be done until it had been allowed to cure for a week. Work it out for yourself – that's half a year just on the varnishing, let alone the other jobs in between. It's slow, back-breaking work and mind-numbingly repetitive. A stray hair, a fly, or bits of dust and pollen blowing in the wind are a constant menace. They land on the wet varnish and there is nothing you can do except wait for it dry, sand it back and start again.

The odd thing is, it never occurred to me to give up. I kept thinking that I had invested too much emotion and money to stop now so I might as well keep going. Also, the fact that it was basic, manual labour was strangely therapeutic. After a week of squeezing every last drop out of my brain and constantly being under pressure to come up with new ideas at work, it was very calming at the weekends to have nothing in my head. The slow rhythm of sanding varnish by hand or painting long strips of wood was mesmerising. It was both a physical and mental release.

Incredibly the day *did* finally arrive when *Friendship* was ready to be launched. After so much work and expectation, it turned out to be a very tawdry affair. Nothing more than an old tractor backing into the water with *Friendship* perched precariously on top of a rusty trailer. Slowly buoyancy took over and *Friendship* floated off. She was a boat again.

This wasn't a time for excited cruises up the river though. *Friendship* might have been in the water but she was still nothing more than a shiny, varnished shell. Now I had to start on the *insides* of the boat. Thankfully this was quicker and easier than the hull so it took only three years to get the cabin fitted out, painted and varnished; the plumbing sorted; the electrics put in and the engine overhauled.

By this point I had been working on *Friendship* for a decade. In the moments when I was honest with myself (which I tried to avoid), I knew that she had drained me of more than just my energy. She had taken me over. I was well aware of the deal I had done with my youth and to some extent I regretted it. While all my friends had been out and about in London, clubbing, slobbing in bed with hangovers, eating late breakfasts, sunbathing in parks and generally living a life of hedonism, I had been slaving over five tonnes of wood. *Friendship* had devoured years of my life and sucked me dry of money that I probably should have spent on fast cars and fast women. On the plus side, I could now varnish really well.

It's ironic that as *Friendship* neared completion, I felt more and more rudderless. With the end in sight I began to question what I was doing with the rest of my life and realised that I had stopped being happy.

To the outside world I had the kind of job that most men dream of: loads of money, lots of fun, sexy women and fast company cars. My 'work' entailed sitting around all day thinking of ideas and making creative presentations. It was glamorous, it was stimulating, I had a PA who looked like Claudia Schiffer, my company car was a Corvette Stingray, our Covent Garden offices looked like a Manhattan loft, I was allowed to park my shiny Lambretta scooter in the reception area and we had a pool table.

To all intents and purposes, I'd cracked it and I should have been basking in smug contentment. Except that I wasn't. Quite the opposite, in fact. At first I told myself it was only stress, a natural consequence of the long hours and the constant pressure to do more, to do it better and to do it faster. Deep down though, I knew the real problem was that I didn't like the person I had become.

Advertising isn't known for its philanthropy, and years of success, back-stabbing and money had turned me into an arrogant bastard. I tried to be a nice guy and quite often I was, but I was just as liable to be offensive, rude, aggressive, opinionated and unthinking. I didn't make time for people, I never listened properly and I never took 'no' for an answer.

It was during this period of moodiness and self-flagellation that I found an advertisement in a magazine and pinned it on my wall:

IF ...
I had my life to live over, I'd try to make more mistakes next time.
I would relax.
I would be sillier than I have been on this trip.

I know of very few things I would take seriously.
I would take more chances.
I would take more trips.
I would climb more mountains, swim more rivers and watch more sunsets.
I would eat more ice-cream and less beans.
I would have more actual troubles and fewer imaginary ones.
You see, I am one of those people who live prophylactically and sanely and sensibly, hour after hour, day after day.
Oh, I have had my moments and, if I had to do it over again, I'd have more of them.
In fact, I'd try to have nothing else.
Just moments, one after another.
If I had my life to live over,
I would start bare-footed earlier in the spring
And stay that way later in the fall.
I would play hooky more.
I would ride on more merry-go-rounds.
I'd pick more daisies.

I would love to say that this advertisement was for Voluntary Service Overseas or Cancer Research but it was actually for a Harley-Davidson. Nevertheless, it did really get to me. No, I didn't rush out to buy a Hog but I did start thinking about who I was and what I wanted.

It's no coincidence that it was around this time I fell in love with Shiv. She was carefree, intuitive, spontaneous and she laughed a lot. I fancied her immediately but it was an office party that was the catalyst. The theme was Bollywood and she was dressed in a green sari. How could I resist?

Soon I was spending time in places other than the boatyard and starting to live like a normal person. At first I felt hideously guilty; I should be using the time to oil the decks or paint the coach roof. It felt like an act of betrayal not to be completing those jobs. Abandonment even. Yet I also felt an enormous sense of relief. Freedom ...

That year I would occasionally drag Shiv up to the boat and potter about on the last few jobs while pretending it was a romantic weekend. Sometimes it worked, sometimes it didn't, but little by little *Friendship* was integrated into our lives. Shiv was there on our first trip up the river. She was there when I first slept aboard and she was by my side when we first ran aground.

By the time Shiv and I got married, *Friendship* was undeniably a huge part of my life (our lives even) but she was no longer the focus of my free time and when we had Noah, *Friendship* dropped even further down the pecking order.

This was a strange feeling for me. After spending a quarter of my life getting *Friendship* back into the water, I was now less and less able to actually use her. By the time India was born it began to dawn on me that this wasn't going to be a short-term state of affairs.

Now we had *two* kids under three. India couldn't walk and Noah couldn't shout 'Help I'm drowning' even if he needed to. They both fell over every time the boat rocked with a wave and neither knew how to swim – hardly the ideal companions for a boat trip. Was I ever going to use *Friendship* now? Had it all been a waste of time?

Almost as bad was the fact that I had absolutely no idea what to do about it. Common sense (ugh) said I should sell *Friendship* but there was no way emotionally that I could do that. Yet at the same time, I couldn't see how we would use her enough to justify the mooring fees.

My angst over *Friendship* was mirrored by my feelings about work. Since having Noah and India, I had found life at the agency harder and harder. I struggled with the way I was behaving and more than ever before I was questioning my own value system. Nevertheless, even though my insides were churning about the person I had become, my bank balance was telling me that until Noah and India turned eighteen I just had to keep the money coming in. I was the provider so this wasn't the time to do something stupid. Instead I should be giving my career one last push. One that would see me through my forties and then I could hang on until retirement.

I was stuck, both at work and with *Friendship*. My heart

said one thing and my brain said another. After being *so* driven, for *so* long, I didn't know who I was or where I was going any more.

CHAPTER 4

If Damian's heart and brain were at odds, mine were courting, holding hands and ready to swing off up the altar. I knew exactly what I wanted – and it wasn't this.

Tidying away Noah's train set one gloomy September night, I heard the key in the front door and braced myself for an even gloomier Damian. He dragged himself in looking a particularly dark shade of grey. Almost before his bags were flung down in the hallway, our 'What if?' conversation started again. For the past year this topic had been our favourite, along with 'How much money do we really need?' Usually these talks laboured long into the night, especially after 'No Going Back' programmes on television. We rarely arrived at any reasonable conclusion. This time it was different.

'What if?' Damian proffered, swilling his red wine, staring at the ceiling, collapsed lengthways on the sofa, 'I take a year off? A sabbatical? We could go have some fun, a real reward for all my slogging at the agency. I've never had a year out, like you have. We could do some travelling. Shift down a gear or two but we wouldn't have to worry about money as I'd be going straight back to the agency afterwards.'

'Great. And come back to this again?' I sighed as I chopped vegetables aggressively in the kitchen. 'You getting in exhausted. Waiting for the weekends to live and simply existing during the week?'

'Well I'm sure it'd be quite different when we got back. We'd relax away from all this and probably return revitalised. Think of all the sex we'd have!' Damian sighed and visibly changed colour.

'What if we didn't come back?' I said, annoyed that even such a huge topic as this could be so simply brought down to sexual encounters. 'What if we just left? A one-way ticket.'

'What do you mean – one way? You mean not come back?' Damian gulped the rest of his glass, jumped off the sofa and poured another without looking.

'Well, I don't think it'd be the same if we knew we were coming back. Our minds wouldn't be open or nervous enough to enjoy it in the same way. I know you – after six months you'd be counting down to starting work. Gearing up and thinking about suits, deadlines, new business strategies. Anyway, I can't believe "they" won't contact you in an emergency to help on a pitch or something. We'd never be able to get away from emails and mobiles. You'd be sucked back into it and we'd never really be free. We wouldn't really be away.'

'Can you really imagine me leaving? I might never get back into advertising afterwards. You know what the industry is like; if you're over 35 you may as well be dead. I'm not sure what I'd do next. You've got to be really sure about this, Shiv. It can't be one of your whims. There'd be no going back.'

'I'm serious about you leaving work. For good. Not just a break. Break free. I really think it's now or never while the kids are still small. You're still young enough to reinvent your career. Aren't you?'

'We'd have to live on a lot less money,' Damian warned quietly.

'Oh come on. I've never cared about the money, have I? If anything, some of our happiest times have been when we were broke. Remember camping in Devon, swimming across the Thames in Richmond, cycling in Skye? That's what we need more of. Can't we just head off somewhere, into the unknown, with no plan and no inkling of what's to come? Something would turn up. That'd be the fun, the edge, not knowing.'

'Okay. Let's say I do leave the agency. Then what? What would we do? Where would we go? I've always wanted to live in New Zealand. How about going to live there?'

'Are you joking? I couldn't live on the other side of the world.' My mouth went dry at the thought.

'Where then? You can't keep saying we'll just head off. You've got to think about where. And why? How would I earn a living? I can't just drop out and be a hippie. What about our future?' Damian fired questions at me as if he was in a strategy meeting at work. 'You've got to have a plan. Something more concrete.'

'Why do we need to KNOW what's going to happen? Something will turn up if we believe it will. Let's stop worrying about the future.' More loud gulping of Damian's wine.

The sound of water boiling covered up the discomfort both of us were clearly feeling. Damian looked like one of those people whose home has been blown away by a freak hurricane. I was irritated at being forced to come up with a concrete plan (plans have never been my forte). So, in revenge, just to stir things up a little, I calmly dropped the bomb.

'Why not sail away on our boat? On *Friendship*?' I wonder if a tiny part of me threw down the challenge to see whether Damian would pick up the gauntlet. I waited quietly, expecting the 'Maybe in a few more years' conversation. The sensible, oldest child talking. But instead there was silence.

So I continued, the second child's voice in me goading, 'You've always said you wanted to do that one day. You've been telling me for years how perfect *Friendship* would be in the Med. So how about it? Why don't we take her there? It can't be that hard. Just because we have kids it can't be THAT much more difficult.'

More silence. Then Damian was as brave and as foolish as I had hoped he might be. 'Would you really go away on *Friendship*? She could be ready to go to sea in a few months, you know.'

'Why not? We could have some real family time before the kids have to go to school. Why worry about money and security? We could rent our house out. *Friendship* will be our home. What more do we need? A bit of food. A few clothes. I'm all for it. In fact I can see us now, sailing off into the sunset, kids running barefoot ...'

'I could grow a beard,' mused Damian. 'Just imagine. *Friendship* bobbing in the Mediterranean Sea.'

And so, that simply, the idea for an enormous voyage was spawned. I can't remember what happened to the dinner that night as excitement and nerves swamped us. By the next morning I expected that the tannins would have settled to the bottom of the glass and we'd see clearly again.

We did. It was with complete clarity that we headed out to our different lives that day, knowing that a new, more unstable world awaited us if we were brave enough to follow what we'd started the previous evening.

That morning, knowing we'd just crossed the 'What if?' line, my daily routines assumed an almost nostalgic air and I revelled in them more than ever, knowing they may soon be over. I scooted past the florist's and crossed over Chamberlayne Road all the while bubbling with suspense. I wondered whether Damian, too, was able to concentrate on the pitch he had on today. I texted him, 'I'm SO excited. Can't wait till tonight to talk more. Love you xx.' As soon as it went, I regretted it. Damian was over-exuberant at the best of times and got carried away with ideas even if he had absolutely no intention of carrying them out. Had I misjudged the situation?

I bought a large cappuccino at the Queen's Park Café, treated Noah to an apple juice and strolled over to the bandstand, where I could safely carry on daydreaming without bumping into any other mums. While Noah charged up and down the steps, India snoozed in the double-buggy, rugged up against the autumn wind, and my mind wandered.

Ever since university I had wanted to travel. So, after several years backpacking around the world I finally unpacked my case in London at a friend's place in Golders Green and joined the travel industry. My twenties and half my thirties were spent at airports as I visited more countries than I'd had boyfriends. I'd watched the sunset on Borobudur crater, canoed down the Zambezi River and camped out with the stars. I'd trekked up to 3,000 metres in Nepal, photographed lions from a hide in Africa and smelt the burning bodies in the ghats on the Ganges. I would rather have been adrenalin-rushed in New Zealand than plan a new kitchen. Pension and career plans weren't words in my vocabulary.

I always assumed I would never be rich, as earning big money was not my goal. Knowledge, experience, a life well lived – these things had always been my aims. Certainly I had always believed that if I made my decisions emotionally, everything would always be okay and something would always turn up. That modus operandi had worked for me so far.

Never in a million years did I imagine marrying an advertising man. In fact, if it hadn't been for *Friendship*, I'd have been living another life altogether. You see, I'd met Damian through work and had instantly written him off as potential boyfriend material. He was too slick, too eager to offer advice on the latest restaurant opening, too citified . . . just 'too'.

Then late one Friday afternoon as I messed with my in-tray and stifled a yawn, my eyes drifted towards a figure chatting to our receptionist. Scruffy trousers, ancient canvas shoes, a paint-covered smock and ruffled dark hair. My kind of man altogether.

Just as I was inventing a reason to visit the reception desk – a package that ought to have been dropped off perhaps – this apparition turned around. I was embarrassed to find it was none other than clean-cut Damian looking very rugged. It was only much later I learnt he was on his way to Essex to spend the weekend with his first love, *Friendship*. He clearly was not as one-dimensional as I had thought.

I became intrigued by this man. I learnt that on weekdays, he was a slick, arrogant ad-man, and at weekends he morphed into a guy who lavished varnish and love on an old wooden boat. He was a man who had dreams, who didn't seem to care about money, who had once cut off his eyelashes and given them to a girl on Valentine's Day.

One wintry, very unromantic, ice-cold weekend I finally met *Friendship*, his weekend lover. It was a look into Damian's inner core. She must have liked me too as I was invited back on increasingly frequent occasions as my relationship with Damian progressed.

Five years, three engagements (all to Damian, whose persistence finally paid off), a wedding and two babies later, I was no longer watching sunrises over volcanoes. Since changing from paid to voluntary work, or, as most people would call it, becoming a full-time mum, my world had shrunk to a microscopic area covering five by three centimetres squared on the A to Z. I had pounded those seventeen streets up, down and sideways, imbibed 840 cappuccinos, pushed my two kids at least 4,000 times on the swing, brushed my hair a handful of times and had no more than three uninterrupted conversations on my mobile.

Every morning I used to dress Noah, India, and on a good day, myself, and whatever the weather, we'd head out. Most mornings, before my coffee, my head would swirl with my 'Holy Grail' question of how to get more sleep. That quest was only interrupted by shopping lists, the number of washes I had to put on, and the odd panic about what to wear to Damian's work do and whether I had anything interesting to say when I was there.

With Alison and Sasha, two other perpetual mums (the only ones who frequented the park all year round through hail, snow and drizzle), I had passed month after month in a round of feeding times, trips to the park and changing nappies.

Was it simply a case of post-natal panic that propelled me to suggest that we should all cram onto a boat that had never been to sea and sail away with no plans and few possessions to an undetermined destination?

I don't think so. I was happy being a mum. Not happy in a skip-down-the-lane, won-the-lottery sort of a way. But happy in a deep, quiet rose-coloured-daybreak sort of a way. Having Noah and India had made me feel deeply centred and at one with the world. However, I was equally unsettled by the future. A nagging feeling at the back of my mind would not go away, even on good days. Like an ex-boyfriend loitering in the shadows.

Deep within me, I feared what might become of Damian (of us) if he continued the high-octane, selfish lifestyle of the advertising world. Somehow, the more successful Damian became at work and the more comfortable we were at home, the more unsettled I felt. I suppose we were a pretty typical middle-class family. Plastic toys piled sky-high around IKEA and Habitat furniture, Damian and I having punctuated conversations over hurried morning cups of tea, then collapsing exhausted at the end of our very different days. I guess typical would sum us up. Ordinary, conservative even.

I desperately wanted some excitement. Without a doubt, I wanted to test my theory that life with children doesn't need to be life on hold.

As I pushed Noah and India back home, I found myself praying that Damian had meant what he said the previous night.

That evening, as seven o'clock approached, Damian burst through the front door and immediately I knew it was all okay. He kissed me impatiently, thrust armfuls of books into my arms and said, 'I've bought a takeaway and a bottle of red – we've got a lot to talk about.'

As he uncorked a Rioja he started, 'Well, I've spent most of the day on the web looking up possible routes to the Med. There's the sea route, down around Portugal and through the Straits of Gibraltar. Or a hundred different ways through France on the canals and rivers only.' Damian was in his element, with Post-it notes and lists oozing from every pore.

'Wow! Do you think *Friendship* is up to the sea route? We've never taken her out of rivers. Even I know that the Bay of Biscay is the mother of seas. Do you think we could do it on our own? When should we leave?' I had more questions than breath to get them out.

'Actually I reckon we should go for the canal route and I've worked out that *Friendship* could be ready in six months but I have to give a year's notice at work. We could use the time to stockpile some money to last us the year or so that we'll be gone.' Damian was a steamroller on a downhill slope – there was no stopping him. 'I've already worked out that we could rent out the house and live frugally off the income. Then there's all the stuff that needs doing on *Friendship*. We'll have to get GPS, lots of safety equipment. That'll take a while to sort out.' He'd clearly done nothing all day but plan.

'A year? Or so? How long do you think we might be away?'

'Who knows. Once we've left we could be gone for ages. Look at this book I found about a couple called the Purdeys. They travelled around the Med for years living off a bit of writing and odd jobs.'

'Wow! Did they have children?' I grabbed the book and rifled through, looking for clues to our future life.

'Damn, they didn't have children,' I said, a little morose. 'Do you think we are being foolish going with the kids?'

For some reason the rational part of my brain, probably the part that took hold once I became a mother, began struggling with my fanciful, emotional side.

'Well, we can't really leave them behind, can we? Look at this picture.' Damian opened a page of *The French Waterways* by Hugh McKnight. Serenity beamed back at me in the shape of a still river, trees swaying gently, a lone boat and two people on deck in Seventies clothing.

'I'm being serious. Noah's what, almost two? India's five months. By the time we leave they'll still be in nappies and buggies. Are we crazy? None of these books mention children.' I'd already looked up 'Children' and 'Kids' in the indexes. 'Are we being selfish dragging them into this?'

'Remember that barge you house-sat once in Battersea? Well they'd raised kids on it and the parents said it's all a matter of training. Living on the water is no different to living by a road – you just have to teach the kids that it's dangerous. Anyway it'll be character forming for them and incredible for us.'

'I guess you're right. I'll worry about water instead of cars. They can wear lifejackets all day. In fact, they'll have to sleep in them in case they wander out of bed. We could get netting put up along the sides of the boat, fit carbon monoxide alarms, gas alarms . . . any other alarms we can find.' I had gone into safety overdrive.

By the end of that second night the number of safety gadgets we wanted had reached the hundreds and our plan was set.

In July we would leave Walton-on-the-Naze, cross the Channel into France and head southwards through the canals to the Mediterranean Sea.

During that winter we feverishly prepared the boat and ourselves for the trip. I ordered the books we would need, including a family book of first aid, a French-English dictionary and *The Complete Winnie the Pooh*. Quick-drying, non-iron clothing was hunted down, even in the smallest of sizes. I voted Le Creuset as the safest kitchenware to use on board as it's so heavy the kids couldn't possibly lift or tip it over. Stacks of paperwork were needed including passports, E11 health forms, insurance and medical papers in case we had an emergency, particularly important if anything happened to one of the kids.

I can hardly remember when Damian formally resigned but I think we celebrated with a Thai takeaway and a bottle of Chablis. He hauled *Friendship* out of the water, repainted her bottom, revarnished her hull, had canvas covers made to save her from the sunshine and spent hours at bedtime ordering essential equipment from catalogues.

India and Noah were moved into a small box room together so they could get used to the proximity of their bunks on board. Their heads would be only one metre apart, so getting used to each other's noises was imperative. Their former bedroom became the 'Operations Room' and the phone and ADSL connection buzzed through the days and nights as we flew closer to D-Day.

Damian and I passed exams in safety and survival and practised how to give CPR to an infant. We took a ship's radio course, learnt the rules and regulations for the French canal system and got a tick from the examiner on a CEVNI course (this is like a driving test for the canals – you need to know which side of the canal to drive on, who takes priority at junctions and what the signs mean).

One sweltering spring day, I spent eight hours inside *Friendship* cleaning her out and readying her to be loaded. The cabin temperature was unbearable. All our planning had been done during the winter months. The possibility of cruising in the heat had been overlooked.

After that Damian ordered even more equipment to cope with the inevitable heat of a summer in central France. Mosquito netting for hatch covers, cabin fans, lightweight tropical sleeping bags, solar showers.

I spent what felt like days on a hard chair in the Nokia shop on Peterborough High Street, understanding how to access emails afloat. It was a tricky brief. No fixed address. On a boat. Maybe France, maybe Italy, Spain or even Greece. Definitely NOT England. Megabytes, memory, download time – these foreign syllables spewed out of the sales guy's mouth. Nodding, hoping it'd all make sense, I couldn't wait to get to a real foreign country where I'd understand people.

Ten months flew by. With all boundaries pushed aside and our minds electrified by adventure, we existed on takeaways, adrenalin and a lot of Post-it notes. We were embarking on a family adventure. The way of living that I'd always imagined for us, more John Lennon and less Paul McCartney, was in sight. Having less money and more time. Being more chaotic and less aware of what might happen next. Having time to read poetry, watch new leaves blossom and play hide-and-seek with our children. More the 'good life' than the 'fast life'. I hoped the journey would bring about a 'cleansing' of our possessions. Unsurrounded by our goods and comforts, we'd soon get to our core as a couple and us as a family.

Just when my 'to-do lists' were out of control, the wall space in our house was Post-it yellow and the departure was being pushed further into summer, my dad died, suddenly and unexpectedly.

My excitement dried up overnight. My *joie de vivre* lay wasted on the floor. How could he leave now? He, of everyone, understood what we were doing, and why. He understood the time-and-money equation we were trying to rebalance. He had inspired me in so much adventure without knowing it. I couldn't possibly go now. We'd have to postpone the trip. Maybe in a few more years, I thought.

At the wake to celebrate Dad's life, a lot of whisky was sunk and even more talking was done. He was from the land of the Blarney after all. It was there, that night, that his words rang in my head. 'Don't look back. There's nothing you can change there.

Look forward. It's the future that matters.' Strange, although he loved history, he never looked back on his own past and urged us to do the same.

I knew then that we had to go. I had to carry on, for him as well as for us. He'd have been so disappointed to look down and see us still in port.

Those last few months are blurred. I must have ticked a lot of things off my lists, probably forgot a few too. We threw a leaving party. I cried a bit but felt pretty angry too. Not sure why. Maybe because my dad wasn't around to send me off. Whatever it was, the emotions were heightened by the imminent pressure of departure.

By the time we eventually set off, India was 15 months old. She couldn't walk but crawled like an SAS guy on an obstacle course. If we didn't watch her every moment she'd be likely to get into hot water or, worse still, canal water. When she was tired or hungry or both, or, come to think of it, just whenever she felt like it, she screamed like a banshee and flailed her limbs furiously and mercilessly. She was likely to go off for the most innocent of reasons – like not being able to lick the last mouthful from her yoghurt pot, being passed the wrong-coloured beaker or not liking the length of the grass. She was still very much a baby with an unrestrained, crooked-tooth smile when she wasn't pouting or fuming about some minor error we'd made. Her clothes were smeared with the day's adventure, giving her a grubby 'don't get too close to me' appearance. Rather haughty too though, with killer rosebud lips and huge mahogany brown eyes.

Noah was two and a bit when we set sail. Sturdy, blondish hair and a real man's man. He still had that sticky-out tummy like a malnourished African village kid. But he could at least aim daytime wees (and worse) in the right place (more or less) so we didn't need nappies for him (one thing off my list).

Noah was obsessed with diggers, books and making things. And un-making things. He could look at Richard Scarry books for hours, yet spend no more than a few seconds concentrating on any practical function, such as washing his hands. He could ferret out a hammer from our best hiding place and mess spectacularly with any equipment in his reach. He knew the difference between a flathead and a Phillips screwdriver. He, too, wanted to do everything himself. He loved collecting bits of piping, stones, anything someone else had discarded, and wouldn't part with them for weeks. Within feet of his bunk on *Friendship* would be the GPS, ship's horn, ignition keys and wheel. I could only imagine what horrors lay in store for us.

He also woke like clockwork at 7 am and had *never* slept in, which I wasn't sure was going to fit into our new life.

And so it was, finally in mid-July, our kids only slightly more grown up, and me only slightly less angry, that we crammed our life, our undies and our hopes into *Friendship* and left the shores of England seeking adventure. My heart bristled with emotion. From happiness or sadness, I can't really say.

CHAPTER 5

Eight days into our voyage and still only just past Watten, I grudgingly accept that we aren't going to be listening to birds singing and the gentle lapping of waves on the canal bank. Instead, as I sit in the cockpit with India on my lap, all I can hear is our engine and the sound of rain drilling onto the coach roof.

Brum-brum-brum-burumm-brum-brmm-brmmm-brum-burumm-burumm-brmm-brmm-burumm-burumm-brmm-brmm-burumm-burumm-brmm-brmm-burumm-burumm-brum-brmm-brmmm-burumm-burummmm-brmm-brmm-brmmm-burumm-burumm-brmm-brmmm-brum-burumm-burumm-brmm-brmmm-burumm-burumm-brumm-brmm-brmm-burumm-burumm-brmm-brmm-burumm-burumm-brummm-brmm-brmmm-brum-burumm-burumm-brmm-brmmm-burumm-brum-burumm-brmm-brmmm-burumm-burumm-brmm-brmm-burumm-burumm-brmm-brmmm-brum-burumm-burumm-brmm-brmm-burumm-brmm ...

'... ing ...' says Shiv from the wheel.

'WHAT?'

'I SAID ... IT'S ... RAI ... AGAIN.'

'I CAN'T HEAR YOU OVER THE SOUND OF THE ENGINE – CAN YOU SHOUT?'

'I *AM* SHOU—!'

'WHAT??'

Damian and I battle through what feels like 'old people's conversation'; the sort that couples have who are both going deaf, when they have been married for 50-odd years. Although I'm shouting, a sudden surge of love and admiration for Damian rushes through me – an image of the two of us flashes through my head, 40 years hence, married forever, still yelling at each other over the top of a boat engine.

The rain continues its merry drumming on the canvas cover of the cockpit. Thank goodness Damian lugged it on and off the ferry at Calais. Like a dead body he had carried it for miles when I had, eternally optimistic and at the same time completely unrealistic, insisted on dumping it in England with the famous last words, 'There won't be that much rain, we'll probably die of the heat.'

Huh, just as well Damian rarely listens to my advice.

Perhaps we brought this whole weather thing on ourselves. What were we thinking, setting off in a wooden boat, jammed with supplies to withstand a siege, with a boy called Noah?

Brum-brum-brum-burummm-brumm-brmmmm-brum-burumm-burumm-brmm-brmm-burumm-burumm-brmm-brmm-burummm-burumm-brmm-brmm-burumm-burumm-brum-brmmmmm-brmmm-burumm-burummm-brmm-brmm-brmmm-burumm-burumm-brmm-brmmm-brum-burumm ...

So it goes on for hour after hour. The monotonous thumping of the big diesel engine is drowning out all conversation ... all thoughts ... all sanity. What was a reassuring and steady throb on the English Channel has turned into a form of torture in the silent and still environment of the canals.

The engine isn't the only thing we've suddenly realised is less than perfect. The bed has also turned out to be a complete pain in the neck – and not just literally. Every night I have to assemble it from nine different pieces of wood. Every night I make a mistake and have to start again. It's worse than an IKEA flatpack.

Then there is the oven. I say 'oven' but it hardly lives up to the name. The whole thing, including the two gas rings on top, is smaller than the microwave we used to have at home. All our trays are too big to fit inside it because Shiv didn't think to test them out before we left. I've learnt that if a meal can't be made in two pans, it's not worth cooking. To my surprise, even I'm getting bored of spaghetti bolognese and tuna pasta.

The 'wardrobe' is also proving a frustration. This is a long locker that lies *underneath* one of the bunks, so even getting into it is a palaver. The clothes for all four of us are in here so we've tried to impose order by using colour-coded bags. (Mine are all blue, Shiv's are red, Noah's black and India's are yellow.) Clever in principle, but every morning I end up having to open *all* of my blue bags to find what I want. To make things worse, Shiv continues to find it impossible to put *away* any of her clothes, so there are loose knickers and tops everywhere . . . it's driving me crazy.

Then the water keeps running out because we are using far too much. It also smells if we forget to add the purification tablets . . . I won't even go into the fact that my back aches because I have to walk with a stoop inside the cabin (I'm just one inch too tall to fit snugly beneath the roofline). Or that there is a burgeoning dirty-washing bag that hangs in the shower area. Every day it looks more like a boxer's punchbag and I have to duck around it just to get washed . . . And what about the lack of visibility because of the bikes and buggies on the front deck? Or the fridge that has already proved to be far too small? Or the . . .

Uh-oh. Time to stop. It's easy to get caught in a spiral of negativity, especially with the constant rain. Living like this should be absolutely awful. The kids should be screaming, Shiv should have left me and I should be regretting the loss of my expense account. But strangely it's not like that. There have been good things about the boat too.

Shiv's book-storage idea has been a hit. We knew that books would be a great form of entertainment on the boat;

they take up very little space and keep Noah and India occupied for up to ten minutes on a good day. Before we left the UK, I spent hours in my shed creating special shelves that tuck between the mahogany and oak beams in the cabin roof. They have enabled us to bring over 20 large-format children's books with us, something for which I (and the kids) give daily thanks.

The plastic step up to the Porta Potty (made out of an upturned orange crate) has been life-changing. It means Noah can now go to the toilet on his own. It also has the double advantage that it can be hosed down (as he frequently misses the target) and it can be unscrewed from the floor if the boat starts sinking and we need to get into the bilges.

Then there is the padding in the forepeak where the kids sleep. This bit of the boat is surrounded by pieces of wood that protrude in all directions to support the roof, anchor, mooring posts and bulkheads. I once spent three months stripping back and varnishing this whole area to turn it into a minor showpiece. Now, to prevent the kids banging their heads, I have had to cover everything with foam. I suppose the fact that India hasn't split her head open compensates for all my previous hard work being completely hidden from view.

Finally there is the 'diorama'. Our beautifully varnished mahogany engine cover now sits underneath a large piece of laminated card. On it I have created an aerial view of a village complete with railway track, pond, houses and roads. The children love it, even though, at just under a metre tall, Noah can barely reach it and India is so small she has to be sat on top of it.

Feeling more upbeat, I look around me at Noah and India, having fun as only kids can: making a den out of the laundry pile. Shiv's at the wheel, taking photos every now and again, quietly smiling to herself and scribbling random thoughts in her notebook. And me? I'm just relieved. Relieved that we're here and that finally we're doing this. But I'm not relaxed yet. I guess I'm still feeling ... uneasy.

It's only been eight days since we left England but it feels like months. This is partly because every single part of our new life is different and partly because I'm doing everything I can to completely reinvent who I am. The thing I want to focus on is living for the moment, instead of constantly planning and building for the future. I've set myself goals for the last 20 years (rebuilding *Friendship* being a major one), so now I want to be more free. To let life 'happen'.

I'm not finding it easy but one significant step forward is the fact that I've decided not to keep a ship's log (Shiv's going to keep a diary though) and am refusing to do any more than take a cursory look at our charts or guidebooks. We're not in London and we're on a canal heading vaguely south. That's as much as I need to know.

What I could do with is a guidebook on the parenting front. It's a real struggle learning how to be a 'Daddy who is at home'. I'm no longer restricted to bedtime kisses and pushing prams at high speed on a Saturday to make the kids scream and squeal in delight. Now I have to be responsible and think about mealtimes, nappy changes and spare beakers of water. Maybe I've just swapped one kind of planning for another ...

I'm shaken out of my thoughts by a sudden crash. All the noises on the boat are still new and unfamiliar so I'm not sure what has happened. This one sounds like a huge sack of potatoes has fallen onto the floor except I know we don't have enough room to keep a sack of potatoes. There is only one other answer – Shiv must have hit something.

'I knew I shouldn't have left her to her own devices,' I think to myself. She has the spatial awareness of a teapot and is still very nervous at the wheel (even though all she has to do is keep us in a straight line). I rush forward to see what has happened and it's at that moment I see Noah crumpled in a heap on the cabin floor. He's not moving much. Even I know that's bad.

I feel sick. While Shiv has been steering, I've been 'in charge' of the kids. I'd only left Noah on the bunk for 20 minutes but he's already fallen off and hit his head. I can't see any blood and pray that he will start screaming. All I can remember from the first-aid course we went on is that screaming is a good sign – it means the patient isn't slipping into unconsciousness. On cue, the screaming starts. As I try to console him, I wonder why this racket could ever be interpreted as a good thing.

I check his head for damage but can't see any obvious cracks or gushing blood so I think he's just had a massive fright. However, this isn't going to stop him becoming absolutely hysterical and I'm sure Shiv will be too if she finds out what has happened. Luckily, the engine is drowning out all the screaming so I may get away with it. Then India joins in with her own wailing. It seems that while I'd gone to check on Noah she'd crawled into a tangle of ropes in the cockpit and now she is stuck. She looks like Houdini in a nappy. (I'm sure Shiv left the ropes lying around earlier. Her messiness may send me over the edge.)

Both kids are crying at the same time and it's about the tenth time this has happened to me in the last hour. As I gather them up in my arms and try to remember the words of Humpty Dumpty I realise how naïve I was before we left when I'd told Shiv's friends how much I was 'looking forward to spending so much time with the children'. I'd even said that I thought 'being on a boat would simply add to the fun'. Now I understand why they had all looked at me with that contemptuous 'just you wait . . .' expression.

For the last two years I have done what all fathers seem to do: I've blithely dished out advice to my wife on how to be a better mum. You know the kind of stuff: 'John's wife said to try this' or 'Andrew said that this always works'. I never had a clue whether they were right but having built a career on talking very confidently about things I didn't know anything about, I was sure the same rules would apply to parenting. What an arse.

Now that I'm in the same boat as Shiv (so to speak), I find that if she even so much as *thinks* about offering me advice

on how I should handle the kids, I want to rip her head off. Fortunately, this time Shiv has wisely decided to say nothing as she watches me clutch our two sobbing children out of the corner of her eye. She is still at the wheel but I can see she is biting her lip. She's obviously resolved not to say anything about my inability to watch the kids properly. She knows she doesn't need to say a word; she has said it all too many times already. I guess when it comes to being a mum, I'm a slow learner.

After the 'incident' that Damian thinks I have missed, he takes the wheel for a break while I set up camp on the foredeck – at least there I can pretend it's peaceful. Noah and India are glued to my hip. As their sobbing subsides, we all gaze around at our moving world of trees, cows and the odd crane. They slowly inch away from me, continually checking on their lifeline – me – their constant in a new world.

It's soothing being here, at the furthest point away from the engine. Like being on a very slow train. The soft thrum of the engine lulls me into a catatonic state.

Leaning back against the canvas, I feel my body giving in to tiredness. India wriggles on my lap, chewing the ends of my hair. Noah spins one of the bike wheels. The tyre is slowly rubbing the skin off my leg. I barely notice. I am exhausted.

It took me ten minutes to get here from the cockpit as I had to hold Noah's hand first, then strap him to a bike lock in case he fell overboard. Next I returned for my tea and wedged it in a bike basket so Noah couldn't knock it over. Lastly I carried India. I unlocked Noah and finally reached for my tea. It reminds me of that puzzle we used to do as kids. A river to cross. One boat that can carry only two people. A fox, hen, a cabbage. I'm definitely the cabbage.

'What a lovely scene,' Damian yells forward above the engine noise as he snaps a photo of us. I'd like to throttle him as I sip cold tea. Not least because I'll look dreadful in the picture.

Damian is steering, still wearing that hideous white vest and has now added to the 'vagrant look' with a wide-brimmed white hat. I'm sure he's having a quiet crisis about leaving work. It has started with his clothes. Guess I should be thankful it's not leather trousers. I must remember not to take too many photos of him in that vest.

To distract myself from Damian's outfit, I pick up the Navicarte guidebook again and point out things along the way. I've been swotting up at night as Damian is feigning a lack of interest in where we are or where we are going. We could just as well be in Outer Mongolia as far as he's aware. I almost feel as if I have to remind him we're in northern France. Very unlike him.

We're travelling on the Aa au Grand Gabarit, which means large-gauge waterway. It's a wide canal that's been made for big commercial barges. With grey-white concrete sides, it's certainly not pretty but Noah is entranced.

The canals in this region get lots of polite lines of sympathetic copy in the guidebooks but they seem to miss out on the limelight. Their crime, it seems, is that they are too dull, too grey, too industrial. Everyone who's anyone heads south for the Burgundy-soaked wine trails – they do not waste precious time here. To me, however, as yet uncorrupted by the class system of the French canals, this is a brave new world. It's *all* worth a look. The derelict factories and former glories dotted along the canalside are enchanting simply because they aren't lined up on Cricklewood Broadway. Location is everything and here, too, it seems to be true.

Just like in Cricklewood, the kids are smiling and occupied. Location doesn't seem to matter to them. India is now chewing her way through her safety line. Noah looks at ease, mesmerised by the moving scenery.

We're nestled together on the foredeck, which is about six feet across at the wide part, narrowing off to a point at the bow of the boat. Relaxing here is tricky, as shoehorned into this space is all the paraphernalia we need for the trip that can't fit below deck. If you saw us from the air, it looks like we are marooned on a roof in a flood, an odd selection of salvaged possessions around us:

- Two new bikes lying on their sides (these and shanks's pony are our only transport on land).
- Two Maclaren buggies.
- Two baby seats to carry the kids on the back of our bikes.
- Two baskets for the bikes to carry shopping back to the boat.
- An inflatable dinghy for when we reach the Med and anchor off in small coves.
- A buggy board for Noah so we can, at times, use only one buggy.
- A spare anchor in case the main one gets ripped off in a storm (at sea, of course).
- Green canvas boat covers that are damp, smell of mould and are covered in slime around the edges.
- An eight-metre-long wooden oar, as recommended by some boat club member who travelled the canals previously. Goodness knows why on earth we might need it.
- The boat's mast, which had to be taken down so we can fit under all the bridges along the canals.

Months ago I had made the decision not to question Damian's judgement on kit and where it should go on the boat. It gave me free rein in the galley and with my personal stuff: my guitar, yoga mat and oil pastels. I could see right from the start what pleasure he took in selecting and ordering boat bits. Now I feel like I'm living in an overstocked junk shop.

I watch Shiv in the bow and I get a touch romantic. After so many years slogging away, trying to bring this old wreck back to life, it's an incredible feeling to be in France watching my wife and kids scramble over the foredeck. They look so relaxed and happy. I'm overwhelmed by a sense that *this* is what life is all about. Everything else will sort itself out ... this is special. Being free, being able to enjoy time together, being at one with nature. Just the fact that we are travelling at four miles an hour means we have the time to unwind, time to think, time to take in more of the details around us.

Farmhouses, black-and-white Friesian cows grazing, a church spire behind a hill – these all glide slowly past. Trees are spaced ten feet apart along the canalside. It suddenly looks quite bleak as a cloud passes in front of the sun; a landscape that was riddled by wars still holds some of its solemnity in the air.

'Bois du Ham is on our left.' I point to a wooded area on higher ground.

'What that Mummy? Budderham? Is it a cow?' asks Noah, looking into the distance, searching for cattle.

'Bois du Ham. It means Ham Wood in French.'

'Hamoodinfinch?'

'No. Ham Wood.'

'Hamoood. What's that?'

'A wood made of ham.'

'Can we have some ham, Mummy?'

'Aaaammmm,' joins in India.

'Maybe for lunch.'

'When's lunch?'

'Damian, do you want to swap again?' I plead.

'No, you enjoy it. Just relax,' he says, without comprehending my desperation. At this rate we shall be divorced by three o'clock this afternoon.

As I watch Shiv in the bow, I realise that all the people I love most in the world are crammed into a space just four foot square and my thoughts turn to the dangers of taking two children who can't swim on a thousand kilometres of French waterways. After a few moments of tortured images, I console myself with how much I have done to make *Friendship* the most child-friendly vessel in France.

For a start, all along the sides of the boat there's netting that makes her look like some kind of lifeboat (which I quite like, by the way). This means the kids can't fall overboard without climbing up the side rails and making a desperate lunge (something I'm sure they have considered more than once already).

I have also bolted a long strip of webbing to the decks.

Whenever Noah or India want to go up to the bow they have to be clipped onto the webbing so they won't fall in. (Fine in theory except the straps are constantly getting tangled, meaning that quite often at least one of our children is strung up like a Christmas turkey, crying for help.)

If the kids *do* fall overboard, they will probably die. Neither of them can swim and they aren't big or strong enough to clamber back on board. To make things a *little* safer, I have attached a rope all around the outside of the boat, just above water level. If one of them *does* fall, they can grab onto the rope to save themselves. At least that's what I'm hoping our two-year-old and sixteen-month-old would have the presence of mind to do if they fell in.

Falling into the water isn't the only danger facing our children. Simply getting around the boat is enough of a challenge for India. She's still at the stage where she can only walk if she's holding onto something so throughout the boat there are now handholds set about two feet up off the floor. These are actually towel rails from IKEA that India can grab onto and walk the length of, before reaching out for the next one Tarzan-style.

My mind wanders like this all the time, especially now that we are pottering along a canal that is nothing more than a straight, watery line through endless fields. It's only when I look up that I see Shiv is looking tired and fraught.

'Shall we call it a day?' I ask. 'We've travelled a full ten kilometres. Let's look for a mooring where we can spend the afternoon and kip down for the night. After all, we've got no deadlines, nowhere we need to be.' I revel in trying out what is new vocabulary for me.

Fifteen minutes later we arrive at Port d'Arques, a basin under a bridge off the main canal. It's full but we are told we can squeeze on the end of a floating pontoon.

By using our rubber fenders like a protective shield, we bounce along the pontoon without doing any serious damage to the boats around us and then pull into our allotted space with only minimal risk to life and limb. As a bonus, we only

have to shout at each other a few times so we're obviously getting better at this.

Surprised and pleased by our success, I make an athletic leap off *Friendship* to tie us to the mooring cleat. This turns out to be a big mistake, one that I appreciate only when my feet hit the wooden pontoon. As soon as I land, I'm bounced back into the air at horrific speed. I have just turned the whole pontoon into a massive diving board. Only a large motor cruiser saves me from going into the canal (if hitting the side of a boat at great speed can be regarded as being 'saved').

After Damian's trials for the high-board diving team, I realise being moored on the end of a pontoon means we won't be able to reach an electricity point. Our cable is too short, even though Damian bought the longest one in the shop, about 30 metres. Which means no fridge again. No cold milk. The look on my face mustn't require translation when I reach the capitainerie (an office in the marina where the guy in charge hangs out).

The capitaine hands me a *ralange*, an extra-long lead that'll reach to the electricity. I thank him profusely. Never thought I'd be this ecstatic over cold milk.

Later I'm glad I didn't have a tantrum over the *ralange* as I discover that the capitaine is in fact Mr Action Man from Phnom Penh. A boating Bruce Lee with a glamorous wife. Tall, slim, arched eyebrows, mascara and pressed clothes, she exudes welcome from every pore. They are a photogenic team. They met in the city of Amiens 18 years ago at the dance hall where her granddad taught her to rock and roll. How exotic they must have looked way back then, swinging to Glenn Miller. I wonder how they ended up opening a marina and whether they still dance at night.

The canals seem to be a magnet for people we'd never meet at home. I wonder whether we'll become more like them – more odd – as our new life flows into our system.

It makes sense to stop here and get a decent night's sleep.

Not only because we're both a bit frazzled by the newness of everything, but also we need to prepare ourselves for the infamous Les Fontinettes lock, just a kilometre ahead. It's a lock so big that it has become a local tourist attraction.

I don't want Shiv to know it, but I'm nervous about Les Fontinettes. We haven't done many locks yet and still we haven't got the hang of them. My stomach turns at the thought of making a mistake in a lock that is bigger than most office blocks.

My plan is to get up very early and try to pass through the lock before the kids awake. At least then we'll have two fewer problems to deal with. However, if something *does* go wrong, I'm not quite sure how we'd get to the kids' bunks, wake them up and get them to safety before the boat is dragged under by the swirling currents in the lock. It crosses my mind to make them sleep in lifejackets but I realise they might not respond too well to this.

Damian seems tense. To take his mind off tomorrow's big lock, I suggest we unload the bikes and explore the area. After half an hour of huffing, lugging and clicking kids' bike seats together, we are ready to depart. We follow an overgrown cycle track along the canal to the town of Saint-Omer. An odd place by all accounts; apparently many people there continue to speak a local Flemish dialect of Dutch and still wear the traditional costumes.

Damian is silent and I'm sure he spends the entire three-kilometre cycle-ride visualising each and every moment of tomorrow morning in his mind instead of noticing the things around us like the two swans that glide past, necks long and eyes low over the grey canal.

Once in Saint-Omer, we cross back into our previous world – the one on dry land. Over the centuries, the town has been fought over by the French, Flemish, English and Spanish. These days they probably fight for the best deals in the Vodafone shops, parking spaces in the square and the attention of the waiters in the restaurants.

In the town square we settle into a frontline staring spot in the Au Spiey Brasserie, ordering omelette and frites. I hope the kids will eat it. In fact, until recently, India has existed on a ridiculously organic, home-made diet of Annabel Karmel recipes. I don't think she's seen a chip before.

'Here's to surviving another day,' Damian toasts with his glass of Saint-Omer beer.

'Here's to our kids being alive,' I joke, meaning it more than he can imagine.

The tension in both of us is palpable. We're still not sure whether we're enjoying this journey or not. Being in charge of the kids as well as handling the boat – it's giving me a daily headache. And Damian too, judging by the speed at which he reaches for the plonk at night. I feel like someone on *The Apprentice* – fully qualified, pretty competent at the outset – who is shredded by Sir Alan Sugar's tasks. The kids don't swear like he does, but by golly, life on *Friendship* is equally as testing.

Later that evening, beers drunk, slightly mellower, we cycle back 'home' with a mild breeze on our faces. India is snoring in her bike seat behind me, her tiny hand firmly gripping my fleece in her sleep. Ahh, now this is starting to feel like an adventure, a life away from London. As the night claims the towpath and turns the canal water into shiny glass, we bundle the kids into their bunks.

Exhausted, we do not bother to make up our own bed. It's too much hassle and neither of us wants an argument now. I sleep on the port side and Damian throws the cushions on the floor and crawls into a sleeping bag. Tomorrow we face our first huge lock and our fears, but tonight we need sleep and no rows.

The sun has just come up and we are about to set off when I have a desperate urge for a pee. It must be the nerves. Having just emptied and cleaned our Porta Potty, I don't want to start refilling it straight away when there is a perfectly good toilet I can use in the capitainerie so I jump off the boat and run over.

It's early, around 6.30, so the capitainerie is locked. Instead I dart over to the woods at the edge of the picnic area and

begin to relieve myself against a tree. At almost the same moment a Labrador appears out of nowhere and begins sniffing my leg. I can hear its owner fast approaching.

I imagine the impending scene: me unable to stop peeing (I'm absolutely desperate) while the owner fights to pull away his dog, which is still frantically pawing at my leg.

I decide the only course of action is to start walking and pretend that I'm not urinating at all but have just popped out for a stroll. This proves quite difficult as I have to push my way through thick undergrowth at the same time as aiming straight and shaking the bloody dog off.

'All right?' asks Shiv when I get back on board.

'Yeah, fine,' I reply.

I daren't tell her that I have been peeing all over my leg for the last five minutes.

I didn't sleep a wink last night. Damian was snoring (which he only does when he's drunk) and the tropical sheets, made from shiny man-made material, kept sliding off me onto the floor, on top of Damian. My body feels like I have been beaten up. Everything aches.

But I'm ready for this lock. I have been creeping about since six o'clock making cups of tea, trying not to wake Noah and India with every creak of the floorboards. If we are to get through this lock swiftly, we need to be at the lock gates for their first opening at seven o'clock.

Before we get to Les Fontinettes, we pass the lock it replaced. Its massive iron structure, looking very sorry for itself now, reminds me of an abandoned Yorkshire mine. According to Shiv, who has read all about it, the old lock was built in 1887 and is still regarded as an absolutely remarkable piece of engineering. Effectively it was a giant set of hydraulic scales. Two enormous water containers sat beside each other and when one was filled with water and boats it lowered to the bottom of the hill, thus pushing the other uphill. Simple.

At least it would have sounded simple on paper when its

English designer first presented the plans, but the reality of building it was a different matter. The lock was longer than a football pitch (much longer) and a full 11 metres wide. The holes for all the machinery had to be dug out with spades and the earth shifted by wheelbarrow. It took hundreds of men working ten hours a day, six days a week, almost four years to build (reminds me of working on *Friendship*). Tragically, after all that effort, it now lies abandoned – replaced in 1959 with a lock of more conventional design. Somewhere deep down inside me, I think about all the niggly problems we have had with *Friendship* and hope that the same fate won't befall her.

I'm glad it's 2005 and that it's the new, fully automated lock we're about to enter. No men heaving and sweating. Just us. Sweating, that is. The light drizzle adds to my sense of foreboding – things always feel worse in the rain.

A monstrous grey barge called *Organza* is lying ready to enter the lock. She motors ahead – eight times our length of metal slides past us. Then *Luchar* follows, another giant, bumps into *Organza* and spews out a churn of smoke and fumes. We hover tentatively in the river, building up a head of nerves to enter the lock. We back off. Although this lock is capable of taking six barges we shall wait till we're on our own.

Finally it's our turn. No-one else is in the lock so we motor forwards with trepidation. Les Fontinettes truly lives up to its reputation. It's absolutely enormous. Two huge towers reach into the sky on either side of the entrance, making it look like a fortified castle. The difference in water levels is almost 14 metres but I couldn't get a feel for that when Shiv read it aloud from the Navicarte. It's only when we gingerly enter that I begin to understand just how deep that really is. As I look up, I have to lean backwards to see the top and almost fall over. *That's* how high it is.

It's like entering a very, very realistic film set for a *Star Wars* movie. Remember the part where they are all left in a giant metal rubbish container, and then the sides begin to squeeze together? Well, as I hold onto the rope, tightly securing the middle of our boat to a metal bollard embedded in the lock wall, I imagine the last breath being forced out of my lungs. Whatever the phobia is for being stuck in a metal walled space with water underneath, I've got it. The dark black gates heave closed behind us with a long, slow screech and a beeping sound begins, like a truck-reversing sound.

I'm gripping onto the wheel so hard I'm cutting off my circulation. I want to be absolutely ready for when the water rushes into the lock and *Friendship* is thrown about like a scene from *Perfect Storm*.

After a couple of minutes I wonder if something has gone wrong with the lock mechanism. Then I realise that we are actually gliding upwards. Yes, 'gliding'. For all its brooding presence, Les Fontinettes turns out to be the easiest lock we've come across so far. The bollards we're tied onto inside the lock are rising with us, meaning there's no messing about with ropes or adjusting heights and panicking about getting lines knotted. Shiv and I don't even have to scream at each other (much), although I suspect this is because the combination of the early start and our nervousness has exhausted us.

Forty seconds later we arrive at our new altitude, having travelled thirteen and a bit metres upwards. I peek into the forepeak and find that Noah and India are both still fast asleep. It's just after 7.30 am.

After the drama of Les Fontinettes, we shuffle on through scenery that is pleasant, although it certainly wouldn't make the tourist brochures. We're in the Parc Naturel Régional de l'Audomarois. It's an area of marshland, tamed through drainage by the monks centuries ago. Now birdspotters and small towns rub along in harmony with nature and farmers alike. I pop down below for mugs of tea, bread and jam, and shrink-wrapped chocolate croissants (the kind that will last for 20 years).

Low grass hugs the banks and attempts to cover the concrete edges. Beyond are lines of trees, deep green, and fields. Grey herons add grace to the landscape as we chug on past. The monotony of the scenery suits my mindset today. I couldn't cope with too much excitement right now. All our focus is on the boat, how it works, handling the kids on board – all inward-looking. We are learning so much every hour it's exhausting just being on the move.

We keep motoring as we're embarrassed at having only moved ten kilometres the previous day. The kids are still asleep, and it's now just past eight o'clock in the morning. By the time we get to our third cup of tea, both of us are on deck, enjoying being together without the need for chatter, Damian resting one finger on the steering wheel and me staring out at France. This is the loveliest moment we have had together since we left England.

An hour later and I have India asleep on my lap. Noah is now hooked on to the safety line, wolfing down croissants and slurping milk from his beaker.

'What's that, Mummy?' he asks, pointing to a derelict factory with a metal chute overhanging the canal. Before waiting for an answer, 'Look. A crane!'

This is far better than a *Noddy* video. Even *Bob the Builder* will have a tough time beating real cranes, monstrous barges and people waving. The pace is so slow that Noah gets to look at the same crane from different angles for at least five minutes. That's a long time for a two-year-old but for Noah this is like surround-sound television. In fact, it's like being in a live show. A cross between *Thomas the Tank Engine* and *Know Your Dilapidated Building*.

Past Béthune it starts drizzling again, just light stuff, but it means Noah is now in full rain jacket and trousers and India in an all-in-one rain suit. India wants to put it on and as soon as it's on, she wants to take it off. Great game and one that occupies me for a good hour while Noah sits harnessed on deck watching tractors and an odd assortment of farm machinery go by. I've never seen him so absorbed and quiet for so long, so I take over at the wheel, while India nestles down below back in bed, clutching her bear and muslin, rain suit firmly on.

Our next stop is a rather practical one. Shiv has declared there's a supermarket ahead, right next to a mooring point. I can't think of many better combinations so we agree to rest there and stock up with as much as we can carry. Which basically means as much as *I* can carry because Shiv will be laden with India in the pram and Noah on the buggy board.

A pontoon situated within sight of a huge supermarket is like finding El Dorado. The exercise of getting vast amounts of tinned food from an out-of-town supermarket and onto *Friendship* has already proven tricky and time-consuming without a car. I'm determined to take advantage of this opportunity and load *Friendship* to the gunnels with food.

I'm quietly concerned that Shiv happens to be at the wheel when we arrive. A prime spot like this will be packed with hire craft and people on boating holidays. Will she be able to elbow her way into a space? Will she be quick enough? Should I take over? Maybe not. I don't want to shatter the fragile confidence with the boat that she has gained over the last few weeks. Maybe we'll be lucky and no-one else will be there.

As we round the corner, I realise there will be fierce competition for the prime mooring spot. I can see one pontoon, one mooring space and two boats steaming towards it. Then there's me.

Suddenly the gentlemanly pace of the canal is charged with a Formula One frenzy. I can almost hear the crowds cheering, the revving of the engines, see the chequered flag as we all put our foot down to get to the pontoon first. Beyond lies Intermarche, a supermarket so close you can wheel the trolley right up to the boat.

My nerves are on edge. I'm terrified of pranging *Friendship* and so far have only relaxed when steering in a straight line.

This manoeuvre, however, requires a turn to port. The pressure's too much. I bottle it and hand over the wheel, too late, to Damian. We lose out by a whisker to a German U-boat. Well actually it's a German boat doing a U-turn. Begrudgingly we tie up close behind them, our stern line far out on the bank, tied to a line of railings and a tree branch. We have to pray that a large boat doesn't pass whilst we're inside shopping as our stern might bash into the concrete bank. It's worth the risk.

Once inside, the pressure subsides. Noah and India shriek hysterically as between us we push two trolleys around every aisle. Tins of cassoulet, fresh baguettes, tubs of Petits Filous, rosy apples, a sack of potatoes, dozens of bottles of wine, tinned peas, pasta and rice are all grabbed off the shelves.

India prises her way into the Petits Filous. I pretend not to notice as she smears her way through four pots. Noah chases imaginary flies with a red plastic fly-swatter. India starts hollering so I grab a yellow one for her and plonk her on the shiny supermarket floor.

They look like kids with Attention Deficit Syndrome, crawling and chasing up and down aisles, blotched in yoghurt. Sometimes it's such a get-out-clause being a foreigner – thank goodness the English are expected to be eccentric.

Somewhere in between the bread and cheese, India takes two and a half wonderful steps on her own from the trolley to Damian. Not quite the romantic image we want to pass down through generations, India making her first burst for independence in the aisles of a supermarket, but it's a memory that shall be treasured alongside the image of our ADS kids.

All 187 euros' worth of shopping are loaded on board. There isn't enough space for it all so we have bags of food hanging off the rear deck and vegetables in baskets on the coach roof. I wonder if they will attract rats? Best not to think about it. Let's just eat them quickly.

Damian coaxes me to take the wheel again to get over my

nervousness of *Friendship*. Noah and India's need for me is inversely proportional to the amount of food they have in their stomachs. Now, full of baguette and yoghurt, they will stay down below with Damian and will not pester me.

So far they don't really like being left in any part of the boat without one of us. I guess it's still a strange environment for them. I suspect Damian has been finding it quite tough too, dealing with the kids' everyday tasks like feeding, sleeps, bath and playtime. I'm sure it will be good for him to have some happy, calm time with them. So far, whenever he is 'in charge', the kids seem to fall, yell, scream – anything that can be performed loudly. Playdough should help – they are always happy when that comes out.

I watch in a daze as Noah sticks playdough in the gaps behind our bunk and India grinds the rest into the seat covers (on exactly the same spot where she poured her Weetabix and milk this morning). I'm like a broken man watching my life's work being destroyed in front of my very eyes.

I realise how displaced I'm feeling at the moment. I'm not quite sure what I'm supposed to be doing, which is an odd feeling for me. I'm slowly accepting that I have just thrown away the whole edifice of security and self-confidence that I have carefully built around me for the last 15 years. I've gone from being a big cheese in a big job, with people who listened to me and respected me, to being a bumbling father who isn't quite sure what he's doing and who even a two-year-old finds quite easy to ignore.

In my head, Shiv and I have always been on a par. Yet when I watch Shiv deal with Noah when he refuses to eat, I marvel at how calm she is. When I see her handle India when she's scared, I wonder why I'm never quite as understanding. It's just so obvious that she's been a full-time parent for two and a half years while I've been playing at it over the weekends.

Take this very moment, for example. Shiv is at the wheel, handling a 32-foot boat while drinking a mug of tea and

navigating our route. Meanwhile, I'm on the floor of the cabin struggling to keep our children from destroying everything around me.

One of us is doing a good job and it isn't me.

CHAPTER 6

Light fades and the rain clears – the clouds clot into soft grey-white clumps blocking out the blue behind. Signs on the canalside come into view for Lille and beyond, rather like motorway signs. Lille, Belguique one way. Douai, Valenciennes the other.

We're following the Canal d'Aire and caught up in the realisation that we're in Europe. No edges, just one country easing smoothly into the next. I just want to keep moving, not sure why as we don't have any deadlines, and nowhere we need to be. It's addictive, watching the distance build up. Damian is so used to moving fast that I suspect, only once we're several hundred kilometres into the journey, will he start to unwind.

Tonight he seems very quiet and pensive. He hates not being the best at things and he's clearly finding each day quite tough with the kids. For my part, sympathy seems hard to muster – he may finally understand just how hard it is to look after children. And, best of all, that steady stream of patronising advice he used to dish out to me in Queen's Park seems to have dried up.

It's raining again. This is starting to feel like a caravan holiday in Wales. I know we are only 60 kilometres from Dover but because we are in France, I had imagined it would be sunny every day.

Shiv is studying the charts and suggests that we forgo the

Canal du Nord as it's supposed to be a lot more commercial, and instead head for a place called the Bras de Paillencourt. It's a bit off-piste, veering away from the linear canal we've been on, but Shiv reckons it's worth the detour.

'In the guidebook there's a little château symbol, a church and two towns, Estrun and Paillencourt, plus lots of wiggly waterways and a large water basin. It looks inviting,' she declares.

I'll never understand how her mind works. She hasn't even considered checking for water taps, fuel supplies nearby or the depth of the mooring.

'Sounds good. As long as there's power and water we could spend a few days there,' I say diplomatically.

'Why not?' agrees Shiv. 'It feels like our kind of spot. Away from the big barges on the main canal. There's a playground only minutes from the boat.'

Always the mum, I think to myself. Shiv thinks about the kids without even realising it. I can't imagine ever being like that.

The basin is a fascinating place (with an electricity point and water tap, so Damian is happy). Nothing much now, but oh, what a past. Le Bassin Rond, where we are moored, is more like a lake than a canal. It's about 90 metres wide and several hundred metres in length. It could accommodate hundreds of barges in its heyday, between the two wars.

There was money to be made then and life sprung up with the speed of seedlings after the first spring rain. Crammed around the water's edge, 28 bars buzzed night and day, servicing the clientele from the barges. Three restaurants fed bargemen looking for a break from their own cooking. Two ballrooms held the itinerant community on festival days, a hand-driven organ providing dance music. Two cinemas showed the latest films every Thursday, in a matinée and an evening show.

It must have been the Notting Hill of the region. Lovers must have revelled in the lightness and joy of the place. In winter, when the canals were frozen, barges would have been stuck fast and men would pull up tables and chairs on the ice to play cards outdoors. Ice-skating and jollity ruled again.

I *love* being here. It's the first place we have moored where I can almost smell the way life used to be lived on the canals.

Now the barges have been superseded by high-speed delivery trucks on motorways. The road is king and has pushed barge transport out to the fringes. There is no sound of dancing, the organ has stopped grinding. But if I squeeze my eyes shut, I swear the chatter and buzz of café society by the water's edge resonates from the glory days.

It's not just Shiv. We are all charmed by the Bras de Paillencourt. Shiv loves the history, I love the rusting barges that still line the edges of the basin and the kids love the café we visit each morning because it has a funny French squat-toilet.

Despite the constant drizzle, we stay for several days and discover other joys. My highlight is discovering a plaque on the wall of a château, dedicated to an RAF fighter pilot (Michael H. Shelton) who died in the town during the Second World War. Who was he? What did he do? Why was *he* so special when so many thousands of other men also gave their lives in this area? There are no answers to my questions.

Shiv's highlight is the row of fading black-and-white pictures that line the side of the Basin. Each depicts life here as it used to be and she is captivated by the images of old men in long beards, dungarees, pipes and hats. I aspire to look like this myself by the time we reach the Med (apart from the dungarees, of course).

Noah's highlight is finding a snail on the pathway near *Friendship*. He is so worried about it 'getting home' that for 30 minutes we have to follow its excruciatingly slow progress back to the safety of the grass verge.

India's highlight is discovering the goat that lives in the field behind 'our café'. Every time it moves, snorts or looks at us, India waves and giggles in delight.

When there are no creatures to watch, we escape the rain by spending hour upon hour in the Café des Sports in Paillencourt. Noah scribbles on the Rapido betting slips, India crawls under the Formica tables, getting filthy and trying to chew the cigarette butts strewn on the floor.

A television in the corner shows the Tour de France and the whole bar is engrossed. The clientele consists of us, the bartender, his chain-smoking wife and two boys drinking beer, their noisy motorbikes resting outside.

It's not where we would choose to be normally but the weather is dictating where we spend our time. It seems to be affecting every part of our daily lives. Not only are we losing whole days in strange bars, it's also making life on board even tougher. For one, we don't have a washing machine and certainly not a tumble dryer. We are reliant on the sun to dry our clothes. So, after four days of rain we are running low on clean things to wear. I had imagined long lazy days of scorching heat, living in a bikini, without worrying about the laundry. How could I have forgotten that Damian was an ad-man when he sold me this dream?

In a rare pocket of sunny weather, proudly I hang my underwear to dry. A long row of white boxer shorts now dominates the line that I have just strung from the radio aerial on the cabin roof to a bicycle wheel in the bow. I have been waiting for this moment for quite a while. Before the trip I bought a whole new set of underwear from a specialist traveller's shop in London because it promised to 'wick moisture' and 'dry quicker than any other material'. I figured this could only be a good thing on a boat with a washing-line that is only seven foot long.

Shiv didn't welcome my new underwear with the same enthusiasm; before we left the UK she contrived to tell everyone we knew that I had been buying 'quick-drying underpants'. I cannot begin to explain the misunderstandings this led to. Now at last, however, with only sporadic opportunities to dry any of our clothes, my foresight and ingenuity can be demonstrated to one and all. I know it's sad but I'm fighting

the urge to text my friends and tell them, 'quick-drying under-pants are the future'.

I wish I had wicking underwear too – a sure sign of how low I have sunk (though Damian loves the fact that I have now run out of knickers).

The kids live in full rain suits, our shoes squelch with damp and our faces are washed pale with the insistent drops. I can't remember having days like this when we lived in a house. Now, on a boat, after weeks on end with every view swathed in drizzle, I wonder exactly why we are doing this.

'I think we should head south,' proclaims Damian loudly one night as we listen to the rain on the cabin roof. 'It's already late July and it should be hot now. I'm pissed off with this bloody rain.'

Hugging him tight, I agree, and immediately we ready the boat for an early start the next morning.

That night we are all woken by the sound of powerful engines and splashing water. A large motor cruiser decides to moor right next to us. The whole basin to go for and they come right alongside. I poke my head out and see a German flag fluttering on the stern. 'Right,' I think to myself, 'two can play at that game. You just wait till morning . . .'

At first light we set off. The alarm clock we have brought with us (in the form of two small children) is beginning to pay off. I gun the engines and smile to myself as I think of our neighbours regretting their decision to disturb our peace last night. I decide to power across the end of the basin in a large, loud arc.

It's when I'm about halfway across that I realise I'm not going to make it. I slam the engines into reverse but it seems to take an age before we lose our forward momentum and come to a halt. I now face the prospect of a 15-point turn to get out. I throw the boat backwards and forwards but we continually end up in the same place. No matter how much the boat turns when we go forward, it always straightens up

again once we reverse. I can't work out what is going on until from the dark recesses of my mind I dredge up the memory of 'prop walk', a technical term which means the boat turns one way far better than the other, particularly in reverse. What I have just discovered is that *Friendship* can't turn to the right in very small spaces. Oh great. Several hundred miles ahead, countless small marinas, hardly any experience between us and now we have to avoid tight right turns.

I whip the wheel round to the left and we slowly loop back to where we started. We pass within a couple of feet of the German boat and see its inhabitants are now all on deck, bleary-eyed, wondering what the hell we are doing. I'm not quite sure what to say, so I wave ... smile ... and then ram down the accelerator.

We steam on towards Cambrai, a large town where there is hope of a launderette – and dry clothes. By then we'll need diesel too. In the rain I get lost in my own little world. The thing is, I'm really missing England – my old daily life seems so dreamily easy and comfortable compared with this. Damian, I suspect, is wondering how on earth he will manage without burying one of the kids under a patio. Luckily *Friendship* doesn't have a patio.

The countryside isn't monotonous but it doesn't change much either, so it comes as a huge injection of excitement when we sight our first lock of the day. It's an excuse to rush around like headless chickens for a few minutes and get the adrenalin pumping. Maybe I am missing the on-the-edge-of-the-seat-tension of work after all.

We scrape against the walls on our way into the lock, shout and blame each other, then snap to a stop as the mooring lines stretch tight. At that precise moment of confusion and chaos, we are surprised by two men who look down at us from the top of the lock.

It might be the funny angle or the fact that they don't look as pale and pasty as I do but they feel threatening. I dismiss the thought and mentally note that being with the kids all day is making me paranoid. I'm turning into one of those mums who worry about absolutely everything and see everyone around them as a potential danger to her brood.

In a stout attempt to regain my manhood, I salute the men with my friendliest wave and shout 'Bonjour' in the deepest voice I can muster. The men look back at me in silence and then the largest of the two pulls a courgette out of his front pocket. It's huge. I have never seen a courgette like it and he's holding it as if it's the weapon of choice in these parts.

Slowly (and sinisterly) he points at the courgette and then at me. At the same time he says something in a deep voice (much deeper than mine) and then contorts his face into an ugly smile. I nearly wet myself.

All I can think of is the movie *Deliverance*, the only film I have ever seen about people going up a river. As I stare back at the man with the huge courgette, my mind is filled with images of inbred locals, duelling banjos, buggery and squealing pigs.

My fear is compounded by Shiv shouting eagerly, 'Oui, oui monsieur, bon idée'. It takes me a second to catch up with what's going on (Shiv's French is much better than mine). These two are in fact the lock-keeper and a mate, who are keen to sell us the produce from their garden. Once I have worked things out, I overreact and in my embarrassment buy more courgettes than Tesco could sell in a week.

I guess I simply got caught up in the moment. Far from being threatening, this is the stuff of my most romantic dreams about the trip – buying home-grown food from the locals at picturesque little locks. It's enough to make me want to crack open a bottle of wine there and then.

By midday we've moved only five kilometres, notched up 40 corrugated roofs and twenty-three courgettes. Being on red alert about the kids the whole time, as well as the restless nights on our spine-killing bed, means I'm already tired when we reach another lock. I look in the guidebook, which informs me of a 3.94-metre rise.

After the excitement of the 'courgette-lock', Noah and India are both determined to stay put on deck throughout the manoeuvre. I'm not sure how to manage both of them on deck, unattached to me, while I race from bow to stern handling several ropes simultaneously. Worried that something dreadful might happen to them, I realise that concentrating on their safety as well as the boat's is overload for me right now.

Deciding that it's better for my nerves to risk a screaming fit, I return Noah and India to their cabin below and rush back up on deck to help Damian. In their bunks, secured behind the netting I can hear India kicking the sides of the hull in frustration. Noah is making 'dee dah' sounds with his fire engine. At least they are both safer down there than up here with me.

As the water fills the lock and we rise to the top, I come into eye line with a fat, haughty man, sporting a peak cap emblazoned with the Dutch flag, leaning over the railings, puffing on a cigar, eyeing Damian with sympathy.

'Your wife is stressy, yah?!' he says, with a knowing wink to Damian.

My insides surge, Incredible Hulk-like, into a raging river of emotion. Part of me wants to burst into tears. The other part wants to shove this bloke over the railings into the swirling water below. I am so angry I want to scream out loud, flailing my arms and legs like India does. I wish I was two and could have a tantrum. How satisfying that would be. Instead, all I can do is simmer while the lock doors engage and open in slow motion, let go of the ropes and pull the wet ends back on board, all done under the smug gaze of the fat man.

As soon as we are out of earshot of the lock, I explode at Damian for going into the lock so fast, for not waiting for me to get the kids down below, for not punching the lights out of the fat Dutchman. My ranting and raving is a very satisfying, if juvenile way, of releasing my anger about the haughty Dutch man. Damian simply stands, stock still and silent, staring at me. At once, with sudden clarity, I realise that the fat man is right. I am 'stressy'.

After Shiv's little fit, we leave the lock and she grabs the wheel, announcing it's her turn again to steer. By now we have both learnt that the only way to get any peace on the boat is to be at the wheel. It means you can't look after the children and you don't have to talk to anyone either. This is because the best way to steer *Friendship* on the narrow canals is to stand on the wooden battery box and poke your head through a hatch in the cabin roof. We've realised that from this position above the roofline, not only do you have a perfect 360-degree view of the world around you but you're also cut off from the din below.

Underneath the level of the hatch, all hell could be breaking loose (and generally is when I am in charge), but the person at the wheel hardly even notices it. The best bit is that even if the screaming of the kids (or each other for that matter) *does* intrude, you can't do anything about it because you are 'driving' the boat. It's the perfect excuse to cut yourself off and we both cherish it.

I knew perfectly well what Shiv was up to when she grabbed the wheel. The Dutchman was right. 'Yah, she *is* stressy.' She's also tired, fed up and frustrated but at least she's wearing no knickers.

Two hours later, still fuming about the Dutchman's comment, we pull in to the diesel pump at Cambrai Basin. A beautiful cream-painted wooden yawl pulls out and delicately motors down-river.

'C'ést fini,' shrugs the thin capitaine who is leaning against the diesel pump, chewing gum and checking us out, eyebrows raised. 'You must wait till our next delivery. Probably in three or four days.'

'Bloody hell. That's all we need now. Snooty Dutchman, rain and now no fuel,' I snap and slump down on the engine cover, shoulders hunched.

I gaze over longingly at the yawl again, sat low in the water with 'our' fuel, puttering quietly southwards. At that moment, the rain takes its cue to double its pressure on my hat so I duck down below the soaking canvas covers, leaving Damian to secure our lines. It looks like we'll be stranded here for several days. If this rain continues, I might well be on the next train home. It's only a couple of hours back to England.

I climb back on board feeling like a drowned cat. India and Shiv have been smart enough to go below but Noah is still sitting on the engine cover. He wanted to watch me tie the boat up. By now I'm furious that we're going to be stuck here and rage about the diesel pump to my son as he is the only person who'll listen.

'What is the point of having a sodding diesel pump if you don't keep it full of sodding diesel? I mean how hard is it, for Pete's sake? Bloody incompetence if you ask me. Surely all they have to do when they see that it's getting low is give Esso a call. Then surprise surprise, the next day a bloody great tanker comes round and drops off another 30,000 gallons of the stuff. It's just irresponsible. People shouldn't be allowed to have sodding diesel pumps if they can't sodding manage them properly. Drives me bloody mad . . .'

Noah gazes at me quietly with his big blue eyes and then says, 'Can we go to the playground now?'

CHAPTER 7

**The less than promising start to our arrival in Cambrai is
mitigated by the marina itself. It's enclosed by wide banks of
freshly mown grass and enormous willow trees on one side
and a large cobbled quay lined with bars and restaurants on
the other. At the far end is the capitainerie and, joy of joys
for Shiv, a brand-new shower block. This is the answer to my
prayers. It might be the very thing to lift us out of our gloom
and get us back on track with this voyage. I scoop up India
and Noah in my arms and tell them that we're going to
explore while Mummy has a bit of time to herself.**

While Damian drags Noah and India around the marina following a great Horner family tradition of admiring moored
boats, I sprint through puddles on cobbles to the capitainerie
office to buy tokens for the *douches*. My excitement is uncon-
tainable at the prospect of an endless hot-water shower without
Damian yelling, 'Shiv, what are you doing in there? It's been five
minutes already. Think of the water you're wasting.'

The modern shower block is a hedonistic blend of sparkling
tiles, porcelain and glass. Space to run around if I fancy it, tonnes
of hot water, mirrors I can see my whole body in, and, best of
all, I'm alone. That's one of the advantages of being a woman on
a boat. Because we seem to be a rarer breed on the water, the
women's facilities are nearly always clean and empty, whereas the

men's are usually tired, with a queue for the shower.

Damian, I know, is doing everything he can to make life more comfortable for me on *Friendship*. But honestly I don't think he can ever understand how meagre a two-minute shower is, cramped into a 'coffin-sized' bathroom, when you're a woman. Like my sisters, I have yards of long hair to wash, armpits to shave and legs to loofah.

Where am I supposed to stretch out to apply my body cream? Or examine the growing crow's-feet around my eyes? Or check if my eyebrows need plucking again? He thinks I am above all that beauty stuff. He's never realised I do it all in secret. It's impossible to have any private bathroom time as negotiating limbs, wax strips and a mirror with the doors closed in our tiny space is nigh-on impossible. Plus the fact there's always: 'What's this for, Mummy?' as Noah holds up a tampon or India scoots off with my toiletry bag and chews the end off my only lipstick.

Standing with my back luxuriating in the searing hot power-shower, I relish the healing water running down the plughole, taking with it much of my tension, and I give in to my exhaustion. With the loosening of my shoulder blades comes a realisation that I have been edgy most of the time since we left England.

I scan the moorings and note the boats that are most interesting, most unusual and most demanding of my attention. Apart from the usual selection of white fibreglass motor cruisers (nothing more than floating caravans), there is a long, traditional English narrowboat in immaculate condition (how on earth did it get across the Channel?), a converted Torpedo cruiser (flying a British flag), a characterful old beast called *Tinker's Tug* and an immaculate barge with deckchairs and flowers all over it called *Chouette* (either it's a hotel barge or they're absolutely loaded).

The highlight of the marina, however, is an incredible 'gentleman's cruiser', a smaller version of the boat that Tony Curtis used to seduce Marilyn Monroe in *Some Like It Hot* (surely you remember the boat?). This one has a beautiful hull with a mahogany cabin and teak decks. Inside, it's filled

**with plants pressing up against the windows and I also count
seven cats and two pigeons. We head straight for it. I carry
India while Noah holds my hand and sets a quick pace. They
can't wait to see the boat with 'the jungle inside it'.**

Fresh from the benefits of my therapeutic shower and 15 minutes
on my own, I step cautiously back on board *Friendship*. There's
a beep from my mobile, which startles me. I was beginning to
think it was broken.

'Sorry to miss your call. Feel weird and sad that you aren't
here.' It's a text from my best friend, Caz, in Hertfordshire. A
dreadful sense of loss washes over me as I read the words through
watery eyes. Loss of my old life, my friends, my family, my dad,
my independence. Tears well up and spill over quietly as I stand
in the cabin doorway dripping in rain again.

When Damian returns, he rightly thinks some terrible news
has burst through from suburbia. When I explain, he sighs.

'Listen, why don't we eat out tonight and celebrate?'

'Celebrate what exactly?' I say as the rain trickles down my
back under my coat.

'The fact that the mobile works. The fact that we're in a place
with a Lidl just 100 metres away. The fact that I haven't worn a
suit for over a month . . .'

I chuckle, duck down below to dry off and as evening falls on
our first night in Cambrai, we troop off together to the promise
of the town centre.

**'Did you know that the Germans occupied Cambrai?' I say
to no-one in particular. I know Shiv isn't listening. 'What's
incredible is that right here, where we are walking, is where
the British used tanks for the first time to break through the
enemy lines.'**

'Can we see the tanks, Daddy?' asks Noah hopefully.

**'They're not here any more. We can pretend the buggy is
a tank if you like.'**

'Yeah!' cries Noah.

I race the buggy up the streets, pretending to be a German

invader, blasting fake bombs out of pretend guns. I'm desperate to liven things up a bit. Shiv is obviously feeling low but at least India and Noah are now squealing with joy.

I find a pizza restaurant which is warm inside (perhaps the one thing in its favour) and we hang our coats up to dry. Noah is quickly absorbed in drawing a tank on a serviette while India is chewing her muslin so I jump off the deep end:

'You okay?'

'Not really,' Shiv sighs.

'I don't know what it is.' More sighs. Damian takes a huge glug of his wine and pushes my glass closer to me.

Hot tears start streaming down my cheeks and I blurt out, in no particular order, my well of emotions.

'I'm finding it really tough. Claustrophobic even. Having no space. Physically and mentally. The boat seems so much smaller now. We seem to be on top of each other 24/7. It takes us ages to make up the bed every night, there's no space to chill out and I can't stay in the shower for longer than two minutes without you yelling at me.' I pause for breath, snuffle up some tears that have run down my nose and continue.

'We're arguing all the time. At every lock. Every mooring. Every moment of the day seems to create tension between us.' I pause and sip my wine, which sears my dry mouth.

Damian's facial features have frozen.

Christ ... Shiv's falling apart and I hadn't even realised. Perhaps I shouldn't have joked so much about the knickers. I knew she was a bit down but I'd blamed it on the rain. I guess I hadn't really thought it through. I imagined a good shower would solve everything. I suppose I always assume Shiv will be fine whatever we do. She always seems so strong and independent.

Now I feel bad; guilty for dragging her through this. It's supposed to be a magical time but it's not. It's turned out to be exhausting, stressful, emotional, frustrating and hard

work. The worst thing of all is I don't see how it's going to get any better.

Damian stares in silence into his wine glass, probably wondering how we are going to manage this life for months on end. Then, in a way only a man can, he offers me a barrel-load of practical solutions.

'Well I think, first of all, I need to sort out our bed. You're right, it takes far too long to put together every night. And if you want to call your friends I can always go out for a beer in the evenings. Also, I must take the kids off a little more and give you a bit of space.' I'm racking my brain for ways to cheer Shiv up. I revert to what I do best.

'I'll make a list of the things I can do to make the boat feel more spacious. It's probably a good thing we're forced to stay here for a while. It'll give us a chance to take stock.'

I go quiet again. I've been so busy with my own problems handling the kids, I hadn't noticed Shiv's crisis. I think radical thoughts. Should we turn back? Should we go full throttle for the south and the sun? My head is spinning.

Later, I lie in bed for hours wondering and worrying. I'm sure Shiv is doing the same but we're both pretending to be asleep.

The next morning Damian is a worker ant, a Trojan with a Protestant work ethic that wins medals. Whenever Damian is stressed, he defaults into producing order around him. He is great at taking control, making lists of jobs and ticking them off one by one. I feel a wave of sympathy for him and, even though it's raining again, I determine to be more positive. There's no better way to forget about the eternal, infernal rain than by focusing on Damian's lists.

Having spent most of last night making lists, I turn breakfast into a blizzard of ideas and suggestions. 'The first thing we have to do is make the boat a nicer place to live in. We should

take advantage of being in a decent-sized town with facilities, water and electricity. Why don't I scrub the boat clean, especially the galley and bathroom, while you find a launderette and sort our bloody mountain of washing. Then we should reconnoitre the area; locate interesting places to visit and most importantly of all, find a café for a stonking morning coffee. We should also see if there is a playground or slide for the kids. Indy will be beside herself if we can't find one.' I pause, realising that I sound as if I am back at work again, firing orders and not letting anyone speak. I shut up but rather than getting angry with me, Shiv quietly gathers the mounds of dirty clothes and puts raincoats on Noah and India so they can face the pelting rain once more.

Feeling forlorn and guilty, I turn to the bathroom, although I use the term 'bathroom' in the loosest possible sense. It's best described as a small cupboard with a sink, toilet and shower inside. It measures four foot by three and a half foot and I can't stand up in it because of the slope of the roof.

Before we left, I spent months trying to make this space workable. The door opens outwards to maximise space and reveals nothing less glamorous than a plastic Porta Potty (extra-large deluxe model in grey with white piping – nice). We had to go for a Porta Potty as, unlike boats on the sea that discharge their 'waste' directly overboard, on the canals we have to 'store things up' until they can be emptied into a toilet at a marina.

Above the toilet is a small window that was intended to let in light and fresh air but so far has proved more useful for passers-by to peer inside while we stand naked in the shower.

To the right of the door is a sink. It's the smallest one in France. You can barely get two hands into it at once. Above it is a mirror. The only one on the boat and it's also tiny. I can just about see the whole of my face in it but not much else. Next to the sink and pathetic mirror is the shower. This is a little more impressive than the rest of the 'bathroom' as the floor of the shower is handmade in teak and looks like it's been stolen from a posh London flat (except that it's only two square feet).

To get round the fact we can't actually stand fully erect in the shower because of the low roof, I have attached a plastic fold-down seat halfway up the bulkhead (wall). This means we can sit down quite comfortably while we shower and then fold it away afterwards. A neat solution, I thought, and one that I first came across in a disabled toilet on the Isle of Wight (no, I don't know why I was there either). Finally, for creature comforts, there are a couple of Tupperware boxes on a shelf for us to keep our toiletries dry.

So all in all, it's not a big space but it's fiddly to clean; full of edges, curves, shelves, hooks and small corners. I get out the Cif and a green scourer and make a start on the shower. Best to leave emptying the Porta Potty until last ...

Quite sneakily I have pulled the 'weaker sex' card and feigned lack of strength for carrying the Porta Potty. As far as I am concerned, no lady should ever, ever have to even think about cleaning out one of these. It should remain one of life's little mysteries as to where the contents go. So, although we have been egalitarian about the jobs, with me sometimes refuelling, Damian sometimes cooking, I revert to type and tackle the laundry pile.

I slew two bulging bags of dirty washing into the buggy on the bank and hitch on the buggy board. Noah walks, holding onto the string of the washbag ('helping' is how I put this to him), and India stands on the buggy board, unable to see through the laundry but clinging on for dear life. In this precarious position we all move like one giant hermit crab looking for a warm shell to live in.

Pushing my cargo uphill away from the marina and towards the town, we pass a dog-grooming parlour, an artisan boulangerie and then stop for breath in front of a tall grey stone church, Eglise de Saint Géry.

My dad's name was Jerry and seeing this church, with the same name, seems to be some kind of sign. For the past few days I have been thinking about him and wishing he was around to talk to. I struggle over the wooden doorstep with washing, kids and all, glad of the gloom to disappear into. Inside I light a small red-cased candle for my own Jerry and think back on life and my family, the Galvins. As I stare into the slim fragile flame, I realise how lucky I am to have this open-ended time with my own, new family; how brief life is and how I should be revelling in every second of our incredible journey.

The stale, cool, incense-tainted air seems to drive calm into me with every breath. The past few weeks, I tell myself, were bound to have been the toughest as we adjusted to life on board. Where have my *joie de vivre* and usual optimism gone? There and then, a resolve grips me to make the most of the trip, to be happy, to shake off this anger and gloom that seems to be hanging over me. I even pledge to take up jogging in order to get off the boat and make some space for myself.

'Mummy, is Jesus going to wash our clothes?' asks Noah rather too loudly.

Restored to my French world, we stride out to the light and bump the buggy board and laundry noisily down the stone steps in front of the church. I draw deep on the fresh air and make a mental note of the kids' need for proper religious education and my need for running shoes.

It's no use, I've cleaned everything else. The time has come for the dreaded task of emptying the toilet. Usually this job is preceded by Shiv saying something like this: 'Damn, the toilet's overflowing. And Noah's just had a wee all over the floor. Please can you sort it out? Thanks.' (Noah's 'aim' still needs work – something I am trying to teach him with the utmost urgency but it's difficult knowing how best to pass on this art.)

For me, emptying the toilet is fast becoming the worst thing about the whole trip. It involves unclipping the top half of the plastic toilet (which is the water reservoir for the flush) and taking the bottom half (the waste tank) to the nearest lavatory where it can be poured down the loo and flushed away.

It all looked so simple in the brochure but ten litres of excrement weighs a ton and often I have to carry our stinking tank several hundred yards from our mooring to a marina clubhouse. This would be fine except for the fact that as I walk along, the water in the tank starts to slosh about, slowly building up momentum as it rolls from side to side in a wave formation. (If you have ever carried a cup of tea very far you will know the effect.) The further I have to walk, the bigger the wave becomes until eventually it starts to burst through the lid on the top and spill over my hands, splash down my legs and trickle into my sandals.

Horrible though this is, it feels like nothing compared to the nauseating experience of arriving at the bathroom of the clubhouse, opening the tank and waiting for my family's waste to glug into the toilet. It comes in fits and starts depending on what is inside but all of it stinks. I simply stand there, my back aching, holding my breath until it's over and desperately trying not to gag.

Then I am washing, flushing and bleaching before dragging the clean, new tank back to the boat, ready for everyone to fill it up again with indecent speed. Is it any wonder that I insist on us using the toilets in bars and restaurants at almost every opportunity?

The moment the job is done, I lock up the boat and hare up the hill into town. Unexpectedly, I see Shiv coming out of a church, looking like a vagrant with her buggy full of dirty clothes. Oh no, have we sunk that low? Then I notice that she's beaming and happy. Has she turned to God? Either that or she bumped into Daniel Craig in there.

My new-found inner happiness expands when I see Damian racing up the hill towards us, even more so when he offers to take the kids for a while. Then, miraculously, around the corner from St Géry's Church, a gift from heaven awaits. A launderette.

Few pleasures in our new life are better than the sheer luxury of clean, dry underwear. None of the guidebooks mention there's a haven on Rue de Victor Hugo. One with crunchy dry air, filled with the slow, tumbling repetition of machines whirring that lull you into a warm sense of security. It's womb-like and comforting.

Hours later and I am still cross-legged on the floor, with my back to the wall, in peace and solitude, lost in my new book *The Seven Roads to Happiness* and listening to my underwear drying. There's a rustle from my left and suddenly I realise I am not alone.

Oh God. Some bloody pervert is here watching my undies too. I hope those lacy black ones aren't in this spin. Hopefully Damian's wicking pants will scare him off.

The rustle turns out to be the owner of the launderette filling up the washing-powder dispenser. Not a pervert. Just a middle-aged, hunched-up bloke with thick glasses that rest on his shiny nose. He is clearly dying for a chat. Probably doesn't have many women in here for hours on end. Come to think of it, no-one else has been in here all morning.

We get around to talking about the journey on *Friendship*. I describe the weather we've had, how we have all run out of clothes on the boat. How I am a lady and I can't go around in a waterproof coat for days on end. He seems quite impressed with my French, although it might be the wide range of sexy underwear Damian persuaded me to buy for the trip. But this is France, the land of the mistress. Surely he must be used to a surfeit of fancy underwear.

'Cambrai has been famous for making lace since the four-teenth century,' he tells me as I pile up my dry knickers non-chalantly on a bench. He shuffles over to me and sits down carefully within inches of them.

'In fact, it's fine linen, cambric, was used to make beautiful lingerie,' he adds. Clearly he's spotted my pink ones. Am I ever going to get out of here?

It's now been three days since our first day in Cambrai but already we seem to be happier. It's amazing what clean under-wear and an empty Porta Potty can do for contentment on a boat.

Since we've been forced to spend time here waiting for the fuel, we've made endless walkabouts and are now getting to know the people on the other boats. Every single one has a story to tell: Bob used to fly Vulcan bombers; John was a jeweller at Hancocks, the place where they make the Victoria Cross medal; Horace was a naval bomb disposal expert; and the man on the traditional narrowboat is supposed to be a spy but not surprisingly we never see him. There is a worrying military theme here but it's the owner of the 'boat with the jungle inside' who trumps everyone else. She is Countess Tatalini, a woman who used her influence and a 16-cylinder Bugatti to drive downed pilots from France to the safety of Spain in the Second World War.

I can see why all the boat owners love it here. Cambrai is a tight, friendly mooring. Everyone has time to chat and to show us around. In 'normal' life we'd have nothing to bring us together but being on boats connects us. It's uplifting to be in a community like this and be part of something. I can almost imagine staying here.

With no locks to manoeuvre through, no noisy engine to shout above and hot showers within easy reach, 'staying put' begins to be good for us. We start to relax and find new ways of doing nothing. Mostly we spend hours messing about with the kids, inventing games. One day when we finish our picnic lunch on the grass by *Friendship*, I move away the plates and plonk Noah and India on the picnic blanket. Then I grab one end of it and run like hell.

They are both thrown backwards and hang on for dear life as the blanket slides across the grass, slithering like a car on ice. I don't think I have ever heard them laugh so much, so loudly or for so long. It's the most beautiful sound in the world and I spend the next hour running through the grass pulling them behind me until eventually I have to stop because either they are going to throw up or I am.

One mat. One bit of grass. Two kids. A dad who can spend some time with them. Maybe this is what the trip is all about.

Our days slow down and some of the tension seems to slough off Damian and I as we hang around the marina, laze on the grass and play with the kids.

'D'you know what?' I say to Damian one night as we both read in the soft cabin light after dinner. 'I really like it here. I'm beginning to love the simplicity of our new life, obviously apart from the fact that I'd kill for a washing machine and tumble dryer.'

'Really?' says Damian. 'You're not just saying that to make me feel good?'

'Really. I think I'd got hung up on the idea of a sun-kissed dreamy cruise along the canals. You know, like all the books we've looked at. I imagined being in my bikini all day, drinking red wine on deck in the evenings, kids playing on the banks till all hours. I think I've been focusing on the wrong stuff. That's what you expect on a holiday. But this isn't really a holiday, is it? We're in a strange uncharted zone. We are always passing through places. The boat is our home, stability and our roots. Our community is the boats and the people we find in the marinas. This isn't a holiday, it's just life.'

'Hmmmm. I think you've lost me,' mumbles Damian.

'Well, what I mean is I'm starting to really enjoy the daily rubbing along with people. You know, just moseying around the marina chatting to everyone, having cups of tea. It makes me happy. Having time. Having time together as well. As a family. Being, not doing.'

'It's odd to have time, isn't it? I keep feeling like I should be doing something big. I can't get used to the fact that I've got nowhere to be, nothing to do, no deadline to meet. It feels odd, a bit debilitating. I feel a bit disconnected with life,' admits Damian.

'Dame, maybe we needed to cut off from all those things in order to connect again ourselves. The two of us. And to connect with the people around us. To appreciate the small things. The human kindnesses that don't feature on the daily news or in dramatic tellings of great journeys. I think we'd lost those moments in our crazy-paced lives in London.'

'Well I know I can start to feel boat life seeping into my veins. There's definitely a change in us both I think.'

This is how we while away our nights in Cambrai; pontificating about our life, wondering where we'll end up. Mentally and physically.

One morning, many deep conversations later, we hear that the diesel tanker has arrived. We have no idea why it has taken so long to replenish the pumps and we haven't felt the need to ask, but now that the diesel is here, we know the time is right to leave.

We are a hive of activity on board. I scurry around filling up water tanks, solar shower bags and scrubbing down the deck, making the most of the endless water supply. Shiv tidies away clothes, sorts Lego and packs away food.

The moment we depart the marina I feel a sense of loss. At the same time as wanting to explore what lies ahead, I miss the comfort and warmth of what we have just left. I wonder if this is how it will always feel on the canals. Everywhere is home yet nowhere is home. It sounds wonderful and magical (which it is) but it's also very disorientating and even quite sad.

I suppose it's a good thing the diesel has finally arrived as any longer and we may have ended our journey here in Cambrai. I wave goodbye to the Russian countess with a kind face, to John and Val on *Tinker's Tug* and to our neighbours on *Chouette*, the smart hotel barge. They seem to be waving rather too enthusiastically, probably relieved there'll be no more screaming and giggling on the banks. Cambrai Marina can breathe a sigh of relief and settle back into its leafy shaded torpor. As we set off again, I feel invigorated and positive. Cambrai was good for my soul and my inner garments. For the first time on the journey we've truly relaxed and opened our minds to a different way of passing time.

CHAPTER 8

After 11 locks, it feels like we've moved a long way but we're just 18 kilometres south of Cambrai. I'd forgotten how slow travelling on the canals can be. Towards the end of the day, I insist that Shiv steers us out of a lock on her own for the first time. So far she has only steered *Friendship* on the straight stretches. I know she's nervous but it'll be good for her confidence. I've come to realise that I cannot keep *Friendship* in pristine condition while we all live aboard. I'm going to have to give in and let Shiv have more control of her (well, maybe just a little bit).

My stomach is in knots, not because I can't handle our boat but because I'm absolutely terrified of damaging her. She is like a precious, restored, antique chair. One I would never, ever choose to sit on, scared that my childhood clumsiness would return.

No matter what Damian says, he will wince in pain at any undoing of his work. I take a deep breath, grip the steering wheel too hard and motor out a little too fast from the lock, bouncing rather too much off the fender that Damian holds to cushion *Friendship* from an encounter with the metal lock gates. Damian glances back at me from the side-deck and gives me a thumbs-up sign. My shoulders relax.

I stupidly insist on steering us into our next mooring on the banks near Vaucelles Abbey. The water level of the canal is high here, which means it's hard to tell where the water ends and the grass verge begins. At an angle of about 45 degrees, I approach the bank, feeling a bit too confident that I know what I am doing.

All too fast, the section of the bank I am aiming for disappears under the bow of the boat. I freeze, my hands locked on the steering wheel, unable to turn either way. Damian starts hopping up and down, shouting directions from the bow and pointing.

'Right hand down,' he yells. 'I said, *right* hand down,' he repeats, this time a little more desperate and a lot louder.

While I try to work out what he means, there is a painful crack of wood on concrete from our port side, followed by a never-ending scraping sound. I feel sick.

I feel sick. To me, the sound of the iron pilings on the bank ripping into the wood and varnish is like fingernails scraping down a blackboard. I leap onto the grass to inspect the damage. The varnish on the plank, low down just above the waterline, has been slashed open. I can see the bare wood. It's gnarled and splintered where the iron has bitten into it. The poor wood. The poor, virginal wood. Wood that hasn't seen the light of day since it was cut into planks by David and I and then lovingly drowned in 23 coats of varnish.

I could murder Shiv.

Instead, I decide to remain motionless. If I see Shiv right now, I'll do or say something I'll regret. I'll just lie here on the grass and wait until I calm down. I look again at the gash in the varnish. It looks worse than a flesh wound. This has gone right through the muscle. The pale iroko wood looks like bone. Bloody Shiv. Why does she always have to be so damn reckless and independent? She *never* listens to me. I was telling her in perfectly simple terms how to steer into the bank and she wilfully ignored me. Christ, it was all so much easier when I was at work. I used to dish out orders and people simply followed them. I scream silently inside my head and continue to lie on the damp grass. I look like someone who has had a heart attack.

'Mummy, you've crashed!' exclaims Noah with glee, looking up from his zoo animals.

'Cash, cash,' joins in India, clapping.

There are times I really wish the kids couldn't talk. I feel guilty about *Friendship* and even worse when Damian climbs back on board and says absolutely nothing. If only he would talk more. All my pleasure at getting us single-handedly out of the last lock evaporates.

To add to my sense of uselessness, I notice three fishermen seated quietly along the bank, who have seen the whole debacle. They nod in sympathy towards Damian and berate emancipated women everywhere, I'm sure.

Damian prises me away from the wheel, shuts off the engine and ties up the boat in silence, hammering out his frustration on two metal mooring spikes.

Twenty minutes later, I attempt to break the *froideur* with a cheery suggestion to visit the abbey. I am dying to get away from the scene of my crime and the knowing fishermen. They're too quiet and unassuming. I'm sure they'll be talking about me in the bar tonight – the Anglaise who smashed a beautiful varnished boat into the side, while her husband lunged onto the bank to avoid further damage.

Luckily the sound of monks chanting as we approach the abbey has a catatonic effect on us all and we stand transfixed, feet on gravel, surrounded by burgeoning pink and white rhododendrons, staring up at what remains of the beautiful beige stone edifice. I hope that Damian's anger is receding in this magical spot.

'Who's singing?' asks Noah, breaking the spell

'Monks in the monastry,' I reply quickly.

'What are monks?'

'People who live in monasteries and do good things.'

'Can we see them?'

'No you can't, they're praying. But you can listen to them.' (I haven't the heart to tell him that it's a tape playing and that these monks from the 12th century are dead.)

'I like the music,' says Noah as he joins in, swaying, chanting and making a prayer shape with his hands.

For the first time in my life I can see the appeal of being a monk. All that silence, the tranquillity, the calm, the communing with nature ... the absence of messy children and stubborn wives ...

That night it starts to drizzle again. Victorian drizzle, the type I remember from film noir shots in dingy cities. Clingy rain. Romantic rain. We are both huddled under the green canvas awning that wraps the cockpit and secures it from the elements. There are see-through plastic squares on each side. It's like being in a tent with windows. Damian hangs up a paraffin lamp and we lean together on the engine cover under the flickering light and crinkle our eyes to see out. The warmth slowly returns between us.

Instead of seeing the rain as an enemy, I am now starting to enjoy it. The strumming sound of the rain on the roof of *Friendship* when we are inside is beautiful. It confirms my basic need to be cosy, warm and safe. We are cocooned. I have everything in the world I love dearly here in this boat. It doesn't matter that it's raining outside.

The next day Shiv checks the charts and tells me that we are halfway between Calais and Paris. So after weeks of travelling we have only got as far as no-man's-land, the area that everyone whizzes through in order to get to the more interesting parts of France.

Today we are aiming for the famous Bony Tunnel on the Saint-Quentin Canal. At 14 kilometres in length, it's the longest canal tunnel in the world. Yes, 14 kilometres. I can't get my head round the idea of travelling that far in a tunnel. Even in a car it would take forever.

The building of the tunnel at Bony was, rather appropriately, ordered by Napoleon and it opened up a whole new supply route between Paris and the north coast. Originally a gang of eight men had to haul boats through the tunnel from the towpath, an operation that usually took around 15 hours. Nowadays an electric tug tows a

long line of boats behind it but the journey still lasts 45 minutes.

We arrive at the back of the queue for the tug and join an assortment of motor cruisers. As instructed, we all turn off our engines to avoid filling the tunnel with fumes. I realise we can't actually see the beginning of our group and it's only when we round the bend that we see the tunnel itself. Not surprisingly, we can't see the light at the other end. Set into the ceiling every 20 metres or so are long strip lights. They create an eerie effect as they reach into the distance, seemingly floating in the dark.

I had assumed that being towed would be quite easy but it turns out to be impossible to handle *Friendship*. We are the last boat and as such are at the end of a long tail, flicking about wildly from side to side while the boats nearer the front move about much more slowly and much less violently. Every movement they make is exaggerated ten-fold by the time it reaches us, so we are swinging from one side of the canal to the other and I have no control over the steering.

At first I wrestle with the wheel and try to counter the movements of the boats in front of us but my antics achieve nothing. We are completely at the mercy of the tow rope. After a while I give up and go onto the foredeck where Shiv has been trying to push us off the sides of the tunnel using a six-foot boat-hook, with just as little effect.

Ever on the lookout, Noah quickly clambers onto the empty captain's seat. As turning the wheel has no effect on our movement whatsoever, I leave him there. He can't believe his luck and I can just make out his face in the darkness, grinning from ear to ear as he spins the wheel round and round.

Friendship is taking a pounding. The sound of wood crunching and splintering seems to echo throughout the long tunnel. All I can do is listen to it. Listen and wait until we get out of this god-forsaken hole. We can't turn around and we can't unhook ourselves from the boat in front. There is no escape. We have to carry on taking this beating.

It's another half-hour before we blink into the sunlight like convicts released from the cooler. The second that the tow rope is undone, I jump ashore to see how badly she has been hurt.

It's bad. But bizarrely, not as bad as I had thought it would be. Perhaps the tunnel's bark was worse than its bite. Sure, there are scrapes and scratches all along one side of the boat but actually, they're relatively superficial. The sides of the tunnel have cut their way through just 15 or 16 of the 23 coats of varnish on *Friendship* (as opposed to Shiv, who went the whole hog when she smashed into the bank last night).

I should be crying but in fact, all I feel is an enormous sense of relief. There is no broken wood, no split planks, no leaks to worry about, no holes to repair. Maybe the crash last night was a good thing? It might have given me a sense of perspective (although obviously I can't let Shiv know that).

I look again at the damage and think to myself that *Friendship* is starting to look like a boat that is *used* instead of one that turns up at boat shows looking for admiring glances. I'm not quite ready to fully embrace this shift, but I'm starting to accept that this is what follows when a boat is turned into a home. Even so, I resolve that we have to buy more fenders. I can't do this to *Friendship* again. It's cruel.

While Damian coaches us slowly towards the next big town, Saint-Quentin, it hits me that we actually have three children on the journey with us. And one of them has just been in a terrible accident – *Friendship*. Damian will not fully recover his peace of mind until her scrapes have been healed with his sandpaper and varnish.

Popping down below after a lock, I check on our two real children. For 20 minutes there has been near silence with the odd trickle of laughter filtering up. I am just congratulating myself on my skills in picking the right toys for the journey – playdough has kept them quiet, without squabbles, for many an hour – when I see the devastation.

India is stood up in her bucket seat, still strapped in, nodding her head and singing, holding several postcards that have been ripped off the walls. Noah is moulding something intently on the tiled galley surface.

His eyes light up and with a Cheshire-cat smile he announces proudly to me, 'I've made a stew.' In front of him there is no playdough to be seen. Instead there is the copper kettle, smeared in soft cheese with florets of broccoli protruding from the spout. A sharp knife and chopping board lie at his side. His clothes, face and most of the galley are littered with black coffee granules, already melting and seeping into parts of the boat only Damian has seen. There's no blood anywhere obvious. I don't know whether to be cross or to hug him so I praise his cooking skills, eat a floret, say it's yummy and clear up quickly before Damian spots the mess. This might just send him over the edge.

Indy's mouth, I notice with a start, is bright red. But she's giggling. It's not blood, thank God. She's been eating the fire-engine-red playdough.

India and Noah are glowing. They've been free. Letting the kids go a little, unable to watch over their every move while we are in locks, has been a strange experience. It's good for me, though, and for them.

Motoring into Saint-Quentin, we pass behind old mills and derelict factories, rows of bins and boarded-up windows. Semi-industrial and semi-abandoned wasteland now used as impromptu car parking and a canvas for graffiti artists.

It strikes me that our perceptions of towns are completely different to anyone else's. When we approach by water we tend to see the extremes. Either the prettiest and richest parts that have lovely houses lining the water with long gardens and willow trees, or we see this, the forgotten industrial past that the town has turned its back on – the decay of local industry that used to rely on the canal for its survival.

We probably wouldn't have bothered stopping here if it hadn't been for 'the beach' that Shiv read about – effectively a huge sandpit created in the centre of Saint-Quentin each summer.

To be honest, I didn't have high hopes of 'the beach' as we cycled up the hill towards it. But now that I'm here I'm stunned by the sheer balls of the people who first thought of it and then made it happen. This truly is creative thinking; a fantastic piece of marketing for an old and tired town. I can't think of any other reason why someone would want to talk about this place, let alone visit it, were it not for this.

The beach is huge. It fills the massive town square with soft powdery sand; there are boardwalks, palm trees, beach bars, benches, sand dunes, trampolines, bouncy castles, fishing ponds, tables and chairs, volleyball, water jets, a swimming pool and water slides. Incredible.

We cycle to 'the beach' every day. It's all free and India is obsessed with fishing small plastic ducks out of a pretend pond using a bamboo rod. Noah stands close by and eyes the kids on the bouncy castle but refuses to get on.

On one of our lazy mornings, I choose a seat on a bench by a plastic palm tree as India and Noah dig in the sand. The sound of waves and seagulls pipes through loudspeakers. A blonde woman in a practical brown cardigan and tartan skirt sits next to me and leans over. Her son is also out there somewhere on 'the beach' and in a way that only mothers can, all the world over, she starts speaking to me, knowing that I'll be happy for some conversation.

In embarrassingly good English she asks me why I'm here and I try to explain. It turns out she is a local French teacher who has been to England once, to show her children what it was all about.

'Ah oui, we went on holiday there last year. We went to Felixstowe.'

'Did you like it?' I ask, not expecting a positive answer, and wondering what on earth made her choose Felixstowe.

'Well it was raining a lot, like here, but I loved, you know, your big shop Tesco. Ah amazing. They have toilets with free nappy wipes and a special mat to change your children. Wonderful.'

How curious it is to be in a foreign country. Here I am marvelling over Auchan, Monoprix and all things French – croissants, stylish kids' clothes, 17 types of yoghurt – while she lusts after Tesco.

'You know in France they would steal the nappy wipes. And Tesco, fantastic clothes. So cheap.'

I wonder whether we are programmed to love all things foreign, to feel that somehow other countries have got it sussed, to get bored with things at home. I wonder if that's what we are doing here on *Friendship*. Looking for another life that we could find at home.

I ask her what French people think of the English. 'We think you are very cold, very polite people. You eat awful food, really terrible. But you have the best tea in the world.' I think about it. One trip to a grotty town in the south-east of England and she's summed up a nation.

I could talk to this lady for hours but the beach is closing, attendants herding children along wooden walkways and away from the pool. Noah and India want to stay here forever, caught in groundhog day with never-ending sandcastles and fishing.

Our next stop is a little different; a riverbank in the middle of nowhere. I set up a bed for Shiv and I 'outside' in the cockpit so we'll be able to lie and look straight up at the night sky. I dig out the duvets. Although it's August, there's a chill in the air after dark.

We've been away a while now and it's the first night I feel really free and pioneering. We're moored close by a tiny hamlet called Tugny-et-Pont, two ropes attaching us to a grassy bank by looping through marlin spikes. The engine is silent. It's a beautiful summer's evening. Light is throwing an orange coat on the barley fields behind us. A few rogue poppies flash red. I set up the barbecue, and cook local sausages and ripe tomatoes while Damian uncorks a two-euro bottle of Corbières.

He has set out two green camping chairs and we're snuggled low in our seats, my feet stretching out onto his legs. The smell of bananas and rum cooking on the last embers of the Cobb barbecue is intoxicating. Tonight, for the first time, an ease with our journey washes over me. I know why we are doing this.

It's not all trial and tribulation, not all squashing and squeezing. It's for this. The freedom to sit out in nature, moored to a bank, no marina fees, no bureaucracy. No office deadlines to wake up for in the morning. Kids snoring in the bunks after overdosing on fresh air. I want to bottle this feeling, this feeling of being at peace with the world. A bird chuckles. Black bats twirl and tumble over the water as the night wraps us up in its black blanket.

As I lie in bed under the black sky, I mentally file tonight as one of my 'Top Ten Most Magical Nights'.

Even our impromptu singalong with the kids had been wonderful. Shiv had dug out her guitar and I found my clarinet. Neither of us had played either instrument since school but we'd decided the trip would be the time to re-acquaint ourselves with them. The racket when we played was terrible but Noah and India don't know what a clarinet or guitar is supposed to sound like so they absolutely loved it.

It's silent now. The kids are asleep and Shiv and I are outside on our temporary 'cockpit bed', snuggling under the warm covers and looking up at the sky. It is utterly romantic ...

Sex just felt too much like hard work before we left London. What with my job and Shiv at home looking after two kids under the age of three, we were the stereotypical couple who were too tired to make love (the kind you read about with shock and horror when you are in your twenties).

Of course, it was utterly normal (I hoped). I didn't know any new fathers who were having sex. It was the opposite of being 18 when everyone exaggerated about how much they were getting; now we joked with each other about how many months we had gone without.

When we set off I have to admit I wondered if sex might sneak back onto the agenda. But I also worried that maybe

my sex drive had gone for good. I was nearly 40 after all, long past my peak.

I guess I can relax on that score now. I look over at Shiv, who is fast asleep next to me. I should be flat out too but I don't want this day to end. I'm sleeping outside in France. My family are all around me. I'm on a boat I rebuilt with my own hands. And I have just rediscovered my libido. Life doesn't get much better.

This morning feels like the right one for baptising my new running shoes from Cambrai. Not because I need some space, but because I am bursting with contentment and want to seize every moment. I creep out of the cabin leaving everyone asleep, stepping on the boards I know don't creak.

It's cold at 7 am on the towpath. Long, dew-laden grass and clover flick at my legs. So few people pass this way there's no natural muddy, flattened way to follow. Bushes grow outwards, blocking the way, and within minutes my shoes and clothes are soaking wet with dew.

Two fishermen (God, they get everywhere) raise their eyebrows as I pant past them. I guess my pink bandana and Top Shop jogging pants must be a shock, looming up through the mist.

After two miles there's a lock and a sign reading 'Canal de Saint-Simon Fermée'. There's not a soul around. It's deathly silent.

The mist is still clearing and the bramble bushes seem to be reaching out to grab me. I get a bit spooked, imagining horrors lurking in the deep leaves behind, and sprint back towards *Friendship*, slowing down abruptly when I see the fishermen watching me again. I don't want them to think I'm scared.

I notice large, fat juicy blackberries weighing down the bramble branches next to me and race back to *Friendship*, cold air in my lungs. Minutes later we are out *en famille* dressed in pyjamas and wellies collecting tubs of juicy fruit to have with our cornflakes. More raised eyebrows from the fishermen.

After the diversion due to the Saint-Simon Canal closure, we end up in Longueil-Annel, a proper barge town and a place

I quickly fall in love with. The canal runs right through the centre of it, and along both banks huge *peniches* (barges) are tied up, sometimes two or even three abreast.

These boats rise out of the water and tower above the level of the road. They are like massive grey and black walls of steel punctuated with flashes of brightly coloured red, orange and turquoise paint to mark the bow. They are brutal in construction and yet on every single one, the portholes are decorated with the most delicate and feminine lace curtains you can imagine. They look like the doilies my granny used to put under her cup of tea to protect the table. It must be traditional to hang these curtains but I wonder how on earth it caught on.

Behind the barges, the houses of Longueil-Annel line the canal in neat terraces and almost all of them are built in a deep red brick but many have added peculiar stone decorations and cladding. They look like they have been modelled on something out of a gothic fairytale. In most of the gardens, people have made features out of the winches, dinghies and cleats from barges. Some pieces have been turned into small windmills, others welded together to make weathervanes while some have simply been filled with flowers. Longueil-Annel is not a particularly pretty place but it feels as if the canal is still pumping lifeblood through it.

It's on our first day here that I spot the house. It's a very simple house, by the side of the water. The windows are protected by faded bluey-green shutters and a little wrought-iron balcony sits above the front door. There is a small garden with a few pink flowers and then a gate that opens onto the canal.

Everything about the place feels untouched by the world around it. Except, that is, for the bright yellow sign tied to the balcony which reads: '*A Vendre.*'

I'm instantly seduced by the idea of living the life of an old bargeman by the side of the canal. I can see myself next to an old woodstove, with a long beard, refilling a pipe with tobacco and wearing a smock.

Quietly, I take a series of photos of the house complete with 'For Sale' sign and estate agent details. That way I have all the information I need. Just in case it turns out to be a brilliant idea to live here ...

Damian thinks I haven't noticed him taking copious photos here. I even clocked him mooning into estate agents' windows. The houses along the quay *are* charming. However, the whole town seems to be built from the same Eighties' maroon brick, with white or black detailing for relief. It instantly time-travels me back to my adolescence when I wore maroon pedal-pushers and granddad shirts. All I can think about is teenage boyfriends wearing Paco Rabanne, slow-dancing to Spandau Ballet and revising for 'A' levels in the heat of summer. I couldn't possibly live here.

It's about 8 pm. It's dark and it's one of my favourite parts of the day. Noah and India are fast asleep, I can hear them snuffling and snoring through the thin wooden door that separates the main cabin from their berths in the bow. Shiv and I have just eaten and we are curling into different corners of the warm boat with our books and a glass of wine each. She is on the starboard bunk and I'm at our small table. The cabin is filled with gentle music and the soft light from the small battery-powered lamps in the roof.
We are in our little floating tree house. Our den. Safe and secure from the world and comfortable in the calm that comes with a good book and cheap red wine.

I'm lost in Pavarotti's Caruso when suddenly there is a knock on the side of the boat. We've not had a visitor before so we look up from our books, stare at each other and wait to see what happens next. Another knock. Damian stands up to open the doors and I can see a man, gabbling away in French. I don't think Damian has a clue what he's saying.

French is flying at me from a strange-looking man with a big nose. My brain is frantically struggling to adjust to this

unexpected situation. What is this man doing? Who is he? What does he want? What is he saying? And what on earth is he doing with his hands?

He is pointing at me, then himself, and then to the woods behind the road. My mind flits back to the 'courgette/ *Deliverance* incident'. I tell myself that there has to be a rational explanation and I've got to stop being so paranoid. This has been a strange side-effect of living on the boat. I've felt a bit more vulnerable, a little more exposed than I would do in a house made of bricks with a big front door.

'Non, non, non, merci,' I say as I respond to the man's invitation. Shaking my head and wagging my finger at the same time. Using all the sign language I can think of to reinforce the word 'non'. (Why I say 'merci' though, I'm not quite sure.)

The man won't take 'non' for an answer. He won't budge and instead keeps calling me the 'Englishman'.

'Oui, oui,' I respond but there is something wrong. He stands there and says it again and again, only louder and more rapidly, 'Anguille, Anguille, Anguille.'

I can't take it any more. They clearly need a mediator. Damian is never going to get rid of the bloke at this rate. Grabbing the dictionary, I leaf through quickly and shout out 'Eel', over the top of Damian's insistent '*Non's*.

'He's not saying "Englishman", he's saying "little eel". He wants you to help him with a little eel,' I say, not leaving my comfy seat below deck, desperate to get back to my book.

'What are you talking about?' I snap at Shiv as she tries to help.

'He wants you to go into those woods to get a little eel.'

'Eh? Are you sure? Listen, I'm not going into any wood with this bloke and anyway eels don't live in woods.'

'I think he genuinely wants your help. Why not go and see? I know what he looks like. If he kills you, I'll be able to identify him.'

'Oh great. That'll make me feel better as I lie dying under a tree.'

I look back at the Frenchman. He smiles in a friendly 'I'm not a murderer' kind of a way. I size him up and tell myself that I could beat him in a fight.

'OK, I'll go. But keep your phone on just in case.'

With that I follow the man as he scrambles up the bank and towards the pitch-black woods. I'm wound up like a spring, trying to remember the route in case I have to run back. Within five minutes though, the woods open onto a riverbank. I'm confused because we have just walked away from the canal and then I see a small sign. This is the old River Oise that runs alongside the canal for a short time before snaking away across the fields again.

The man leads me to a bend in the river and onto a pontoon that has police tape and danger signs all over it. He ignores them and walks carefully across the rotting timbers before climbing onto the hulk of an old barge.

At this point I have given myself up to the danger. I want to see what happens. To test myself. To feel alive by being scared.

I follow the man and he leads me to the bow where two chairs and two fishing rods are set up.

I look at him quizzically. The guy doesn't want any help, he just wants someone to go fishing with him. I can't get my head round this situation. I can't imagine going up to someone, banging on their front door at night and asking them if they want to go fishing. Someone who I have never met before, who doesn't even speak my language and probably doesn't know how to fish anyway (which I don't, by the way).

I sit down, pick up my rod and copy what he does. Which isn't very much actually. We simply peer into the dark and try to talk to each other. This isn't very successful as he doesn't speak a word of English and I don't know the French for key phrases like *eel*, *float*, *reel* or *net*. Couple that with our natural ability (as blokes) to be appallingly bad at small talk and I wonder why on earth he invited me out here at all.

After an hour, a little bell rings on the end of the line of my new best friend, Philippe. We both jump up. Philippe grabs a huge net and thrusts it into my hands with a flashlight, then points at the water.

I have learnt a lot about the nuances of Philippe's pointing. It has become our own little language (who needs Esperanto?) and I immediately understand that my job is to hold the net out and shine the flashlight while he reels in the eel.

'This is simple,' I think. Then the torch catches the flashing silver of the eel under the water. As if driven crazy by the light, it arches its back and twists itself out of the depths. Before I know it, the eel is in the air.

I swear the bloody thing makes a lunge for me. It's still attached to the line but thrashing around wildly. Philippe pulled it out of the water too hard and we are now both trying to catch the beast as it writhes about in the sky above us.

I reckon it must be eight feet long but it's hard to tell in the dark. I get smacked on the side of the head by its tail and drop the net but Philippe finally manages to wrestle it into a bucket of water. I shine the torch on it and am stunned to see that the anaconda we have been fighting has shrunk to about two feet. Philippe looks at it, and smacks his lips as if to say, 'Wow, doesn't that look delicious?!'

Even in the dark, without any knowledge of eels, I know that it doesn't look very tasty. I worry that Philippe is now going to whip out a camping stove and cook it for us. I'm not sure I'm ready for that but luckily he simply returns to his rod and we set up for the next catch.

Three hours and four eels later, Philippe returns me to *Friendship*. He offers me two of the eels but I decline. We haven't got a pan big enough to cook them, and anyway, the kids would probably want to keep them as pets. Philippe says goodnight and heads home to the house six feet from our boat, 18 Rue de Canaux. He is our neighbour.

Shiv opens one eye as I crawl into our bunk and mumbles from under the covers, 'Was it gay sex or eel fishing then?'

CHAPTER 9

Next morning we leave Longueil-Annel, debating over cups of tea whether it should be renamed 'Long Eel Canal', my suggestion, or 'Long Oui Anal', Shiv's idea.

We head south once more, still travelling at crawling pace through the interminable dead space between the coast and the capital. We're three-quarters of the way to Paris but it's more like northern England than northern France. The towns we pass through are akin to Doncaster, Castleford and Pontefract. I know they all have their own kind of appeal but they're not places I'd *choose* to visit. I have to remind myself constantly that these canals weren't built for tourists but for industry, which is why they are grim, dirty and dour. But I've had enough of gritty realism now. I'm ready to crack on and get to Paris as quickly as we can.

I've even consulted the Navicarte and worked out we have just 170 kilometres to go. That doesn't sound far, but going at four kilometres an hour with locks to negotiate, it could amount to several days of hard travelling. It's going to be frustratingly slow. I still haven't shaken off the need to set targets and hit deadlines, so the closer Paris gets, the more agitated I am by our speed. I realise that old habits die hard. I'm even irritated by the fact that I can't become relaxed and laid-back as quickly as I want to.

Damian is determined to reach Compiègne today, over ten kilometres away and one step closer to Paris. I'm sure he'd like us to sprout wings and fly there, but I'm really relishing the slow pace of life and want to soak up the insignificant places en route. As a compromise we put our foot down between agreed stopping places (Damian and his damned goals!), so I'm at the wheel belting along.

The family is in the cockpit. Noah's on the potty absorbed in a Richard Scarry book. India's making 'grarrh' sounds and banging a plastic lion on the cockpit floor. Damian is crosslegged on cushions on top of the 'fridge locker' buried in *World War Two for Dummies* (again). For weeks he's been hoovering up facts from that book. Damian loves facts. He spouts them at every opportunity, the more dramatic the better.

I've also become fascinated by the war but I've never been good with raw facts, remembering them only when embedded into a story. Philip Warner's book, *World War II: The Untold Story*, has me hooked. Being in the area I'm reading about makes it so much more powerful and for the first time in my life, history is coming alive.

I'm on 'kid-watch duty' so every now and again I glance up from my book to check they haven't fallen overboard. (Maybe I *am* getting more chilled out after all. A few weeks ago I wouldn't have let them out of my grip, let alone out of my sight.) On one of my quick scans I notice a blue and white motor cruiser in our wake. There is a well-dressed, elderly woman on the bow and she is pointing at us.

The cruiser is flying a royal yacht club ensign. No, that doesn't mean the Queen is on board. It's simply a way of them telling everyone that the boat is from a posh marina in the UK. I've always had a chip on my shoulder about royal yacht clubs so I choose to ignore the lady but discreetly signal to Shiv in order to catch her attention (there's no point trying to shout over the sound of the loud engine). I motion her to look back at the woman and make a 'What's she on about?' sign with my shoulders and eyebrows.

I glance back at the white motor cruiser quivering in our wake. A purse-lipped woman is self-righteously motioning with her hand for us to slow down. She's definitely chastising us but thankfully the noise of *Friendship*'s engine drowns out her words.

I check *Friendship*'s speed. It has crept up to six knots when the speed limit is a firm four. This is to protect the edges of the banks, protect the wildlife, the reeds and the birds' nests that all live there. Typical. The one time I speed I get caught. For the last few hundred kilometres we have crawled along like goody-goodies. I feel ashamed at my London driving, throttle back immediately on the accelerator and pray we don't see that woman again.

The posh old hag is still behind us in her boat so I decide to kill two birds with one stone. We can get away from her *and* feed our new-found interest in the two world wars if we take a small detour up the River Aisne. From there we should be able to moor up and cycle to the famous Clairière de l'Armistice memorial site.

We moor at Choisy-au-Bac, a pretty little village of stone houses with flower-filled window boxes. I unload the two bikes and strap the child seats on, while Noah and India chase ducks on the banks. Then we set off on the five-mile cycle to the site.

India still is a bit nervous in her child seat so she hangs onto the back of Shiv's blouse with one hand and sucks the thumb of her other. She's then quite happy and falls asleep, lulled by the motion of the bike (but never letting go of Shiv).

Noah meanwhile loves strapping on his little helmet and clambering into his seat. He gets so excited he won't shut up as we cycle along. He doesn't stop asking questions and twisting around in his seat to see things. This means the whole bike is being thrown in one direction and then another. Noah is totally oblivious to this, of course, but I'm in a constant state of fear as we wobble dangerously along the road.

Large country houses, gardens down to the river and river-side restaurants all roll by until we turn into a long, deep

forest and eventually (somewhat surprisingly) arrive at a large car park cut into the trees. We leave the bikes and follow the signs through the woods until we arrive at an enormous clearing in the trees.

This is it. This is the place where, on 11 November 1918, the Armistice was signed between the Germans and the Allies, effectively ending the First World War.

I look around me. It's nothing more than a massive circle of gravel with two railway tracks that curve towards one another and then stretch out towards the woods once more.

In 1918 there wasn't a clearing, it was a densely wooded area where two military supply railway lines (hidden by the trees) happened to pass within a few yards of each other. On that famous day, French Field Marshal Foch arrived by train on one of the tracks. (He was in the converted dining car that he liked to use as his field office.) On the other track, the German commanders arrived. The two trains stopped opposite one another and the Germans walked the three metres to Foch's carriage where the peace talks began and the historic signing took place.

In the years after the First World War, the woods around the tracks were cleared and the site became a monument to the victory over the Germans. That could have been the end of the story but then came the fascinating bit. For me, at least.

When the French surrendered to Hitler in the *Second* World War, some 22 years later, I always assumed it must have taken place in Paris somewhere.

But no, Hitler was far too much of a showman for that. He knew the power of symbolism and he chose to make the French return to the scene of Germany's humiliation in the previous war. He forced the French to meet him at the Armistice Clearing and surrender there instead. In fact he made them do it in the very same train where the Germans had been forced to surrender all those years before. He even insisted on sitting at French Commander Foch's old table himself.

As I read about this at the site, I can't help but admire Hitler. I know it's not very **PC** but what a brilliant piece of propaganda. A psychological masterstroke. It must have been devastating for the French. My God, if Hitler had worked in advertising he would have been hailed as a genius.

At the back of the clearing there is now a museum with a replica of the infamous carriage inside. Noah is desperate to get on board and see the 'naughty Germans'.

No-one is allowed to go on the train but we are able to peer through the windows at waxwork dummies of the key military figures. Noah and India are amazed at how long they can sit without moving.

At the back of the museum, the kids finally understand why we wanted to come here. Where I see an interesting display of uniforms, guns and model battle scenes, they see a playground. They're now skidding around the room on the polished wooden floor, pretending to shoot everyone.

'Bang bang. You're a Bomb Head. I'm going to shoot you,' shouts Noah at the top of his voice while standing in front of a mannequin of a soldier.

'Bam, bam, bam, bam, Bum 'ed,' India shouts in support as she crawls across the floor.

I'm not quite sure of the etiquette of this. War games in a place dedicated to the memory of war. I edge away and pretend the kids are with Shiv.

I end up looking through a series of black-and-white photographs of young lads in uniform, surrounded by mud and death. They look like children. I work out that they are closer to Noah's age than to mine. It leaves me humble and mute.

Damian is only this quiet when he's asleep. Something emotional must be going on. I probably need to give him some space so herd the kids outside, shrugging my shoulders at the stern museum curator as if to say 'Kids, eh?'

A flat, grey stone monument lies in the centre of the clearing, its engraved words reaching out more to the lost souls in the sky than to us here on land. I remember how exotic and hilarious

French sounded to me as a child when my dad would sing Frère Jacques to us all. So I read the words out in loud French to a giggling Noah and India:

ICI

LE 11 NOVEMBRE 1918

SVCCOMBA

LE CRIMINAL ORGUEIL

DE L'EMPIRE ALLEMAND

VAINCU

PAR LES LIBRES

ON IL PRETENDAIT

ASSERVIR

Noah climbs on top of the monument to see. I don't stop him. I want him to enjoy history.

We are lucky that it's a weekday, just after opening time, so thankfully we're alone outside. The air is cool and I can smell the dampness and ferns of the forest. Only the grand stone statue of General Foch looks down at us. It's silent except for the sound of birds (and the chattering of Noah and India of course).

At each compass point around the monument, a stone bench waits for contemplators. I walk slowly to each one, read the inscription and try to imagine the horrors:

1915 Les Tranchees
1914 La Marne
1917 Chemin des Dames
1916 Verdun-Somme

I say a little prayer for all these lost people and a bigger prayer for our children. Please may they never have to live through such a thing.

I'm deep in thought as we cycle back to the boat and motor the three kilometres to Compiègne. The town looks pretty enough, which lifts my mood and I'm even more upbeat when

half an hour later, I expertly moor in the enclosed marina. I look around me to see if anyone noticed and immediately spot the white motor cruiser with the royal yacht club ensign. The uptight woman is glaring.

My first instinct is to shout that it wasn't me. 'I wasn't the one speeding on the river. It was Shiv. Look at how well I have just moored up, that's not the seamanship of a nautical joyrider. It was my wife; she's the one behaving like a yob.'

Luckily no words actually leave my mouth. No doubt there will be stories flying around the clubhouse tonight about the rude English family speeding on the river. I will be tarred with Shiv's brush. Thankfully we're only allowed to stay here two nights so we'll soon be able to make a getaway. I'll make sure it's a slow one.

Damian offers to cook his speciality tonight (pasta). I'm sure he's avoiding the battleaxe who told me off earlier on the river. Gladly I leave him to the steamed-up galley and drift around the small, enclosed circular basin for an hour or so. It feels odd to move about without the kids and the noise they carry with them. I actually have time to think.

About 80 large and small motorboats all point their noses at a shabby blue and white shuttered cabin. The clubhouse. Grass banks slope up to a fence and at the end of each pontoon there is a locked gate. Many boaters seem to have appropriated the little patches of grass fronting their mooring and filled them with plant pots, canoes, bikes, even welcome mats. It feels more like a campsite where people make it home-from-home, bringing their garden gnomes for company. I suspect many boaters live here full time. Furthest away from the river are a few rotting hulls giving themselves back to the water.

In the clubhouse I pocket our pontoon gate key and make a note to tell Damian about the photos here. Pictures of boats frozen into the ice, the basin covered in snow. A reminder that we are still a long, long way from the Med.

It's our first morning in Compiègne and the sun has made a rare appearance. Shiv has gone shopping to stock up on food. She jogged there, which was a shock for me, as I didn't think this craze would last. I furtively glance at my expanding stomach and swear to do 50 sit-ups a day from now on.

I'll start tomorrow though. Right now, I've got to get rid of that smell. The sun is heating up the boat and our rubbish bag, full of rotting Pampers, is starting to stink.

I have no choice but to put the kids' breakfast on hold and dump the dirty nappies in the marina bins. Even my morning cup of tea will have to wait (*that's* how little oxygen is left in the cabin). Obviously I can't leave Noah and India on board alone so the three of us clamber off the boat and up the bank in our pyjamas, Noah proudly holding the 'bag of poo'.

It's only when we head back to *Friendship* that I see the pontoon gate has swung closed and is now locked. As I wrench at it, I remember that Shiv has the only key and she took it with her when she went shopping. Bollocks.

My first reaction is to see if I can climb over the gate but of course I can't. I've got Noah and India with me. I could manage it on my own but not with Noah and India on my back. I half wonder whether I could 'throw' them over it, but I just know I'd end up impaling one of them on the spikes.

Hmmm. How bad is this? I think. Shiv will be back in a bit so we'll just have to wait a while.

The worst thing is that we are all in our pyjamas. Noah is in a blue Thomas the Tank Engine set and India is in a yellow number with teddy bears all over it. I'm topless but in a pair of long, grey and baggy Calvin Klein pants that have shrunk and now come to just above my ankles. (I don't think I look like the kind of person he had in mind when he designed them.) All of us are barefoot and all of us have hair like cavemen.

At least no-one seems to be around and it's not cold so all we have to do is potter about until Shiv returns. There is a lot to keep us amused. There are ducklings, abandoned dinghies, old boat trailers, a pile of sand, sticks, an old shoe, wild flowers, a steep slope, a massive puddle and a rabbit hole.

I'm having as much fun as the kids as we make the small marina feel like a massive adventure playground. I like it – no plastic. No electronics. Just our imaginations.

As Noah has a pee against a tree, I hear the melody of my mobile, left in *Friendship*'s cabin. I hear it again after a few more minutes. It can only be Shiv, no-one else calls me now. I wonder whether she's in trouble, or is she just calling to check which brand of yoghurt I'd like? I'll leave it a while and see what happens. Three minutes later the phone rings again. And then again. There must be a problem. I decide to set off into town to find her.

I must look a right state; there is a rip in my pants and my flies are hanging open because the buttons broke long ago. My feet are already black with dirt from the pavement and I realise that I smell. India is cradled in my arms, which makes me look like the Eastern European beggars who walk up and down the tube trains in London. Noah is walking alongside me and I try to make a game out of dodging all the dog poo on the pavement. It turns out he's not very good at that game.

I try to act nonchalant, eccentric even. But after quizzical glances from the beautifully dressed Frenchmen going to work around me, I reluctantly acknowledge there is a fine line between 'eccentric' and 'twat'. Right now I'm on the wrong side of that line.

I am turning into my mum. At only 39 years of age, the thing that tops my 'Wanted' list isn't a pair of Manolo Blahniks but a tartan trolley with wheels. All the French women have one. Well okay, most of the ones approaching their third age. If I could squirrel a wheelie trolley on board I would, but there's not an inch of space to spare.

Labouring under the weight of eight bulky carrier bags of provisions and a supersize pack of nappies from Monoprix, I hover by the exit doors, wondering what to do next. I hadn't thought about how I was going to get this lot back to the boat. On my way round the aisles I seemed to be attracted to all the heavy goods: wine, tins of cassoulet, jars of Bonne Maman jam.

A call to Damian, my first reaction when trouble arises, clicks straight to answerphone. He is probably weeing up a tree or something. Worry scuds across my face when there is still no answer to my fifth call.

Then I relax. He has probably dropped it in the water (he's lost more mobiles than I can remember). With no taxis in sight I shall have to relay the bags the two kilometres back to the boat. It's going to take me all morning.

After struggling ten metres along the pavement, I cave in to my new addiction. It was in Cambrai that I became hooked and strong French coffee is now my drug of choice, driving me out of the boat each morning. I can't get past eleven o'clock without my hit, and seek out bars that offer the perfect *café au lait*. Sometimes we find amazing and quirky places in my quest. The café I've stumbled into now is certainly one of the odd ones.

It's called Bar Le Retro and is decorated like the inside of a 1930s wooden cruising ship. Warm, mahogany walls with maroon- and gold-striped wallpaper above. All around the room are objects, linked only by the fact that they are gold. Horses, candlesticks, a ship's propeller, a cricket bat, two super-sized bullets, fleets of team cups. This place must have spent a fortune on eBay.

I order a coffee from the lady. She's made up for a glorious ball on the upper decks. White hair piled up on her head, full make-up and a dramatic gown. A French Miss Havisham. There's no wedding ring in sight, only an equally grey-white poodle by her side, standing on the bar.

It's undrinkable; definitely the worst coffee I've tasted so far in France. It's so strong I wince. Unfortunately there are no pot plants around (presumably she couldn't find any in gold). So I add four sugars to muster strength for the walk home.

As we get closer to Monoprix, I'm thankful that I haven't 'popped out' of my flies yet (at least I think I haven't). It's a

good thing Noah and India aren't old enough to be embarrassed by me yet. It would appear to them that walking barefoot along a crowded pavement in your pyjamas is not unusual.

I'm thinking about how to drag my provisions along the pavement without tearing any bags or ligaments when I hear a familiar, high-pitched screeching that sounds like India.

A dishevelled tramp-like man appears at the left of the large floor-to-ceiling window pane. It's Damian, clutching one toddler, writhing in his naked arms, and another marching at his side, eyes on the road ahead.

'Mummyyyyyyyyy...' India is yelling. I lock eyes with her and wave, motioning the vagrant inside. What a happy coincidence – Damian has clearly come to help me. How on earth did he know?

The woman behind the bar looks at me as if I'm going to try to sell her pegs. She turns away as I walk in. Shiv on the other hand bursts into laughter, then suddenly stops when she sees my face and hears me start babbling. 'We got locked out ... India's done a poo in her nappy ... I've got no drinks ... No wet wipes ... The kids are both starving ... I'm half naked ...'

I'm hit by a sudden flashback to how I used to be in London, when something went wrong in my day with the kids. I couldn't cope. I'd get myself in a complete state and then download on Damian the moment he walked in the door at night. Damian sounds like I used to.

'Thanks for coming to get me. How did you know I needed you?'

'Because my phone was going crazy. It could only have been you. Who else is going to call me? But what's the crisis? From the looks of it, I'm the one in need here ...'

'There's no crisis. I just needed some help with my bags ...'

On the way back, I relax more. I wonder why I always get so uptight? I should be rejoicing in the fact that I can walk down a busy street in my pyjamas in the rush hour. Christ, until a few weeks ago I was one of those men in that sea of suits. I smile and look down at my bare feet. *This* is the new me.

Later that day, fully clothed and with Damian more tranquil now that I am on hand as back-up, we venture back into town on the hunt for a hairdresser.

'This one looks okay I guess,' I try to convince myself, peering in through the window of Exclusif.

My hair is so long now that each wash is using more than my two-minute allocation of water. I haven't dared cut it. As far as my hair goes I am a creature of habit and have been going to the same guy in London for ten years. I'm scared to go to anyone else.

'What the hell,' I say and throw caution to the wind. 'I can't possibly look any worse.'

As I nestle into a squeaky, faux leather chair and pick up a 1998 copy of *Cosmopolitan*, I fail to notice that all the cutters sport the same hairstyle – just off the shoulder and bouffant. I also miss the fact that this place seems to be a favourite of the over-sixties.

'Sauvage, comme sur la plage.' I'm trying to explain beach-hair, a well-used phrase in central London. They look at me, look at each other, smile, shrug and nod in unison. 'Ah oui, oui,' they say so positively. What a relief. They understand.

Noah is kneeling in the chair next to me licking an orange lollipop he's been given by the ladies. He whiles away the half-hour by pulling bulldog faces in the mirror and warily watching me being attacked by the scissors.

I'm wandering aimlessly around the shaded avenues outside Louis XV's royal palace with India asleep in the pram, trying to kill an hour or two. I hope they give Shiv one of those sexy

French bobs like the girl on the cover of my old copy of *Fair Stood the Wind for France*. I fell in love with her when I was sixteen and still haven't got her out of my system.

While we are wandering about, I spot an old door with a number three on it. The three is hand-carved in wood and all around it radiates an Art Deco sunshine. It looks great. I dig out my camera and take a close-up photograph. It'll make a great 3rd birthday card for Noah in October.

As I admire the picture on the screen of my digital camera, I wonder if there might be a business idea in this? Could I create a whole series of numbers and letters from 'found' objects in French towns and villages? Stuff like door numbers, street signs, shop windows, old posters and the like. I could probably find most of the letters of the alphabet and all the big birthday and anniversary numbers (18, 21, 30, 40 etc). Then I could sell them as greetings cards.

As my mind explores the possibilities I see the shape of an 'N' in the timber of an old Tudor-style house. While I take a photo of it I start to get really excited. This could be my new life. I could be a photographer. How cool is that? I can't wait to tell Shiv and rush back to the hairdresser through the cobbled streets and narrow alleys, babbling away to India about her daddy becoming an artist.

Despite my mild protests and worst fears, I now sport a bouffant, just off the shoulder. The only thing 'sauvage' about it is my emotions. They even use hairspray, not gel. I feel like Joan Collins. Totally out of place on the canals, or anywhere this century. I loathe it. Thank God I didn't get a wheelie trolley too. I have aged 20 years.

Shiv looks like she's about to cry and I can see why. This isn't the Bridget Bardot/Vanessa Paradis sex vixen that I was hoping for. They have made her look like the middle-aged wife of a French town mayor. This woman in front of me just isn't Shiv. I feel weird giving her a hug. It will feel even weirder later. It'll be like going to bed with Margaret Thatcher.

I tell her it looks … nice, but clearly she doesn't believe me (frankly I wouldn't either). She's now scurried off to a toilet to try to 'do something' with it. I think I'll wait until later to tell her that I'm going to become a photographer.

My pensioner hairstyle calls for a long lunch in the sun with a lot of vin rouge.

We choose a brasserie, Au Coq d'Or, with wrought-iron tables and chairs, white linen tablecloths and sparkling glasses. Surprisingly, high chairs and extra cushions are produced with a flurry and we aren't dumped on a table by the loo. While we are waiting for our food, I look around us. The place is packed. People in suits go through starter, main, wine and coffee. Even a single older woman has three courses and wine while reading her newspaper. There doesn't seem to be the culture of 'lunch on the go' or 'grabbing a sandwich at your desk'. Even on the canals, the locks close for an hour or so over lunchtime. It's all so civilised.

The waiter is very attentive and for the first time on the trip we manage a leisurely meal out without the need for mops, trips to the toilet and apologetic glances to other diners. I'm so proud of the kids I forget about my hair. Noah's almost three and India has just articulated her first clear word: 'More.'

Perhaps it's the red wine that has relaxed us. Or perhaps the waiter feels sorry for this bouffant pensioner out with her son and two grandchildren.

A pyjama walk, a new career idea and a bouffant have filled all the time we are allowed in Compiègne. We have to leave our mooring to make room for other visitors so we head straight upriver for the chandlers and fuel barge that are just past the town bridge. (After the long wait at Cambrai, I now fill up at every opportunity.)

While Shiv is sorting out the diesel, I dash into the chandlers. Big mistake. It's an Aladdin's cave of outboards, lights, switches, floats, ropes and anchors. I could be in here for days but with 167 kilometres still to go to Paris, I restrict myself

to buying just two things: a safety harness for India and some more fenders.

The harness is to clip India onto the boat because her life jacket is too bulky. The poor girl is still learning how to walk, still needs to cling onto things in order to move about and yet she can hardly do a thing because she is wrapped in a fluorescent orange buoyancy aid that is bigger than she is. She looks like a small, brightly coloured version of the Michelin Man.

The extra fenders are to protect the sides of the boat from being continually bashed. The day Shiv crashed into the bank still gives me nightmares. To be fair to Shiv though, it wasn't *entirely* her fault. Much of it has to do with the shape of our boat. One of the reasons I love *Friendship* is her flowing lines, particularly the unusual way her bow curves up and inwards while her stern rolls outwards and wide. It's a very special design and very beautiful but just about the worst shape you can imagine for the canals; just as one part of the curve comes alongside, the other bits stick out even more.

Frustratingly the chandler has no small harnesses and no fenders the right size so ordinarily this would be a failed mission. Except for two things: firstly, I don't know when we'll come across another chandler and secondly, the girl serving me speaks English with the kind of sexy French accent you only hear in porno movies (I imagine).

Twenty minutes later I walk out of the chandler with a harness for India that we have to wrap around her twice in order to make it fit. And six fenders that are so enormous they look like spacehoppers.

While Damian struggles to lash down a new giant fender, I look back at Compiègne. Despite a recurrent picture of 'Caveman Damian', Compiègne is full of happy images of the kids: Noah standing on deck, wearing only underpants, a baguette stuck down the side of them like a gun; tearing chunks off the baguette to feed the ducks; India hanging onto the strips of the fly curtain and propelling herself down the steps into the main cabin. Or the pair of them together, with sponges in hand and a bucket of soapy water, being 'pirates' washing the floor of *Friendship*.

The kids seem to be so at home on the boat now. It feels like we've been on board for months and months. So much has happened but it's only now that we're finally beginning to relax and enjoy it. Even the space doesn't seem to be so much of an issue now.

The next stretch of the trip has been keeping me going; the last leg before reaching the Seine and then Paris. What a milestone! There were points a few weeks ago when I didn't think we'd get here.

CHAPTER 10

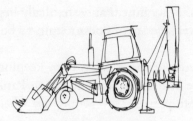

'Feels good eh?' I grin as we join the river again. It feels so familiar now to be chugging through brown water. Clutching a mug of tea and barefoot on the side-deck leaning up against the cabin side, I feel completely comfortable in a pose that felt awkward only a couple of months ago.

'Yep,' he smiles. Damian has finally abandoned his Jude Law white vest for a real shirt and hat. I actually feel a touch romantic when I look at him.

'You missing anything from home?' I ask. 'Go on, give me your top three.' This always gets him going. In a concise way, that is.

Shiv must be in a good mood if she's indulging me in 'list games'. I concentrate on my answer. It's weird trying to remember all the things I've spent the last few weeks trying to forget. The stuff that used to dominate my life in London. Winning a pitch? The adrenalin before a big presentation? The buzz of working on a great campaign? Even as I think of these things I feel numb. I surprise myself with what I *really* miss:

'OK, here are the three, but not necessarily in order:

1) An Indian takeaway.

2) A long, hot, deep bath full of Radox.

3) A big sofa.'

'Oooohhhhhh, yeah. I'd kill for a Koh-I-Nor special. Well, apart from all your three, for me it's gotta be fresh milk, a fridge with a vertical door and a bed I can stretch out in.'

We both fall silent for a while and fondly remember these simple luxuries. I continue, aware that Damian is now hooked.

'How about what you're most looking forward to? Top three again.'

Hmmm, tricky but not as hard as the first question. At least I've been thinking about this for a while.

'Same rules – no particular order:

1) Sailing past the Eiffel Tower on *Friendship*.

2) Endless sunshine.

3) Getting to the point where I am so relaxed, I don't spend my whole time thinking about the future, instead of enjoying the present. I know that *not* thinking about the future doesn't really fit with a list of what I'm looking forward to in the future but you know what I mean.'

'Yep, I get it. Well for me, it's simply Paris. Ooh! Paris. I can't wait to go crazy in a city again. The galleries. The art. The cafés. I can't think beyond Paris. Paris is all of my top three.'

Paris is definitely the goal for both of us now but it's still going to be days before we get there (140 kilometres to go). We press on. At Sarron Lock, a kind German couple help us with our ropes and push us off the side. Noah is unusually silent as I wave goodbye but then he starts tugging at my leg.

'Daddy. Will they kill us?' he asks.

'What do you mean, Noah? Of course they won't kill us, they were really nice,' I say, trying to hide my shock.

'But they kill *everybody*, Daddy,' Noah exclaims adamantly.

At first I don't know what he's talking about but then the penny drops. He's thinking about the war. Since the V-2 rocket factory near Watten, Noah has been obsessed with killing, who's doing it, why and how. He loves the war monuments we find in every town while places like the Armistice Clearing have simply added fuel to his fire. I guess I haven't helped because I've been caught up in it all too. I don't think you can avoid it in this part of France.

It's a challenge to explain how and why so many people died here but I think it's important he knows what went on and how we must avoid it happening in the future. Clearly I've failed though, for despite my noble efforts, it seems the only bits Noah's interested in are the guns and death.

I decide it might help if I called the Germans from the war 'the Nazis' from now on. At least that might stop some of the confusion and save us further embarrassment in the locks ahead.

Damian has got himself into a pickle explaining the war to Noah in a sensitive way. I know I should be more sympathetic but really it's hilarious watching Damian being a full-time dad.

In London, when he was only around at the weekends, Damian used to go into overdrive from 7 am Saturday to 7 pm Sunday. As though, in those 36 hours, he could cram every anecdote, every cuddle, every loud-music moment that the kids had missed by being without him in the week. Sometimes it would drive me to despair that he could be so wonderfully 'on' all the time, when I seemed mostly to be 'operating on standby'.

Now, though, it's a relief to watch him struggle with a simple conversation, worry late into the night about decisions he's made with the kids and end the day rather monosyllabic.

As we get near to L'Isle Adam, a huge navy blue gin palace passes us. I'm sure that big boats like this are a sign we are getting closer to the capital. There is a red ensign hanging off the back so we know it's English and I crane forward to look at it more closely. It's very flash, with a young woman in a bikini on the deck and an older guy steering from the upper wheelhouse. It never fails to surprise me that no matter how old you are, you can always get a sexy young girlfriend if you have lots of money.

I strain to read the name of the boat as it powers away from us and it looks like *Guinness*.

'Probably one of the original family,' I yell over to Shiv, 'or maybe it's some corporate freebie for the top execs that work there.'

As I muse about the luxuries of the corporate world I have left behind, we turn towards L'Isle Adam and look for the pontoon marked on the Navicarte. Within a few minutes we round a corner and see that the gin palace has taken the prime spot. There is a small space behind it so I challenge myself to manoeuvre into it. We may not have a super-yacht, I think to myself, but *Friendship*'s beautiful, she's a classic and I can handle her like a dream (well ... sometimes). Let's see what the girl in the bikini thinks of that.

As I edge *Friendship* in, two young kids run out onto the deck and hug the bikini babe, then an older but cool-looking lady wanders out of the cabin and adjusts one of their ropes. It's a family: grandparents, yummy mummy and children. Now that we are closer, I see the boat's name is *Gallivant*. I was wrong on just about every count.

L'Isle Adam is an old Gallic town, described by Honoré de Balzac as 'paradise on earth'. And it sure is. We are moored only a few minutes' walk from the beautiful, tidy little town, packed with restaurants, an old church, riverside gardens and an artisan ice-cream shop. Apparently rich Parisians drive up in droves on the weekend.

To Noah and India's delight we stumble across a vast riverside beach area, with two enormous fluorescent-blue swimming pools, soft white sand and truckloads of high-pitched screeching children. I poke some euros through a tiny glass ticket-window as the matronly clerk points to Damian and then a sign on my left with a raised eyebrow.

'Pour la baignade les shorts et Bermudas sont interdits.'

Damian reluctantly (very reluctantly) abandons his knee-length, flowery surf shorts for a regulation pair of blue Speedos, sold to us with glee by the clerk. Now there is no doubt we are in France. Speedos are so European, so old-school, so uniform-like, whereas surf shorts are American, loud and scruffy. You can't hide behind a pair of Speedos.

Nevertheless Damian tries to, even though it's impossible to blend in with the crowd, given his knee-length tan mark. His Speedos are a tight fit and I'm sure Damian spends the whole afternoon breathing in. He even seems to walk a little differently.

Despite my best efforts to catch him unawares with the camera, Damian forbids me to take any photos of him and I sense a rewriting of history creeping in. Luckily we can call it quits now. My haircut and Damian's swimming trunks shall never be seen in print.

Later that afternoon, the 'yummy mummy gang' invite us for drinks on board. Presumably they didn't notice Damian's outfit.

Over a chilled white wine and nibbles on *Gallivant* (their deck is the size of our whole boat), I start chatting with Christine, the grandmother. We quickly discover a shared passion for old boats. When she lived in the States, she helped restore a classic yacht with a varnished hull just like *Friendship*'s, and like me she'd fallen in love with Epifanes, a particular type of varnish. Whenever she came to Europe she used to smuggle tins of the stuff back to America in her suitcase. This kind of madness is something I can relate to. We are soon lost in a discussion about the finer merits of restoring old boats.

When I talk to her husband Trevor later, the conversation is very different. He is a wily sea dog from South Africa and is the first person on the trip to challenge what we are doing. Not the trip itself but how it might fit into the rest of our lives. Most importantly, what we do next. I guess that although I want to be free and dream of becoming a pho-tographer, I'm not sure it'll *really* happen. My dark belief is that this is a really big holiday and one day we have to go back.

Trevor tells me he also thought that when he left his big fat job to go on a year-long sabbatical. That was 20 years ago (when he was 42, a couple of years older than me).

Since then he has sailed the world and raised a family but still managed to turn up at his old company for board meetings.

While I imagine the glories of his life, he looks at me intently and then with eight words turns my world upside down: 'You know, you don't *have* to go back ...'

Damian looks like he's just won the lottery – stunned into a silent imagining of a brighter future. Trevor's urging for us to 'keep going' takes root in my head too.

Christine also throws down a gauntlet. Something she says really gets to me, and settles in my mind next to Trevor's comments.

'You know, so many of our friends have died lately. When I turned sixty, I made myself a vow. From now on, I am not going to do *anything* I don't really want to do.'

I wonder whether I can make the same vow on my 40th?

These two retirees are unlike anyone I've met before. The fact that they've sailed all over the world while having three children and staying married, seemingly happily, gives me a sense of what I hope Damian and I might become in the future.

That night, in our own single-sized bed, back in our own mini-sized boat, *Gallivant* and our conversations on board her seem to have taken on mammoth proportions. We are both restless.

We lie face to face, going over Trevor and Christine's exact words. Turn onto our backs, remember an anecdote, laugh, sigh. Turn away from each other in an attempt to sleep.

I'll never sleep tonight. My mind is alive with possibilities. It feels like someone has shown me a door that I didn't know was there ...

We say goodbye to *Gallivant* in the morning, both of us knackered but also slightly changed since the drinks last night. Lost in our thoughts about the future we quickly come upon Cergy, a small group of buildings popping up out of the woods. The semicircle of modern apartments is clustered around a

new marina. All around the edge are cafés and restaurants populated by working men and women.

I get a tingle of excitement. This is no longer a small town in the neverland of northern France. This is the edge of Paris, which is now only 79 kilometres by boat. I can sense the buzz in the air and it's quite intoxicating after weeks of meandering through wheatfields.

Shiv is excited. She's ecstatic, in fact. Right here in the marina is a place that does leg waxes. I've never quite understood why she gets so bothered about having her legs waxed. I was expecting that the Porta Potty, the lack of a fridge, the limited water supply, the tiny and uncomfortable bed or the living out of bags would have caused most distress but for Shiv these are nothing compared with the thought of arriving in Paris looking like a gorilla.

I leave Damian chatting to Rudy and Yytte, a Danish couple moored next to us, and rush off to the beauty salon for my leg wax. Okay, not the usual first point of interest for most tourists, but not all tourists have my genes.

It was Noah who inadvertently forced me to hide my shorts under the bunk and get out my hideous, beige, three-quarter-length, and truly unfeminine, trousers. Four days earlier, as he had snuggled into my lap for a story he had asked quite matter-of-factly: 'Mummy, why are your legs all spiky?'

'I need a leg wax.' I had decided to go straight for the truth rather than invent a long tale about a magic cactus I'd eaten.

'What's a leg wax?'

'It's when they make your legs all smooth.' I really want to spare him the ugly details.

'What's smooth?'

'You know, like Mummy's face.' A risk, I know, but I am only 39 after all.

'You mean brown?'

I capitulate. He'll never remember after all. 'Yes, a bit like that.'

While Shiv is in the beauty parlour, I am keeping India and Noah amused in the small square between the restaurants.

For the sake of something to do, I try to get India to walk a few steps. This has been my favourite game recently. Even though she is perfectly capable of walking by my side when I am holding her hand, she simply flops to the floor if I let go.

My latest technique has been to get her to stand while I crouch in front of her and hold out my arms. Then as she steps towards me and the apparent safety of my embrace, I slowly back away so that she is forced to take more and more steps to reach me.

So far, this approach has generally been met with slumping to the floor. I've also been worried that I am nurturing some deep-seated distrust within her. After all, here I am, a supposed haven of security, yet as soon as she lurches towards the safety of my arms I'm snatching them away.

As I ponder whether I am training India to believe that all men are bastards, she suddenly takes three steps in a row and then ... just keeps going.

I stumble backwards and roll out of the way (I'm not sure she can turn yet) and watch in amazement as Indy walks right across the square. There is no build-up from three to four to six steps. She just keeps going.

I whoop in delight and clap. Even Noah, who has been running around to emphasise the fact that he can *already* walk, stops to cheer.

I can't believe I'm the one seeing India walk for the first time. I'm not hearing about it after work or looking at a photo. I'm right here in the moment. This is my first 'First'.

I keep picking Indy up, carrying her back to the same start-point and watching her set off again like a wind-up toy. It's a joyous feeling.

Leaving the salon into the bright sunshine again, a warm and feminine glow all over me, I can now hold my head (and legs) high in front of my two-year-old son.

Noah shouts loudly across the marina: 'Mummy, are you smoothy brown now?'.

A young couple nearby shoot me a look, smile in sympathy, probably wondering how much it cost to have an all-over tanning session and some Botox.

I am saved from having to answer by Damian hopping up and down. 'You'll never guess what happened. India can walk! She can walk, she can walk. Look!!'

Damian winds India up, places her on the concrete marina floor and we watch over and over. It's such a momentous occasion – her finding her feet. It will never again feel miraculous that she can walk. I am happy Damian got to see this 'First' in our little girl's life. There are so many others he missed.

When we leave Cergy, Shiv and the kids clamber up to the bow. They are all craning forward to see where the river takes us, to see the Seine for the first time (it's just five kilometres away), to see Paris in the distance. I don't think I have ever been so excited about looking for office blocks and traffic lights.

Along the Oise, we arrive at a watery T-junction with the Seine. To our left is Conflans-Sainte-Honoré and beyond, Paris. If we turn right we can follow the Seine past Monet's Giverny and out to Le Havre. We swing towards the capital, feeling the slow current of this ancient river against us. We are now on the Seine and only 70 kilometres from the Eiffel Tower.

Long lines of barges, some ten deep, are rafted together along the quay at Conflans-Sainte-Honoré. Most of these are no longer working barges, their heyday long past. Behind them, tall houses stick tightly together huddled in awe of the tall-spired church behind, stood up high on a hill in watch.

Damian is transfixed by a different place of worship. It's a barge that's been converted into a church, all brilliant white with a grand cross and even stained-glass windows.

Noah and India are agog at the array of watercraft; some of them straight from Richard Scarry pages, mechanically weird and wonderful. There's a blue and white medic's boat, a fire engine boat, a police boat and even a mini submarine.

By dusk we realise we are too late to pass through the Ecluse de Bougival – it's gone 7 pm. It's getting dark now and the river suddenly seems more hostile. We need somewhere safe for the night. We spot a cutting off to the right, with 1.5 metres of depth highlighted on our chart. Hopefully, tied up here, off the main river, we'll be safe. We nose along. There's a string of houseboats and the smell of wood smoke. This is tantalising. Soft orange glows suggest cosy evenings are being enjoyed inside.

We tick slowly to the end of the cutting looking for a space to moor. There's nothing. We turn back and choose the rustiest, biggest, least homely barge to tie on to as there doesn't seem to be anyone aboard. I hope they don't decide on this very night to come back.

We are almost in central Paris. It feels like the night before Christmas – laden with expectation. A moon silhouettes the trees on the opposite bank. We hear muffled laughter waft over the still, black water.

The next morning at almost first light, we motor back up the cutting. Peering into the different boats is just wonderful. I love houseboats but I have never seen so many in one place that are so incredibly beautiful.

Every one is different, but they are all finished to an impeccably high standard. It's as though each is trying to be more special than the last. We see boats with gardens on the roof; boats with wrought-iron pergolas and sundecks, swimming pools on the deck and expansive glass windows all around. Inside we glimpse enormous oil paintings hanging on the walls, Corbusier chairs and spiral staircases. Houseboats are usually owned by people who can't afford houses and as a result they usually look run-down and rough, but these boats are like penthouses crossed with art galleries. God, I could live in any one of them.

I feel like a spy, staring into houseboats from the water – the side where the people aboard don't expect anyone to be. They have let their guard down. I glimpse a woman staring into the mirror applying mascara, a man pouring boiling water into two mugs. Private cocoons, with their windows and their souls wide open on one side.

Noah screeches, 'Look, he's got no pants on' and points to a man skidding across the deck. The last thing poor 'no-pants' had expected to see at that hour was a toddler in a blue bandana floating past. I dearly wish we could go faster, but instead twiddle with a piece of rope on deck as we putter past, pretending not to have seen 'no-pants', not sure who's more embarrassed.

It isn't long before we get to Bougival. The Impressionists used to come here when it was nothing more than a village in the countryside. They came for the light. Plus, this was the last stop on the train line from Paris so it was the furthest they could easily travel in a weekend.

La Maison Fournaise in Bougival is the original 19th-century *guinette* where Monet, Manet and Degas used to hang out in their free time. The balcony here is the one depicted in Renoir's painting, *The Boating Party*. Even though I love art, I didn't know which picture that was until I saw it on the wall outside. Then I recognised it. It's the one that's featured throughout *Amélie*, one of my favourite films.

We've moored *Friendship* on the other side of the river. If she'd been here when Renoir was doing his painting, she'd be in the background.

As I stroll round the gallery holding India's hand, for once moving at her pace, I imagine how the Bohemians' laughter, clinking glasses and dancing were framed and captured by these great artists. Once again I am struck by the power of seeing history and place together. Bougival is brought to life. I think we would have fitted in here (now that Damian has binned the white vest).

Next door to the gallery I make a surprising discovery. There's a little boat-building firm making replicas of the rowing boats that were used at the time of the Impressionists. These are available for hire and there are one or two gliding up and down the river. I walk around the barn where they store the wood, the half-built hulls, the coiled ropes and brass fittings. The smell of the varnish and wood oil is intoxicating. It transports me back to my *Friendship* years, the period of my life that was lost to the pile of wood we now call our home.

I feel so comfortable in this environment, so happy. I start thinking about what it would be like to work in a place like this. Maybe I could combine this with my photography? Would that keep us all going? I remember what Trevor said about not going back. I decide to keep the ideas in a drawer in my mind. I'll return to them when I know more about where this journey is taking us and when it will end.

When we arrive at Port Van Gogh that evening, I write '24 kms to Paris' on the whiteboard in our galley, a little reminder of how far we've come and how little there is to go until we get to our first big milestone. This is really starting to feel like Paris now. Gone are the trees and the fields. We are surrounded by modern buildings, fluorescent lights, posters, telephone masts and the sound of car horns.

When we go to bed, the wind starts whipping up the Seine, creating small waves. On any other boat these would wash against the smooth hull and silently slide away, but the sides of *Friendship* aren't smooth. She's clinker built – rows of planks overlapping each other – and right now the waves are slapping against every single one of them. This only happens on clinker boats and only when waves hit them at a certain angle. The noise is ridiculous. Far from being romantic, it's unbearably annoying. Just loud enough to keep us awake, just random enough to drive us mad.

The next day, bags under our eyes from a rough night, we are ready for the city. Markets, shops, treats, comforts, calm nights in a secure yacht basin. I want to savour every one of the 24 kilometres left to go as this may be the only time in my life I ever do this. It strikes me that entering a city from the water is completely different to arriving by car. I've been to Paris many times before, but never like this. It feels like a new discovery, the way the Viking Norsemen must have felt when they travelled up the Seine for the first time. We feel like pioneers, scanning both sides of the river, looking ahead to a string of bridges, like steps leading us into the core of the city.

If they are like steps, they are part of a spiral staircase. I learn that the word 'Seine' comes from the Latin word for 'serpent' and as soon as you look at the chart you can see why. I had never noticed it before but now that we are travelling down the river, I realise that each loop almost cuts back on itself so that the distance we travel forward is almost minimal.

With just 14 kilometres until we arrive at the Eiffel Tower, we pass through La Defense: towering skyscrapers, windows, glass, reflections, mirrors; international companies beavering away as we potter past, two wavelengths crossing momentarily. It's drizzling again and Noah and India are staring through the plastic 'windows' at a world they've never seen. Even in London I can't remember ever going past skyscrapers with them in the buggy.

We pass the large Ile Seguin (11 kilometres to go) and see the ruins of the old Renault factory. It holds a special place in French history. Not only was this the birthplace of the car company but also the workers seized the factory in 1968 during the student riots. Apparently when the students heard this they marched from the Sorbonne to the island to cheer the car workers on.

There is no cheering now. The island is desolate and ghostly. A rusting blue bridge reaches out to it and is greeted by a once-triumphant arch. The Renault logo is still proudly emblazoned across it but behind the façade is nothing but rubble. The whole place is like an eerie tomb rising out of the middle of the river. There have been various high-profile

attempts to resurrect the site – the latest was to turn it into an art gallery, but like the other plans it foundered. Sadly the old Renault factory is still more like the power station at Battersea than the one at Bankside.

Although technically we are ten kilometres from central Paris (a point on the map near Place de la Concorde), I feel like we're in the front garden. We pass to the right of Ile Saint Germain and under the Pont du Périphérique Aval. I can just make out something tall on the horizon.

On deck now with India and Noah, I strain for clues of a Paris I recognise only from the land. As we round the Pont du Garigliano, we get our first glimpse of her on our right: the Eiffel Tower.

'Wow ... there she is,' I shout to Damian, who is also staring. She grows steadily in height and majesty as we motor towards her, drawn as if by a magnet. Superlatives flow off our tongues as we gaze in awe. We are the peasants come in from the jungles looking at our Machu Picchu.

It's as though I have never seen the Eiffel Tower before. It's a structure I could describe with my eyes closed, yet I am marvelling at its size and beauty in ways I never imagined. This is what it must have felt like for the visitors to the Paris Exhibition in 1889. Mind-blowing.

I put my arms around Noah who is standing on the side-deck, hanging onto the railings. He's also transfixed.

'Look, Noah, isn't it beautiful?' I ask him.

'Yes, I like it. I like diggers.'

I'm confused and then I see the building site just before the bridge ahead. Noah has been looking at the bulldozers while we have been looking at the Eiffel Tower.

I laugh out loud. Maybe he'll be interested in the Eiffel Tower if I tell him it's a big crane.

CHAPTER 11

There's an island coming up splitting the Seine in two. The chart directs us to the left of it, *away* from the Tower, where there is deeper water. I am thrown completely. Do we get this close to our dream moment and then have to steer away at the last minute?

No way. *Friendship* doesn't have a big keel (the bit at the bottom of the boat that sticks into the water). In fact, she has only 90 centimetres of her bulk below the waterline so I reckon we are less likely to run aground than most. I peer at the channel of water ahead of us and utter what has become our favourite battle cry: 'Oh sod it.' I throw the wheel to the right.

We edge nervously towards the Tower, expecting any moment to hear a scrape of wood on the river bottom. It doesn't come.

Noah shouts and points at the bank. 'Look everyone! A rubbish truck! Look!'

'Tuck,' screams India in echo, also pointing to the bank from her vantage point of a blue and yellow plastic seat, on top of the coach roof.

We follow their gaze towards a cluster of moored boats and some bins, noticing a grey industrial rubbish collection truck noisily gnawing away. Just in front of the bins lies a prime mooring spot – and it's empty. We can hardly believe our eyes.

Here, under the Eiffel Tower, there's a space for us.

'Do you see what I see?' I ask.

Damian nods, incredulous. 'I guess we're always so busy looking for the obvious but Noah and India aren't. There must be some moral in there. Look for rubbish trucks and ye shall be rewarded.'

I can't believe it. This is what I'd dreamt about; mooring under the Eiffel Tower in Paris. It's on my 'Must-do-before-I-die' list. And it's actually happening. If we'd followed the chart, we'd have missed it. Fantastic. Utterly fantastic. I'm dancing up and down with excitement.

'Let's tie up for a few minutes. We should be able to nip out and take a couple of photos of *Friendship* with the Eiffel Tower in the background before we get caught – I assume this must be someone's permanent mooring space and they've gone off for the day.'

I suppose I should have realised that as soon as I stepped ashore someone would come over. He's tubby, has an impressive moustache (First World War-style) and is wearing an over-sized white T-shirt with equally baggy blue shorts. Despite these handicaps, he has the unmistakable air of someone in authority.

I'm on deck with the kids staring unashamedly at the man strolling towards us with such a friendly, haphazard look. Red cheeks, two wild caterpillars for eyebrows and a face like it's fashioned from playdough. He's such a caricature he cannot be for real. Perhaps *Candid Camera* is about to pounce and the free mooring space is a set-up.

'Don't look at him,' I hiss to Shiv under my breath as we secure the ropes. 'Just keep your head down and pretend we're supposed to be here.'

Years ago I learnt the art of getting away with things by being brazen. Few people like to embarrass themselves by questioning the actions of someone who looks as though they

know what they are doing. Unfortunately, our fat French friend is not one of those people.

'Bonjour,' he says chirpily.

I groan inside but say nothing.

'Bienvenue a le Plaisance de la Tour Eiffel,' he continues.

I look at him closely for the first time and then grin inanely as he explains that this mooring is very new, opens only in summer (therefore not marked in our books), and we are welcome in this space for the rest of the week. It turns out that a barge is behind schedule so we can take its space until it arrives.

Sensing our surprise that the charts send boats round the other side of the island, the capitaine explains it isn't because of the depth but because too many clog up the channel in front of the Tower taking photos.

Then, to top off his fantastic introduction to our new mooring, the capitaine invites us to a barbecue that he happens to have organised tonight for all the local boaters. Incredible. Could there possibly be a better way of staying in Paris than a whole week moored under the Eiffel Tower? It smashes any lingering memories of romantic weekends in Paris with old girlfriends.

That night, while I shower, ten feet away from us on the bank, a three-piece band plugs in wiring while the tubby capitaine lines up sausages over hot coals. This scene plays out to me through a diminutive eight-by-six-inch window. It's like watching the build-up to the Millennium celebrations on a portable television. Dull, but good to have on in the background as a reminder of the party coming up.

The jovial capitaine had been so effusive when he invited us to the event.

'You come for dreenks later? We 'ave mewseek, we 'ave feud.'

'Mais oui, bien sur. Merci,' I had nodded.

'Wonder what type of feud it is? French versus Brits?' Damian quipped.

With Coldplay crooning out of our own mini iPod speakers,

Damian creates a trouser press by sitting on three thick books. I fling clothes out of our locker under the bed, hunting for something equal to my optimistic mood.

Never before have I been invited to an evening soirée on the banks of the Seine. The spontaneity and unexpectedness makes it all the more potent. Last night's rainstorm and the water slapping against the clinker denied us sleep. Tonight we'll be dancing to a three-piece band. This juxtaposition of our days on *Friendship* sets me on fire, makes me come alive.

I pull on jeans (my other boating trousers are not fashionable enough), my lime-green, long-sleeved top and apply a whizz of lipstick, brought along in case of such an occasion. I'm dying to wear the one chic dress I packed. A Vietnamese hippie number in midnight blue silk, embroidered with bright flowers. It's a perfect outfit for the boat. I don't need to iron it and it rolls into a ball the size of my fist. However, it's too cold already to wear it. Even though it's August, the temperature on the water plummets when the sun goes down.

We wait for the party to kick into life, sitting side by side on our canvas deckchairs in the cockpit, sipping our very best bottle of wine (four euros no less). The kids are asleep and the baby monitor is in my pocket. We don't say much. There's no need. This is a special time and we both know it. We are in easy silence, watching the boats slowly chug along the river and the cars rush along the road behind. Two worlds, completely different, yet right next to each other.

We are shaken out of our reverie by Bon Jovi belting out 'Living on a Prayer' through the capitaine's sound system. We both smile and I lean over the side to see that the barbecue has begun. It's got dark in the last half-hour and we hadn't even noticed.

'Come on, let's go for it,' says Shiv, knowing that I always feel awkward in social situations. If it was a work thing I'd be fine because I know I'm good at my job and that gives me confidence, but when it's purely social, I'm less secure. I get those same stomach somersaults I used to get on the first

day at a new school (a feeling I had to go through six times before I was 14). Invariably I fall back on my ad-man skills and wheel out a showman's façade but maybe it'll be different this time.

'So, no babysitter required and no-one has to drive home,' I joke with Damian. 'The perfect night out.' We are capricious teenagers with parents away and no curfew imposed. Even Damian's usual pre-party nerves seem to be evaporating.

Smoke and chatter mingle together as boaters drink and jostle whilst laughter is lost in the air. Two cups of dark red wine are thrust into our hands by the capitaine. Buoyed by our unplanned arrival and the triumphal sounds of U2, my French flows. I drag a metal chair over to sit beside a drably dressed old man. His benign eyes and sad, shrunken body draw me in.

'Je m'appelle Siobhan.' I hold out my hand in greeting, unsure whether stooping to kiss this stranger is crass or expected.

'Enchanté. Je suis Jean.' (Another one. I remember the charming, younger Jean in Watten.)

After only minutes, I'm engrossed. Just as well he's almost eighty or Damian would be getting uneasy. A glance backwards into the crowd and I can't pick out Damian's flowery shirt, so I continue my conversation.

'Oui, je suis née dans un bateau.' Jean was born, grew up and married on a barge. He had three kids who attended 'barge schools' during the winter months.

'I have always lived on a boat. I can vividly remember horse-drawn barges as a child. Oh no, I can't imagine being in a house that can't move. How terrible,' he almost whispers.

Jean quietly recounts how when he was a toddler he was tethered with a rope length, exactly calculated so that he couldn't fall overboard, but could walk along the decks. He began driving the boat when he was six years old, learnt to ride a scooter in the empty hold of a barge and remembers how engines rapidly took over from horses.

'I married my sweetheart and the barge was painted for the wedding feast. We didn't really have a honeymoon. We went downstream to Conflans and there I loaded sand for Maubeuge. We'd never been there before, so that was our honeymoon.'

Jean's eyelids flutter. He's tiring. His middle-aged daughter, who has silently chaperoned our conversation, nods goodnight to me and escorts Jean away into the arms of the night. Together they must have supported each other like this along bank after bank, year after year. First him holding her hand, now her hooking his arm.

All the Jeans I have met so far have been charming and wonderful. If we have a third child we must name it Jean, boy or girl.

God knows where Shiv is. She always does this, disappears off into the crowd and talks for hours to some unsuspecting soul. It's the Irish in her. I'm chatting to Pierre, a gay designer who has lived on a small modern motor cruiser in the middle of Paris for the last ten years. He has an office locally but every night he goes back to his little 20-foot-long plastic boat. Often he takes it for a trip up the Seine after his dinner, just to see the city from a different perspective. It helps him relax, he says. I bet it does. We laugh at how small 20 foot is, but then we work out that because he lives on it alone, pro rata he has almost three times as much space to live in as we do.

I find Damian vigorously chatting with a stringy man, probably retelling his 'getting arrested on the M25' story. The man looks annoyed when I pull Damian away by the hand onto the makeshift wooden decking dance floor. Drums and guitar smash out Bryan Adams' 'Summer of '69'. Eyes shut, arms wheeling, body complying with the music, the sounds colouring an inky night by the Seine, I honour our arrival in Paris. Finally, tonight, Damian and I collide in emotional harmony and our steps work together on the dance floor. Over a hundred engine hours have driven us far enough away from our old life to now embrace this new country with splendour and ceremony, and this new life we are inhabiting.

It's been a long time since I've had this kind of physical and emotional energy. Noah's recently acquired catchphrase rings in my ears: 'I just love everyone in the world.' My heart too wants to scoop up Jean, the capitaine, the orange-shirted singer, Damian, Noah, India and *Friendship* and squeeze them all tight.

The sound of a train crossing the black bridge over the equally black river behind us makes me look up. Every carriage is lit up inside. It looks like a string of fairy lights flying unsupported through the sky. The passengers are looking down at our little party, watching everyone on the 'dance floor' grooving to a live band and either laughing, talking, or both. They must be wondering how on earth you get invited to such parties.

An hour later, it's the end of the evening. There's no more music, the coals in the oil-drum barbecues are glowing dimly and Pierre the designer is motoring back to his mooring across Paris. Shiv and I dance together in the quiet and in the dark. We're all alone. I don't need my life to get any better than this.

Slightly tipsy, we swagger the five steps home and collapse into a beautifully made 'al fresco' bed in the cockpit. Damian's ingenuity and foresight is touching. He will go to the ends of the earth for just one fantastic possibility of a moment made better, made memorable. He has set up an almost-double cockpit bed. Our heads are at the stern, our toes point towards the cabin door and the Tower. The canvas has been rolled back to bring in the night.

Snuggled together, toes entwined under a cosy duvet, our eyes reflect a fully illuminated Eiffel Tower. Then, as though specially ordered for us, lights explode in orange and shatter downwards taking our eyes with them, and I half expect them to spell out 'You made it.'

'We made it,' I whisper, holding back a well of emotion. This is one of those accidental moments of magic that makes my heart grow.

I feel I've barely fallen asleep before I am woken by Noah, wailing for a weewee. I poke my head above the duvet and realise it's morning. Our quilt is wet with a fine spray of dew. It hadn't felt cold in the night, but perhaps the red wine had dulled my senses. With no canvas awning I am suddenly aware that the whole world can see Shiv and I in our bed. Naked, I dash down to the cabin to help Noah. As I do so, the woman on the barge behind us waves at me.

Lifting Noah onto our Porta Potty is even more difficult than usual because the boat is rocking violently from side to side. There is a surprising chop on the Seine and now the barges have started moving up and down, creating waves and rolling us about even more.

Shiv reluctantly gets out of bed too and now we are all crashing into each other. The four of us getting dressed at the same time in the small space between our table and the bathroom is testing my patience. I escape the arms, legs and squealing into the calm of the cockpit, where to my surprise I find a bag of croissants on the rear deck. A note explains that they're from the capitaine to welcome us to Paris. What a nice bloke.

Damian is raving about the capitaine, whose real name we do not know. I wonder if he is called Jean. Everyone calls him simply 'Capitaine'.

I want to share my joy of being in Paris so I leave Damian with croissants, Bonne Maman jam and half-dressed kids, grab my jogging shoes and set off along the quay in search of a phone box.

Because I am breathing the heavy air of a capital city again, concrete and planned trees in my sight, no wild things encroaching, it seems perfectly fine that there are people everywhere. People in smart clothes, people walking dogs, people carrying shopping, people with agendas and Metros to catch. I want to get caught up in the rush; having had so much 'four-kilometre-an-hour time', I crave the speed, the bustle, the nastiness of a city.

When I am out of breath, I settle my shoulder into the corner of a public phone box and, armed with euro coins, call just about everyone I know in England to announce our arrival – and survival – thus far. No-one picks up. I've forgotten that most of the people I know are at work in the morning, not moseying around with two kids on the banks of a river in a foreign country. They're in meetings, grabbing a quick coffee or have their mobiles on silent. I forgot, too, that my mum is also in her own routine of a pre-breakfast stroll for the newspaper. I give up and amble back to *Friendship* past a boulangerie where I pick up a yeasty baguette fresh from the oven, just so I can feel a little like a local. Paris is even better than I remember her. I could stay here for months.

While Shiv goes off to broadcast our arrival to the world, I wander along the riverside with India in the pram and Noah on the buggy board. As usual, we're inspecting our new neighbours' boats.

Suddenly my mobile rings. I assume it's Shiv so am shocked when I see the number – my old office.

I can't believe they've rung me. I turn cold inside.

It's Guy. He needs to know where I left the notes from a client meeting in March. Christ knows. I can barely remember the client, let alone where I filed the notes (assuming I made any). I surprise myself at how much of my past life I have managed to shed without realising.

I fudge an answer and we sort things out. Even over the phone I can tell I'm now operating at about half the speed of Guy (someone I hired as a graduate trainee not that long ago). He makes me feel out of touch, off-the-pace and old. I'm no longer at the cutting edge. I'm just some bloke who 'used' to work in advertising.

Is that how I have to define myself now? I feel like the countless new mums I've met who describe themselves in terms of what they *used* to do because they're not sure who they are any more. Finally I understand how they feel.

Guy interrupts my thoughts by asking where we are.

'Paris!' I proclaim proudly. 'We're moored right under the Eiffel Tower.'

'Paris?' he asks, laughing out loud. 'Is that all? But you've been gone for months . . .'

So much for telling people about our grand arrival.

Damian is in a bad mood and it's only nine o'clock. I knew the ad agency would somehow creep into our lives and hope to God that Damian doesn't get tempted back.

India is still chewing on a croissant when we join a long snaking queue for the Eiffel Tower. Eager tourists and pale teenagers chat and smoke cigarettes. I buy our own drug – hot steaming coffees in cardboard cups. Our equation of grumpy dad plus two toddlers, croissant ends and one apple juice won't add up to a peaceful morning queuing. I hope we get to the front fast.

'Look Mummy, sand!' Noah shouts gleefully, pointing at the ground. I pour half my coffee on a patch of sand at our feet and hand over my plastic coffee stirrer with a time-consuming idea. I have become very good at inventing these.

'Now it's mud. Can you make a mud pie?'

'Me, me,' insists India, and Damian obliges, also sacrificing his coffee for peace.

An hour of early-morning waiting drifts by before we finally reach the lift. It is oozing people. We squeeze in, each clinging to a coffee-stained child. At the second level we spill out to merge with a sea of bodies and move about, not of our own accord. Ninety-six metres above the mud pies we peer down through metal balustrades and wire to the ant people and toy cars in the city below.

'Can I see?' asks Noah every six seconds, as he is buried in people. Damian lifts him onto his shoulders and a few tuts bounce off the crowd. I think we've just ruined someone's photo.

'What's that?' Noah questions, pointing to the roads.

'They're cars on the roads.'

'Tars,' echoes India, who loves to agree with anything Noah says. I am kneeling down next to her so our faces are side by side looking out. Her fingers prod through the wire, and I press my cheek to the cold metal to block out the sense of enclosure.

'They not cars. They are small,' Noah says, disappointed.

'Yes, that's because they are far away,' Damian explains logically.

'Where's the awful tower?' interrupts Noah with a complete topic change.

'We're *in* it and it's the Eye-full Tower,' reminds Damian, smiling softly, slowly coming back to us from his past world.

'The awwwwfill tower,' repeats Noah.

'Filltawaaa,' echoes India softly in my ear, and she nuzzles in close as some brown boots and fat calves close in on her. I don't want to be here, squashed in by tourists' legs, seeing Paris from the air. After last night's magic, I don't want the slog of summer-holiday sightseeing. Jean, the capitaine, our quirky, rocky mooring, the rubbish bins – that's my new Paris. That's the one that I want.

It's awful up here. There are too many people. I must be the only one not interested in the view. You can forget the cultural splendour of Paris; I just want to look down on *Friendship*. I stare at the Seine, tracking the boats along the river until I find her. At this height she is nothing more than a small dot but I take 30 photos so that I can bore Noah and India in years to come with exactly where we stayed.

The warmth of close bodies, the hubble of foreign languages and the fear of losing Noah or India below all these knees is too much. It's much like a sweaty tube journey on the Northern Line in summer. After the open countryside of the past few months, my body is accustomed to its own breathing space or, at worst, only each other to contend with at close quarters. Neither Damian nor I want to ascend the full 267 metres to the top, packed in like sardines, so we grab the next lift back down to earth. And head for the nearest patch of green.

The wide pastoral lawn of the Champs-de-Mars is cut short, springy and firm. Lying on my back on the grass, feeling the softness with my hands, I stare up at the grey tip of the tower against the dull, flat sky. Damian, Noah and India all do the same. We are a family of grass angels.

'The French do lawns well, don't they?' says Damian, his eyes already closed. Within moments he is inert. I envy his ability to drop into deep sleep anywhere. It's also irritating as it means I now have to stay awake to mind the kids. We cannot both fall asleep.

A foot away stands an ornamental fir tree enclosed by a three-foot-high fence. I lift Noah and India inside the barricade, hand them the plastic coffee stirrers that I've saved from earlier (just in case) and present another game.

'This is the best, best digging here. It's your own private area, no-one else can get in. Isn't that great?'

'Yeah. No baddies can get in. Can I be the guard?' shouts Noah.

'Great idea. You keep guard while India digs. I'll lie here and pretend to be dead. You warn me if anyone comes. Okay?'

'Mmm,' nods India.

Rejoining Damian on the grass, I lie back and close my eyes for ten minutes, listening to Noah and India's gurgles and chatter. This is definitely the best view of the 'Awful Tower'.

Damian awakes with renewed energy. He has the power-nap down to a fine art.

'You know what, Shiv? That *was* an awful tower. Why don't we forget the tourist stuff while we're here. Let's face it, sightseeing is tough with the kids and both of us have been here before. Why not come back to Paris when they're older and do the sights then, when they'll appreciate them more?'

'Okay. So what do you want to do in Paris then?'

'Let's just pretend we live here. Hang out and relax like chilled Left Bank artists.'

'Wow, you've definitely slowed down a bit. Six months ago you'd have underlined all the best bits in the guidebooks and written out a timing plan for us.'

'Maybe this trip is working.'

'Maybe . . .'

I'm certainly slowing down. And not just because I'm desperate to become more of a hippie like Shiv (except with a beard) but because we're now travelling around by bicycle, which, with kids on the back, is almost as slow as when we're on the boat. It's funny but both forms of transport have helped us to see things with new eyes – like the symmetry of the trees that line the Seine, the width of the pavements, the smell of the boulangeries and the sound of dozens of different languages mixing together on the streets. I realise that instead of haring past the world at speed, I'm now in it. Going slowly is an antidote to my previous existence. Even so, my nature is to rush ahead and see what's coming next. I'm not sure I will ever *fully* embrace going slowly but at least now I can see there are some benefits. Maybe going slowly is some kind of therapy for me.

I ADORE the bikes – the freedom they give us is like birds leaving the nest. Added to that, moving around independently of Damian is quite a thrill. We can play tag. I can zoom past him on the vast boulevards of plane trees. He can scream up behind me, Noah screeching with delight, and then overtake me dramatically, bell ringing, yelling, 'Come on slowcoach.'

Damian is a travelling circus, laden with bags, props and a heavy child. He carries it all with such panache, as though it's the most normal thing in the world. Everyone turns their heads as we pedal past, India's white muslin flowing behind her in the wind, like a glamorous actress from the Thirties showing off in a new motor car.

On our flying machines, we venture miles from the shell we've been inhabiting to take in the oceanic boulevards, the Champs Elysées, Paris Plage and most of the 20 *arrondissements* (districts). We also cycle nowhere in particular, simply enjoying the movement, letting the wind and smells of Paris penetrate. This is 'being' at its finest.

The only problem with the bikes is that although Shiv and I get a real workout, the kids are very sedentary sat in their

little seats on the back. I'm worried about India. She isn't doing enough walking. She's just grasped how to do it but there's nowhere for her to practise. On board, there's only enough room for her to stagger seven steps before she has to stop so she's not improving at all. The banks of the Seine are hardly the safest place for her to master her new skill, the grass by the Eiffel Tower is too full of tourists and the pavements are simply too busy for a small girl just 60 centimetres high to be lurching about. We need a park.

At once I'm looking at a city I thought I knew quite well from a completely new perspective. I've never looked for large, open areas before. I've always been too interested in chic restaurants and funky galleries. I rack my brains and grasp at vague memories of the quiet gardens surrounding the Louvre.

So it is the next day we saddle up for the world's most famous art gallery. We are the only ones there who have no interest in seeing either the art or the sites mentioned in *The Da Vinci Code*. All we want from the Louvre is the flat grass of the ornate gardens in front of it.

With a picnic of baguettes and cheese we while away hours watching our precious little girl totter about in a huge nappy and a small white cotton blouse. Shiv and I take turns to kick a ball with Noah, read the English newspapers (what a treat now we're in a city) and even just doze off in the sun. Well, *I* doze. Shiv doesn't seem to need as much sleep as I do. It must be because she's been a mum for longer than I have.

While I drift in and out of sleep, I recognise that even though I'm trying to stop living for the future, it'll be amazing to tell India when she's older that she mastered the art of walking in the gardens of the Louvre.

Today we must relinquish our slot on the quay for a new barge so it's time to get on with the chores. I pack away *Cloud Atlas*, which I finished yesterday while Damian was restoring an old tricycle he'd found in the bins. Noah and India help me roll up our deck washing-line, collect pegs and pack away stray ropes that they have been playing with. The capitaine beckons me over from the bank.

'Ici, pour vous.' He hands me the least likely thing. A maroon-red, metal, finely made 'trotinette' – an antique scooter. 'A present from Jean, the man you spoke to at the party, who lives on *Itinerant*. He knows you have to leave today and he wanted to give you this for the children.'

It used to be Jean's when he was a boy. He's too shy to give it to us himself. Tears prick my eyes as Damian's head pokes into view.

'You okay?' he asks.

'I'm happy and sad at the same time.'

Yet again, a community has moulded around us. *Friendship* seems to get us to the core so very quickly, like a time-travelling machine. In only a week on the Quai de Grenelle, we have moved miles into people's hearts as they have entered ours. The loyal part of me wants to put down roots here with our new friends Jean, the capitaine and the rubbish collector who Damian chats to every day. I really don't want to leave.

We both feel empty as we leave Port Grenelle but at least we had a week here and we aren't going far. Hopefully our new home will be just as exciting. We are heading to Port Arsenal, the most famous marina in Paris. Only steps from the Bastille monument, it will be like having a mooring two minutes' walk from Trafalgar Square.

Friendship noses into the Seine once again and heads east to new pastures. We are instantly beguiled – Damian from the wheel, India in her bucket seat, Noah and I from the bow. I have visited Paris so many times before, but never, ever like this.

India sits next to me on the roof, chomping through a banana, happily letting Paris slide by between bites. Crowds of people lean over the sides of the bridges to wave and take pictures of us. We must look a bizarre sight. I imagine what I would think if I saw an old wooden boat pass under Waterloo Bridge,

complete with a two-year-old boy and his mum in the bow, and a dad with a 16-month-old girl sat on the roof next to him.

I can see Shiv pointing things out to Noah on the bridges but I'm drawn to the hundreds of houseboats lining each bank, laden with flower pots, barbecues and sun-loungers. They add a shabby-chic charm to the river. It would be great if they allowed the same kind of community to build up all along the banks of the Thames; a string of boats and bohemians running from Docklands to Richmond.

What a life! To be on the water but also in the buzz of the city; this must surely be the perfect combination. I add 'Living on a boat in Paris' to the list of things we might do when this adventure is over.

We pass under my favourite bridge in Paris, the Pont Neuf. (Actually, it's the only bridge in Paris I could name until today.) The film *Les Amants du Pont-Neuf* is my ultimate love story. A blind girl, her lover and a homeless tramp live in a concave curve of the bridge. Their story seared into me the beauty, wonder, awfulness and hope of true love. I gaze up as we pass below it and I remember that, oddly enough, the lovers end up on a barge sailing off into a black sky. I wonder if that will be us at the end of this journey.

As soon as the gates to our new home open, I sense how different the Port Arsenal will be to our small and relaxed mooring at the Eiffel Tower. This is more conventional, safer and easier than Port Grenelle. There are security gates, electricity points, picnic tables and even a playground. It's true then, there really *is* a full-scale marina in the centre of Paris.

I spot *Gallivant* immediately. It's hard to miss her as she protrudes from the smaller boats around her. I note a German couple we'd seen at Port Van Gogh. I recognise a barge I saw pass us at Cambrai and we see Rudy and Yytte, the retired Danish couple we met in Cergy.

I realise that we're not on our own any more. We are now

part of a boating community, a moving mass of individuals, just like a flock of birds. Except this isn't any old bunch of birds. We're all Jonathan Livingston Seagulls.

'Welcome to the Arsenal,' shouts Rudy from the bank, grabbing our mooring line. 'Where have you been?' (Like everyone else, he had missed out on the mooring by the Tower.)

'It is so nice to see Fender-ship again,' laughs Yytte. At first I think she's simply confused about the name of our boat, but then I see she's joking about the ridiculous row of fenders that now line both sides of our boat (since the tunnel incident).

'Fender-ship'. Very clever, I think to myself, especially with English not being their first language. I guess they made that one up one night as they talked about us. They must do what we do – chat about the people on other boats, trying to work out their stories. I love the fact that no matter what we imagine, the truth is often more surprising.

Within minutes of mooring, Damian strips down to his khaki shorts ready to get stuck into his favourite job: boat cleaning. He's probably embarrassed at our new name, *Fender-ship*, and wants to spruce her up. I am having nothing to do with this and herd the kids ashore to explore our new home and say hello to people we recognise.

After months aboard, I now reluctantly accept that Damian's fastidiousness on the boat is necessary – is a good thing rather than an evil one. Plugs of ham, knobs of mushy bread and globs of honey find their way daily into *Friendship*'s underworld. Without Damian aboard we would probably have rats – fat and happy ones.

Unlike Damian I like mess. I love to pick up a newspaper that has lain untouched for months, only to read something new in it. To find a card from a friend, months old, and re-read it. To leaf through piles of photos that I have left, one day to sort out. It's not that I am lazy about tidying. It's more that I love the chaos and collision of stuff lying around, another manifestation of my childhood – brought up in a home chock-full of books, newspapers and souvenirs from lives lived abroad. My untidiness drives Damian to despair.

I tell myself that I need to tidy and clean the boat because she is small and we can only make it work if we keep her organised. While this is true, it's also an excuse. The real reason is that no matter how much I try to chill out, I'm one of those people who can't relax until everything around me is tidy. It's a curse. Also, if I'm honest with myself, I'm finding it hard to accept that *Friendship* is getting battered by the day-to-day living aboard. Not to mention the seemingly constant smell of urine and wet nappies that permeates the air in our cabin.

'Get over it,' I say to myself. 'That's what it's like having kids, what did you expect?' The crazy thing is I *did* expect this. I just thought I'd be able to handle it better. I've only just managed to accept the Bob the Builder stickers that are plastered all over the mahogany table that took me three months to carve.

After ten years making *Friendship* perfect, it's difficult to stop protecting her. I know she isn't a 'museum piece' and 'she has to be used, that's the whole point' (Shiv's words ringing in my ears), but I'm finding it hard not to don a pair of Marigolds whenever I get the chance (an unappealing trait in anyone, let alone a man).

I have taken everything that wasn't bolted down and laid it on the bank. It's taken three hours to get *Friendship* back to bare bones and the path next to us is lined with the kind of equipment most people would never dream of taking on a boat. If looking into someone's supermarket trolley gives you an insight into their lives, then looking through this man-made mountain must be the equivalent of reading an intimate diary.

Everything in my life is on that bank right now, except for my family. I know it's not exactly minimalist living when you see how much crap we've got with us, but at the same time, it is liberating to think that everything we want in our life is

in that pile. Even better, we can move it around with us and go wherever we want to. That really is freedom. We are like snails and *Friendship* is our shell.

I can just make out Damian's hunched body from across the far side of the marina, where I sit on a wooden slatted park bench in a children's playground.

'Where's Hamish and Lola?' asks Noah, surprised, I think, not to see them here. It is a park after all, and Hamish and Lola are the two kids Noah used to knock around with in Queen's Park. He used to gallop into Lola and hare away with Hamish's ball. They were his friends.

'They're not here, sweetheart. They're in London.'

'Is London near the park?'

'No, London is over the sea. Where we used to live. We are in Paris. You won't see Hamish or Lola in this park.'

'Where's Paris?'

'In France. Here. We're in it.'

'Is France made of sand?'

'Yes, and trees and buildings and museums and lots of French people.'

This is the first time that Noah has referred to London. It's as though being in a park he is back there. So far he hasn't mentioned missing anyone or anything from our life in 10 Amery Gardens, Kensal Rise, London. He lives completely in the present. India too. She probably cannot remember anything of London except for green grass, carpets and lots of feet, as she spent all her time before we left crawling or sleeping.

Our new mooring might be different but we spend our time in Paris in the same way; criss-crossing the city on our bikes; spreading our time between cafés, parks, the riverbank and the marina playground. We also get to know more of our neighbours, including a cool South African couple, a posh American lady who lives on a British tug and an English couple who have left a life in Barcelona for a farmhouse in Brittany that they plan to restore.

Nuser 2, owned by Rudy and Yytte, the Danes, is old but immaculate. Everything is scrubbed and buffed. Even the engine room has a floor so clean it would put most hospitals to shame. Obviously I love it. No stench of urine here.

'So you came here from Copenhagen?' I ask Rudy one day. 'That's some trip. You must know your boat pretty well.'

'Oh no. Ha ha ha. This is our first trip. We'd never been on a boat before,' laughs Rudy in his sing-song Danish accent.

Yytte cuts in, 'Well Rudy, that's not quite true. We did drive to the Canal du Midi last summer to hire a boat. We wanted to see if we liked it.'

'What? And then you just bought one and set off for France?' I interrupt incredulously.

'Yah, pretty much.'

'Blimey. What made you do it?'

'We looked around us at our friends and they all lived the same life; they all retired, they all played golf and had drinks parties. We wanted something different.'

'You got that right then.'

'Yes, in life people often make decisions that close down their options. That is what many of our friends have done. My philosophy is to always make decisions that open up new choices,' advises Rudy sagely.

I ponder this seemingly simple approach to life. Rudy has suddenly become 'The Diceman' with brains.

'Yah, it means all sorts of things happen to us. For example, now we are staying the winter here in Paris. We have just booked in. We just decided, just like that.'

Rudy and Yytte are like two kids who have a surprise day off school. Dressed in matching beige sweatshirts, jeans and boating shoes, they remind me of elves the way they bob and skip around their boat. Their enthusiasm for life is infectious.

'You mean you can stay here for the winter? Wow. Imagine it, Dame. We could hole up here. A romantic snowy cold winter in the middle of Paris. We'd have to take up smoking, drink lots of wine and wear woollen socks in bed to stay warm. Shall we do it too? Shall we stay the winter? What do you think?'

'Oh ho, ho. What a super idea,' chivvies Rudy. 'We could be neighbours.'

I'm a man inspired. 'I'm going to go and book us in right now,' I exclaim, and with that I am off, running to the marina office to get us a slot next to the Danes for a really international winter.

Half an hour later I clamber back onto *Friendship* where Shiv is bathing the kids in the washing-up bowl. She looks up, a picture of expectation – like a child.

'There are no spaces left for winter. The Danes got the last one. The capitaine says there is no way in hell we can stay.'

Shiv's face crashes. In her mind's eye she had already become a Parisian for the winter.

So that's it then. No sending the kids to a local Parisian nursery. I was so convinced I'd be speaking Paris slang by March.

'Maybe we could head upstream and find a little village there for the winter. We could come in every day on the Metro,' I say, trying to console myself. 'Mind you, it wouldn't be the same. It'd feel like commuting. Let's make the most of it for a month or so while we can, before the winter.'

'Um. There's more bad news, Shiv. We have to leave tomorrow. It turns out we're on a temporary mooring and there's another boat booked into this space tomorrow.'

'What! You're joking! I'm not ready to leave Paris. We've only just arrived. I was so looking forward to meandering around all those little bookshops, pottering in the markets ...' I trail off. 'Can we can go back to Port Grenelle, by the Tower?'

'You know we can't. That barge arrived to take our place, and anyway the mooring closes down at the end of summer. I guess this is what happens when we don't plan ahead.'

'We don't need to plan. This was just bad luck. We'll just have to amble on southwards then. There's no rush, after all,' I say, bruised by Damian's dig at me about planning.

'Well there is actually,' says Damian sheepishly. 'The capitaine has just warned me that parts of the canal system are closed off for the winter. Basically if we're not at the top of the Rhone by late October, we'll be in trouble and won't be able to get out. Some of the canals are worked on – repairs, dredging and stuff – while others freeze up because the water is so still. If we happen to be in the wrong place, we could get frozen in till the spring thaw.'

'Frozen in? I can't believe I haven't read about this before. Huh, so much for my research.'

'Yeah. We could be trapped for five months.'

'Ooh. How exciting.'

'What – on *Friendship*? With that Porta Potty and no room to move? Shiv – come on.'

We squeeze tightly together into bed that night but neither of us can sleep. We are restless about the fact that we have to leave Paris and wriggle around noisily, trying to get comfortable.

Tomorrow, reluctantly, we start our journey towards Burgundy.

CHAPTER 12

The motor is pounding and so is my head. I've gone into 'man on a mission' mode, determined to speed to the 'good bits' of the canal system in case we hit another setback. The goal is Sens, the gateway to Burgundy, with a break at Saint-Mammes on the way.

Wallowing in my own little world of loss, I face backwards, stretched out in our port-side hammock, which is strung between the cabin roof and the sternpost. I have spent the morning sulking, teenager-like, about the Paris 'news', annoyed that we've had to leave early from a rip-roaring house party, a bohemian winter in Port Arsenal. Now, mirroring my mood, the beauty of Paris has been replaced by industrial chimneys. She is literally fading away from me as the functional bridges march overhead. Who knows if we will ever return to Paris on a boat and with no deadline?

I'm not in the mood for talking. I'm pissed off. Having to leave Paris before we want to is like reality slapping me in the face. So much for being carefree. If only we had rung ahead or looked at a few more guidebooks, we could have been booked into the marina at Paris for the whole winter. Instead we're scurrying away with our tails between our legs.
  And the irony of it all is that we hadn't thought beyond

Paris. It was such a big milestone it blinded us to what lay beyond it.

Damian isn't the only one who's absorbed at the moment. Last night, crushed against the wooden hull by Damian's bulk, my face inches away from our galley fan, I spent an age in that half-asleep state mulling over life, dreams mixing with reality. Between three and four in the morning, never the best time to make any decisions, I nevertheless made a few.

In those warped early hours I realised that, since getting married and having kids, I've lost my ability to make decisions, simply following in Damian's wake. I never used to be like this. Pre-Damian I was an independent, strong-minded, opinionated woman. Now I become flustered when having to choose which canal to take and go wobbly if I have to steer the boat anywhere but in a straight line.

After last night I am determined to get back to the old Shiv. That means letting go of the kids (a little). Ever since Noah was born I admit I have found it ridiculously difficult to let Damian handle the kids his way. It's been like watching someone holding a hand grenade, unaware that the pin has already been removed. Knowing it's going to explode in his face, but he's clueless.

Now my need to let go is overwhelming. Being jettisoned from Paris has given me perspective on my previous, highly timetabled and settled life.

So, on the decision front I have to stop being a passenger in my own life, and actually do some of the driving. Perhaps I should start with *Friendship*. If I can handle her round corners as well as on the straights, maybe something will rub off on me.

We motor until dusk. The next morning we pick up the same pace. Shiv has insisted on sharing the driving, which has been both unusual and terrifying. At least we haven't hit anything and have travelled much further than we would have done otherwise. The hammering of the engine has been relentless, much like the thoughts in my head. Not being able to stay in Paris has challenged me to define what I really want from

this journey, not only in terms of where we go, but more importantly what I want to learn about myself. Who am I and who can I become? I haven't a clue, but I sense that Shiv also wants to make changes. I just hope that we move towards each other rather than away.

I have ousted Damian from the wheel again and am taking in the engine sounds while avoiding passing gravel-laden tugs. Nevertheless there's lots of time to think up here. Now I know why Damian doesn't relinquish the wheel for long.

Damian – he is an unstoppable force in my life. Without him life would undoubtedly be arid. However, with him, my main concern is being washed aside by the floodwaters. He has this unerring belief in our ability to alter our behaviour if we want to. He spends some days, like New Year's Day, reminding me of his own resolutions and throwing me titbits on how he is to re-invent himself. In the last two days alone I've had 'I'm definitely going to grow a beard' and 'It is time for me to have long hair' and 'I must live for the moment'. It's quite charming really, and remarkable that such a successful career man approaching 40 seeks so fervently to grow long hair. Is his mid-life crisis gaining momentum?

There's a crash from the galley, then a cry. I wince. My legs itch to rush below but my mind compels me to stay where I am. I peek down just as Damian looks up and our eyes lock. I snap my head back and fiddle with the GPS, hoping he didn't see the look of anxiety shoot across my face.

Bloody hell. India has fallen off the bunk in the cabin. It's the second time in the last hour. The boat is tiny and yet I am still incapable of keeping an eye on both kids at once. I might be turning more and more into a mum on this trip but I still haven't developed the X-ray vision and radar-like senses that Shiv has.

Before we set off, I thought that the biggest danger on the boat for the kids would be falling in the water but because we are so paranoid about it, Noah and India can't make a

move on deck without being leashed to a rope, made to hold a handrail or wear a lifejacket.

It turns out that the real problem is that they aren't tall enough to climb on and off the seats in the cabin. This means they're constantly crashing onto the wooden floor, usually head first (or at least it seems to be that way when I'm 'on duty'). India now has bruises on her arms and forehead, making her look very fragile and making me look like a child-beater. I'm not quite sure how to help her. I can't even put a small ladder in the cabin because there's just no room.

I wonder how long it will take for Noah and India to grow a couple of inches. I glance over at the height chart I've carved into the side of the toilet door. Chiselled into the shiny mahogany are notches that record the ridiculous growth of Noah and India over the last few months. I can't believe that children grow this fast in 'normal' life; maybe living on this tiny boat is the equivalent of battery farming for humans.

Damian and I are saved from a 'discussion' about how to stop India falling to the floor by the sight of Saint-Mammes. We round a bend and rows of barges clinging to densely wooded banks come into view, a fraction of the number that would have been here long ago. Our engine cuts through the graveyard quietness and I can sense the ghosts of a thousand bargemen.

The boats lie in state together, seeming to contemplate the bustling, exotic lives of their heyday during the late 19th century. Past their steely tombs, a glimpse of a railway bridge is a reminder of the young guns that shattered their reign.

Once 40,000 bargemen plied the French waterways as we are doing now. The arrival of the train soon shunted the quiet, hard-working, often illiterate men out of the way and now only a thousand or so still pull back the net curtains in the captain's cabin to greet a new day on the river. Some are here in Saint-Mammes, looking out at the two kilometres or so of tree-lined, almost suburban clipped lawn running down to the water's edge.

I panic at the thought of 'parking' *Friendship*, so bail out to Damian. He nudges her expertly between two new finger pontoons. I look towards the town and a strange feeling twists my insides. It surfaces at each new mooring. Butterflies in my stomach – the same ones I used to get as a teenager before school discos. It's fear mixed with hope.

I hope that Saint-Mammes revives our adventure. Now that we need to get to the Rhone by late autumn, we must be so much more careful about where we stay. The next few months are going to be like walking a tightrope. Don't go too fast! Don't go too slow! Where do we stop and what do we miss out? Who knows?

We roll the green canvas awning back over our cockpit to reveal a full 180-degree view of the town. It's like pulling the curtains open at the theatre, except there's no-one onstage. There's not a soul about.

A waddle of ducks is asking to be watched. I lower both the kids onto the pontoon and climb out after them.

While Shiv re-immerses herself with Noah and India, I shoot off to look for the bread shop, butcher and maybe even a supermarket. We've learnt it's best to get ourselves orientated as quickly as we can. I haven't actually found anywhere useful yet because I've come across a shop that is much more exciting; in fact, it's heaven.

The establishment in question is a boat chandler that's been artificially inseminated by an Oxfam store. The hybrid offspring is a cornucopia of the kind of junk that I lust after: there are shackles made from anodised aluminium, captains' hats and brass lanterns mixed with old framed advertisements for Citroëns, second-hand bicycles and vinyl records.

After 30 minutes my eye is drawn to two pieces of polished stainless steel; tubes that have been bent into beautiful semi-circles with a flat piece of metal filling the middle. They are the kind of thing I want to pick up and stroke. It turns out they are door handles from the old Paris Metro carriages.

They were removed when the trains were scrapped and somehow ended up in this shop. As I hold them, I rack my brains for an excuse to buy them. I suddenly come up with a brilliant answer. These could be screwed horizontally onto the side of the bunks in our cabin to make two little steps for the kids to get up and down onto the seats. Small, discreet and stylish.

Within an hour they are fitted into *Friendship* and christened 'The Paris Steps' in honour of their Paris Metro roots. The kids love them – they are fun to climb. Shiv loves them – no more bruises and a little bit of Paris for keeps. I love them – they are beautiful.

In the time it has taken me to explore the length of a pontoon, Damian has reconnoitred the full three-kilometre length of the town, found the one and only curio shop, bought their oldest, oddest piece and fitted it on board. That sums us up. I 'am' and Damian 'does'. He cannot spend a day without building, bettering, creating. My days can pass without much to show for them but memories. Now, between us, we have two 'Paris Steps' and an old piece of orange rope that Noah found in the mud.

We've only been here a day but already Saint-Mammes has been good for me. Maybe it's the sunshine. Or is it the first flush of a new relationship? Albeit on the rebound. I'm still getting over the whole 'leaving Paris' thing. It was like being dumped by a beautiful girl, one I'd fantasised about for years and then finally got the chance to date. At first it had been great between us but then I had to get serious about it, didn't I? So just as I'm thinking about moving in, she kicks me out and replaces me with some Danish bloke called Rudy.

Saint-Mammes is my new partner and she's coaxing a smile out of me once more.

We wake to a crisp Sunday morning. A town this size should be pretty sleepy: old folk in the church and young ones in bed.

I figure this is the perfect day for Damian to teach me the finer points of boat-handling.

Friendship's bulk and sheer power when under way makes me edgy – five tonnes' worth of edginess in fact. I find myself imagining what would happen if her engine stalled. How we would simply carry on ploughing a furrow through the slight wooden pontoons, how the sound of splintering wood and joints giving way would hammer through the air.

Even so I am ready to take her on. I must be rising above the fog of early motherhood, when it was only possible to focus on the next opportunity for sleep.

Although I'm terrified, I now want to push myself. After all, what's the worst that could happen? I'm an optimist, plus I'm not the one who has spent the past decade under her planks, living with varnish in my hair.

Teaching Shiv the trickier aspects of handling *Friendship* is not easy. Imagine a husband teaching his wife to reverse into a small space in a car park. The opportunities for argument are almost unlimited. Now imagine doing it in a 1960s tractor. That's what it feels like in *Friendship*.

The worst thing is that Shiv can't hear what I'm telling her because the damn engine is so loud. I'm reduced to screaming at the top of my voice from the foredeck while at the same time trying to sound calm and reassuring. I don't think it's working.

Damian is bellowing at me again from the bows. Over the rasping of the engine stab it sounds like 'ut, ut!', 'now', 'urn, urn'. There are four fibreglass motor cruisers and an 80-foot barge moored around me, leaving only a few metres of clear water in which to turn.

I yank the wheel over to the left as the barge looms up six feet ahead, realise we are still moving forward and throw the engine into reverse, black fumes covering me, then, thank goodness, drifting over Damian.

From the banks, gaggles of people appear out of nowhere to

watch me unravel. Of course! It's the Sunday market. What a show I'm putting on for them. It's excruciating. I've never been comfortable with attention focused on me, usually pulling a stupid face when a camera is pointed in my direction to hide my inner embarrassment. Well, now I'm the star attraction of Saint-Mammes.

After what feels like forever, when I finally complete my tight turn and return to my start point, two leathery-skinned men in brown cardigans and smart trousers with pleats ironed in, clap in unison.

'Bravo,' they cry, without an ounce of sarcasm. I curtsey, blush, look to Damian, and fill up with pride.

Safely tied to the pontoon once more, we all tumble off the boat to stock up with provisions for the next leg of the journey. Holding India by the hand, I thread through wooden stalls selling blood-red cherries by the handful, pyramids of glowing peaches and bright green bunches of basil.

With Noah and India to keep an eye on between this mass of knees, wheelie bags and hustling grannies, I move at a snail's pace. Noah grazes on handouts from stallholders – a slice of apple here, a plum there. India strains on my arm to stroke two kittens curled up under the egg stall. Chatter mixes with wafts of my new favourite French market smell – freshly cooking, hot roast pork. I look around for Damian but he has disappeared.

He has this annoying habit of marching ahead of me at any new place, whether it's a market, a town or a marina (in fact, the only time he sticks close is at parties).

After a few minutes he returns. In his hands he triumphantly holds aloft three baguettes of *pain artisan* stuffed with wedges of hot pork. 'Where've you been?' he laughs.

He so loves to be the hunter, the bearer of the news, the first to the post. He is a high achiever in every sense of the word.

We should have set off for Sens by now. But even though we're in a hurry, these quiet towns seem to have a way of

drawing us in. There's always something else to look at. It's hard to leave. As we finish our delicious, makeshift lunch we agree to get going at the crack of dawn tomorrow.

At 6 am the next morning, with the kids sound asleep, Damian has already started the engine and untied us from the pontoon. I tiptoe up on deck carrying two mugs of tea, in only a long sweatshirt, knickers and socks. Damian loves me like this, especially when the kids are still asleep. It feels rebellious to start the journey semi-clothed, as if reaffirming that we are not like the rest of the working world.

Saint-Mammes lifted our spirits and today, despite our latent need to maintain some kind of momentum, everything on the river feels comfortingly gentle and slow. All is calm.

We drift into Sens a few hours later. The quay here is pretty impressive. And best of all, the town doesn't charge anything because it wants to attract passing boaters who will then bring income into the area. Simple, enlightened thinking.

Once again I'm amazed at how inventive these small French towns are at marketing themselves. From the beach at Saint-Quentin to the free moorings here, to the new pontoons at Saint-Mammes; they're all looking for ways to breathe life back into the canal system, now that the barge haulage businesses are dying off.

Damian is talking in his 'old agency way' again about innovative towns, lateral thinking and forward-looking civil servants. This place seems to have got under his skin already, even though it was me who really wanted to stop here.

One of the books in our boat library is Ken Follett's *Pillars of Stone* – chosen simply because my dad, usually scathing of blockbuster sell-out novels, had raved about it. In it, Sens Cathedral is mentioned and I really want to see why everyone in the Middle Ages went nuts about it.

As usual, as soon as we arrive I scan the boats around us. Given that the moorings are free, there are several of them. Right behind us is a floating caravan with a peculiar man on board who immediately comes over to introduce himself. His name is Bernard and he looks like he should be in the 118 118 advertisements; a throwback to the 1970s with big hair and a big moustache to match.

He lives on board all year round and never moves his boat, hence the ungainly wooden sundeck he has built on the roof, complete with plastic grass and sun-loungers.

My first impressions of Bernard are worrying. He dresses in tight hotpants, socks and sandals – no-one looks like that without having serious issues. After chatting to him, though, I realise he's actually a lovely bloke who just happened to get stuck in 1973.

While he's telling me how lovely Sens is, another vessel arrives. It's a traditional English narrowboat and the old man at the tiller has a white beard down to his waist. He looks like a pretty cool Santa Claus. I go over to help him tie up. He introduces himself and his wife (somewhat confusingly) as 'Leslie and Margaret'.

I leave Damian on the quayside chatting to what looks like a bunch of charity shop volunteers (baggy cardigans, kindly faces and slip-on shoes). I trundle over the cobbles to recce the town.

Sens is an ancient city that has attracted the rich and famous for centuries, long before we tourists found it. Pope Alexander stayed here a while and Thomas Becket spent part of his exile here. Not a bad place to be exiled, I reckon. There's more here than in most of the towns we've moored at since Calais.

The limestone cathedral of Saint Etienne, one of the earliest Gothic buildings in France, towers above the coffee drinkers below. I try to imagine how it must have felt to be a peasant in the 13th century, dwarfed by the sheer height and solidity of the building, awed by the pointed arches, the flying buttresses and stained-glass windows. With no Imax theatre or skyscrapers in those days, it must have blown their minds.

It doesn't look particularly special to me, though, probably as we have sailed so close to Notre-Dame. But there's one section of the roof that's glinting in the bright August sun. Diamond-shaped tiles of screaming canary yellow, sky blue and maroon grab my attention. I remember reading about these patterned terracotta tiles being typical of the Burgundy region. Wow. Of course – we have arrived in Burgundy.

Shiv's gone ahead while I sort out the boat, secure our ropes and hook up to the electricity point. An Australian couple trap me at the water tap and tell me about their ongoing journey to Greece, before inviting us to their drinks party on the quay tomorrow night. Despite my reticence about parties I assure them we'll be there. We haven't gone out enough on this trip but I guess that's because babysitters are hard to come by when you're on a boat.

No-one is prepared for the freakishly hot weather. Just as well the party is on the quay – even as dark descends, it's still sweltering.

We climb off *Friendship* and stroll six feet along the quay to the big event. Our contribution is a couple of bottles of red wine, our own chairs and two wine glasses.

'Kids asleep?' asks Santa's wife, Margaret. She's a mother of five herself, so gives me a knowing look.

I nod, hoping Noah and India don't show up my mothering skills by yelling, or worse, clambering out of their bunks to find me. I manoeuvre my chair so I can watch the cabin door surreptitiously, and take a sip of cold rosé.

'It's marvellous what you are doing,' adds Leslie. 'You're smart. You've done it early. Didn't wait till you retired. Wish we had. Life's too short.'

'Yeah, yeah,' agree Viv and George, an octogenarian American couple, from a white fibreglass cruiser. 'We've flown back to the States for so many knee uperaashins. Now my harrt is givin' out. My gawd, we've only just started and we may have to give up soon.'

'Yer now, we feel like spring chucks ourselves,' quips John, the

Australian, from *Seabird*. 'I'm fifty-two and we've only met old folk like yerselves,' he nods towards Santa and the octogenarians. 'Makes me feel younger.'

There's an awkward moment of silence as everyone tries to work out whether they've been insulted. Damian breaks it with a topic change.

'So, which canal are you all doing? The Nivernais or the Bourgogne? We can't decide,' he says chirpily and the awkwardness subsides.

'Hmmmm. Well, you have a grand choice to make,' says Leslie. He is so wise, yet humble at the same time. I have so much to learn.

'The Bourgogne Canal really does lie in the heart of France. It passes through marvellous towns like Dijon.'

'If you like your food and wine, this route will give you gout!' adds Margaret, laughing heartily along with Leslie, who is stroking his long beard.

'Burgundy was one of the wealthiest parts of France in the Middle Ages. They got rich from tanning, flourmilling, making cutlery, all kinds,' says Leslie.

I watch the fluid way that Margaret and Leslie operate in each other's company, building on each other's conversation, not seeking the limelight and still laughing at each other's jokes after so many years. Next to them I feel like a crass teenager, stumbling through life naïvely, seeing the world very much from my own perspective.

'Yeah. Most people do the Bourgogne,' chip in the Americans. 'You have to remember the problem with the Nivernais is it's very shallow in some places. We've heard of people who have run aground and have had to wait a long, long time to get sorted out.'

'We could do the Nivernais in *Friendship*,' boasts Damian. 'She draws less than a metre.'

'You're in luck then,' says Leslie. 'Like us. We can do either route in our narrowboat. It's great to have that choice. Not many boats do. But they're both wonderful canals so it's a difficult decision.'

'I guess it's like choosing which school to send your kid to,' says Damian. 'We've changed our dinner party conversation from schools to canals.'

Everyone laughs.

The banter continues till almost midnight when we retire back on board. Already I like the sound of the Nivernais, but then I am always one to support the underdog.

Later, collapsed in bed, the fans are on full blast, doors thrown open wide to catch any breath of wind. It's still desperately hot. When the kids went to bed, Damian hosed down the decks to cool off the boat to reduce the temperature of the cabins below. He also rigged up a special canvas 'sock' to divert any wisps of wind through the hatch into the kids' bunkroom, reducing it from a sweltering, torpor-inducing 40 degrees to a relatively cooler 30.

That night I lie awake in the heat mulling over the pros and cons of the two canals that lie ahead of us. Do we go for the obvious joys and clichéd beauty of the Bourgogne or the subtle charms and quiet aloofness of the Nivernais? If they were women, I know that I'd lust after the excesses of the Bourgogne but fall in love with the offbeat charm of the Nivernais. I ponder this for a while and then realise it isn't helping me at all.

Damian is obsessed about which canal we should take, when it's so clear to me. But if I tell Damian now, he will be untying the boat and preparing for the off at first light tomorrow. And I'm not ready for that.

I like being here, with neighbours again. Wallowing in the heat like lazy seals, soaking up pearls of wisdom from Leslie and Margaret and sipping burgundy on the quayside till it's cool enough to go to sleep. There's something completely 'summer holiday' about being here. I'm not ready to pack up and head to the airport just yet. I'll hang on for another day before breaking the news.

'The Nivernais,' I declare loudly to Shiv, as I hand her a mug of tea one morning.

'What?' she asks, rubbing her eyes.

'It should be the Nivernais,' I continue.

'What should?'

'Where we go next. The Bourgogne or the Nivernais. We're taking the Nivernais. I've decided.'

'I hate it when you do this,' Shiv snaps.

'What?' I ask innocently.

Shiv rages without pausing for breath. 'You can't just wake up and make an announcement like that. Instead of discussing something you come to a decision in your head and then tell me what we're doing as though I'm not even part of it. You're not back in the agency now you know.'

'But we've been talking about this for ages. I just want to make a decision and get on with it.'

'Well, actually I've already made a decision,' says Shiv, seizing the upper hand.

'What do you mean?' I ask, a little surprised.

'I knew ages ago which one we should take.'

'And . . . ?'

She grins. 'I think we should do the Nivernais.'

God, sometimes I wish Shiv was more like a 1950s house-wife, just agreeing with me, and not always wanting to have a point of view.

'Ummm. So . . . er . . . why do *you* want to do the Nivernais?' I ask.

'It's different. It sounds beautiful and remote. And it's a challenge.'

I look at Shiv and smile – she's my very own Nivernais.

CHAPTER 13

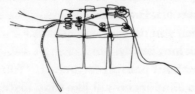

'Bugger' ...

'Bugger. Bugger. Bugger.'

What the hell's going on? The ignition key's turning, the choke is out, the gearbox is in neutral ... I'm doing everything I've always done, but all I'm getting is a clicking sound.

Click. Click. Click. Click. Click. Click. Click. Click. Click. Click. Click. Click. Click.

I wonder how many times I can do this before the starter motor burns out?

We've spent the last two hours saying goodbye to everyone; loading up the final items from the quay like the buggy, bath and bikes; making sure Noah and India have been to the toilet (so they don't start filling my Porta Potty before lunchtime); topping up all the water tanks; and swapping mobile numbers and email addresses with our new friends.

Now that we are finally on board and ready to go, the only sound our normally unbelievably noisy engine will make is a pathetic little click.

I look to the bow where Shiv and the kids are still waving wildly to Bernard and 'Santa Christmas'.

Click.

Click click and bugger bugger bugger click click again.

I glance over at our little crowd of neighbours on the quay.

They aren't sure whether to keep waving or not. Meanwhile, Shiv peers at me quizzically from the bow.

I check the engine is in neutral, reset the accelerator and try again.

Nothing.

I look back to the quay once more and in the faces of our new friends I actually see the moment of realisation that we aren't going anywhere. All of a sudden everyone is very awkward. Their hands drop. Leslie and Margaret smile supportively but everyone else looks down in embarrassment.

Every person there knows how awful it is when your boat fails you. It's not the same as your car not starting; it's so much bigger than that. When it lets you down, it feels like your whole life is letting you down.

This is painful. Damian will be hating this damp squib of a send-off – like an advertising presentation that has fallen flat. He may be cursing now, but later he'll be analysing every detail to see what went wrong. He may have left the pressurised environment of London, but he still has this need to perform, even if the audience is a motley crew of over-the-hill sailors.

Leslie, Margaret and the others all lined up on the quay are probably putting down our spectacular false-start to the ignorance of youth, assuming, I imagine, that we've been too busy with the kids and parties on the quay to properly maintain our boat.

Even I can hardly look them in the eye as I uncurl the bowline and loop it back around the bollard on the quay. They're all staring, quite without shame. Leaning against the heat of the day, chewing the cud and silently taking everything in. Except for John.

'Beck agin thin,' he chortles. 'Did ya missus?'

I hurl him a stern headmistress look. One that spits 'Quiet!' John dries up and shuffles to the back of the watching gang.

John's remark has hit Damian too. He's scowling.

'I'll go put the kettle on,' I sing cheerily.

'Mummy, why aren't we going?' asks Noah with perfect timing.

As soon as we are tied up again, Shiv pops below to save the situation by making a cup of tea, the panacea for all ills on land or sea. At the same time (and uninvited), all the men on the quay climb aboard to offer opinions and advice. Great, that's all I need.

It doesn't take long for everyone to agree that the batteries are flat – all three of them. On the scale of humiliating breakdowns, this is only just above running out of fuel. I can feel the blokes who are now crowding around our cockpit look at me with a complicated mixture of sympathy, embarrassment, disgust and curiosity. They are all reassessing my competence and intelligence. Just like I did with the 'Couple-in-the-know' in Calais who had forgotten to open their seacock and blew their exhaust system apart. These schoolboy errors are akin to putting diesel in your tank instead of petrol. Understandable in a way, but also completely stupid.

I thought I'd taken every precaution possible against getting a flat battery. I mean, we have a battery charger plugged into the mains, a wind generator as a back-up charger and even solar panels on the roof to keep everything topped up. Christ, we are a floating ecological power station. Flat batteries just aren't supposed to happen on *Friendship*. I'd been so conscientious because without batteries we are paralysed. No battery power means no engine, no movement, no lights, no water pumping through the taps, no heating, no emergency radio, no bilge pump, no nothing. I suppose I should be grateful for small mercies. Thank God this happened here and not in the middle of nowhere. Otherwise we would be quite literally cast adrift.

I call the local boatyard for an electrician to check out how this could possibly have happened. Bizarrely, he turns out to be English and even more strange, he arrives an hour later in a restored English lifeboat from the 1950s. It looks remarkably similar to *Friendship*. Spookily similar. Our two classic boats sit next to each other on the quay at Sens. It's the equivalent of two blokes in Morris Minors meeting by chance in Nigeria.

The electrician's name is Simon and after five minutes he diagnoses the problem. We have overcharged the batteries while at the same time not kept them topped up with enough water to keep them cool (I didn't even know we were supposed to do that). I feel like an idiot.

Even though Simon can plainly see I am squirming in discomfort he twists the knife further.

'Couldn't you smell them?' he asks incredulously.

'Um ... not really.'

'Christ, they would have stunk – really acrid, like ammonia.'

'Like wee you mean?' Shiv interjects, raising her left eyebrow at me from the galley.

'Exactly.'

'Ah ... um ... no. I never noticed anything like that,' I say.

I wonder if he can tell I'm lying. Normally I'm a very good liar (you have to be in advertising) but I'm a bit out of practice at the moment. I hope Shiv doesn't blow it now. She's a terrible liar, thinks it's immoral or something strange like that.

I can't face telling Simon that we've been bothered by the stink of urine since Paris. We made the (not unnatural) assumption that it must be the kids; overspray from Noah at the Porta Potty or a stray nappy from India rotting in the bilges. It never occurred to me that the ammonia smell could come from anything else.

As I look sheepishly at the floor, Simon delivers the killer blow – three new boat batteries are going to cost us nearly 900 euros, more than we have spent on food, moorings and drinks in the last two months.

Shiv breaks the silence. 'Oh well, at least it won't take long to get fixed, eh?'

'Um, actually I don't have any in stock right now,' says Simon.

'How long?'

'A week, maybe two?'

So that acrid smell we had blamed on nappies turns out to be the smell of our incompetence. Quietly and under our noses, the three enormous truck-size batteries, with enough volts to curl your hair, have been drying out. Burning themselves out, to be precise. We have been so concerned that the engine should roar into life, that the fridge should be cold, that the fans should cool us down, we have been leaving the batteries on full charge and frizzled them all out.

If this had happened on the Nivernais a week or two later, we might have been stuck there through the winter, waiting for someone to help us out. Romantic as that sounds at the moment, it could've been disastrous.

Knowing how disappointed Damian will be with our long wait for batteries, I cast around looking for something positive to say.

'Thank goodness you put your foot down when we left Paris. It's going to be tight, but even with this delay we can still make the Rhone before the canals close. At least we now have more time to prepare the boat for the Nivernais. We can re-stock with supplies, get *Friendship* serviced and check all the kit that we have taken for granted since Calais. Like the depth meter. If there's an error with that on the Nivernais, sounds like we'll be scuppered.'

Sure enough, simply mentioning the word 'kit' cheers Damian up and sparks a spending spree at the chandlers. Every day he staggers victoriously back to *Friendship* clutching pipes, rubber tubes and plastic packets of filters, all of which I'm sure will lie unopened for the rest of the trip. His obsession with shoring up our cupboards with boat spares is matched only by mine with food supplies. Siege mentality is quickly adopted. I figure that temperatures may plummet, shops may be closed, we may even get stranded for a week or so. The most important thing is to have enough food to keep us happy in any crisis.

After ten days of victualling the boat, discussing how remote 'remote' could mean and filling the cupboards with tins, chocolate and spare parts, we know Sens now like no other place we've moored. Even Sylvie, the buxom waitress in the market café who sports a gold front tooth, knows us by name.

In the last few days, I've sealed the leaks around the hatch in the cockpit and also the ones round the galley window to prevent the rain dripping in; I've rearranged all the lockers so we can get to the standby generator and the engine spares more easily; fitted sun reflectors to the wheelhouse windows to keep out the heat; adjusted the height of the hammocks so we can get into them without needing a stool; aired all the mattresses; and I've sorted out all the ropes on board so that we have extra-long ones to hand if we need to tie up to trees or rocks in the absence of decent mooring points.

Most important of all, I've had a go at re-configuring our bed (again). It's still driving us mad, even though I've tried various improvements since Shiv broke down in tears about it at Cambrai.

The problem is that there is simply no room for a double bed in the main cabin. *Friendship* was built to sleep two people in the forepeak (the triangle in the very front of the boat) but we put the kids in there because we can close them off at night. So while they sleep in luxury (the space in the forepeak is eight foot wide by seven foot long), Shiv and I sleep on a makeshift bed in the cabin that is just three and a half foot wide. (Lucky we are both slim and it has done wonders for our sex life.)

One end of our bed rests on a shelf and the other sits on top of the sink. Oh yes, and because the table gets in the way, the bed has to be positioned above it – four foot off the floor. (I have since realised this is the perfect height for not being able to get out of bed without having to jump.) The height also makes for a terrifying night's sleep for the person on the outside edge; dreams are constantly filled with a sensation of falling.

Today I've struck upon a new configuration for our bed. It's going to run *across* the boat at knee height. For hours I've been cutting, sanding and screwing bits of wood – using some

of the vast supply of spare timber that I brought with us and stored under the floorboards. I even went up to the market this morning and found a man who could cut and shape foam to fit the new bunk exactly. I can't wait for tonight to try it out. I don't think I've been this excited about going to bed since I lost my virginity.

All I can hear is sawing again. Damian is still operating at full speed ahead. I had forgotten how much he loves a drama. Without a TV aboard, there is no *CSI Miami* and, missing the deadlines of the agency, he invents new ones to invoke panic in the herd. The Nivernais is his latest.

I let Damian be, something I'm getting better at on this trip. I don't want to spoil this weird fun he has, preparing for possible crises. As heat bounces off the quayside, I revel in my own pleasures – watching our kids play and being part of a community.

A change is in the air. The long, hot days of our surprise Indian summer are starting to fray round the edges. It is already cooler at night, with no further need for the windsock. It reminds me of my back-to-school days when my maroon school blazer would be far too heavy for the heat. Then suddenly, overnight, the weather would turn cooler, and the blazer would be perfect.

Even though I'm happy here, the fact that soon we have to reach Chalon-sur-Saône scratches away in the back of my brain. We have to be there, at the top of the Rhône, before winter sets in and canals are closed off. Usually this is around the beginning of November so we'll have to get a move on once the batteries arrive. It's a shame we won't have as much linger-time as I would like on the Nivernais.

It is hard to believe that some sailors, usually those delivering boats from England to the Mediterranean, power down the length of France in three weeks. The motor runs almost continuously, they take shifts at the wheel and eat on the go. The locks closing at night provide the only break on the journey.

With the new bed completed, I can now give in to the begging of Noah and India to 'do some painting'. Since we've been in Sens, most afternoons have included an hour or so with our watercolours. Paints, brushes and paper take up very little space so they were an obvious choice when we were deciding what would fit on board to keep the children entertained.

India strips down to her nappy and Noah wears his underpants (the last thing we need is more washing than is necessary). I set them up with everything they need on top of the engine cover. This large wooden box measuring three by four foot is rapidly becoming our equivalent of the dining-room table at home. It's the place where most things happen.

I know I shouldn't be, but I'm still surprised by how many pictures of boats they create. I half wonder if instead of opening their eyes to the world, we're actually narrowing their view of what is around them. I'm sure a child psychologist would have a field day as he analysed yet another painting of a black barge.

Once the painting loses their interest, we get out the blue plastic baby bath and set it up on the quay. As usual, this process is accompanied by squeals of delight and lots of running around naked. While Noah and India get excited, I fill the bath with hot water.

We have three ways to heat our water:

– Heat generated by the engine is used to warm up a miniature hot-water tank (although this can only be used when we have been running the engine).

– Mains electricity from the shore is used to heat water in another tank (although this can only be used in marinas with an electricity point we can plug into).

– The sun heats water in black plastic solar bags that we leave on the cabin roof (although obviously these can only be used on warm days).

Since arriving in Sens, I've been using the solar bags as it's been so hot. The kids always love this as it means I have to lug them off the roof and try to keep them under control. Easier said than done as it's like carrying a wobbling and quivering pair of Dolly Parton's breast implants (an image I can never get out of my head).

Noah and India like to squash into the tiny bath together. They're far too big for it and I try to get them to take turns but they'll have none of it. This special time is one of the highlights of the day for all of us. The laughter is infectious and often their giggles are returned by bemused couples out for an early evening walk.

The children are bathed and in their pyjamas ready for bed when Simon arrives quite unexpectedly with our batteries. Just 20 minutes later, he is gone with his money and I feel liberated (and not only of our cash). With the new batteries, *Friendship* has turned herself back into a boat. She has life again. She has movement. She is free to roam the canals and so are we. We decide to leave first thing in the morning.

Second time round, after a great night's sleep in our new 'bed', our leaving is a more sober affair, rather like a second wedding. A few early risers (Bernard and his moustache) cheer us off but without that certainty and hope for the couple. We have shown our vulnerability.

As we leave Sens, I notice for the first time a wooded ridge in the distance. I know that before long this will give way to endless fields of grapes. I can't wait. I look at the charts. We're heading almost due south, perhaps south-east. The next big stop is Auxerre, which is at the top of the Nivernais and is supposed to be an amazing city to visit by boat. After that we should be able to cruise at leisure and still be able to get out of the canal system in time.

Being on the move, with power again, is like the blood running through my veins once more. Colours are brighter. The loud, life-affirming brute of our engine celebrates with us. For once I don't whinge about the noise. It's a proper send off from Sens.

'Hooray! We're moving. Don't stop till we get to the Nivernais,'

I yell at Damian who mouths 'What?' and puts his hand to his ear, unable to hear above the throbbing 70-horsepower of *Friendship*.

After a day on the move, we can't go any further. There's a lock just around the corner but it's 7 o'clock so it's closed. We pull over, moor up and look around us. The chart says it's Etigny but I don't see much.

There are no signs of civilisation. All we can see for 360 degrees are fields, trees and the river. The silence is deafening and feels all the more powerful after hours of *Friendship's* engine in our ears. I know that this is a special moment. It's rare to be so alone and yet feel so secure. We are miles from anywhere yet with *Friendship* here, we have everything we need.

We go for a walk as the sun starts to set around us. The kids run ahead along the grassy riverbank while Shiv and I hold hands following behind. The silver lines of birch trees turn to burnt pink as the sun goes down. In light darkness we sit together on a log and eat baguettes filled with ham and the fragrant cheeses from the market at Sens. No one talks. Not even Noah.

I look back at *Friendship* tied up to a tree, patiently waiting for our return. I think about how much I owe her. If she hadn't come into my life, none of this would be happening. I turn to my family and then tell Shiv and both Noah and India that I love them more than anything in the world. I'm having what my father calls a 'happy attack', a moment when you stop and appreciate just how wonderful life is.

Being in places like these, which barely make it onto the road maps, at this time between day and night, is a reminder of the wilderness in us all. Of the place we began, without roads, rules and sharp edges.

We are the only ones on the towpath, apart from a few black slugs. This could be Botswana, not a grassy bank only an hour's drive from Paris. I snuggle in closer to Damian as the chilly night air descends on us and the river.

It's happening. It's finally happening. Instead of adrenalin coursing through me at a hundred miles an hour, there is something slower and softer in my veins. Of course it could simply be the red wine, but I'm sure this woozy, chilled happiness is more than that. This is calmness. Mixed with love – real love. Love of life. Love for the world. Love for the future.

CHAPTER 14

I've never met a middle-aged PhD student before, but I imagine the places we moor at nowadays, like Joigny, Etigny and Moné-teau, are just like them. You know the type, still living in dorms, glory days past but still retaining an air of wiseness and hidden depths. They're a far cry from the dirty, grungy, undergrads of Saint-Quentin, Calais and Cambrai in northern France.

At Joigny we tie up next to a clutch of white Locaboat hire boats, their decks being hosed down and insides being gutted after a summer's rental abuse.

Across from us is a large park, mature horse-chestnut trees hurling conkers on the sand below with each brace of wind. In front, dozens of swans flick their necks reaching for bread from passers-by. A symphony of white wings, windblown water and rustling leaves plays out before a backdrop of stone-arched bridge, clustered medieval buildings and a cloud-peppered sky. It's a fitting overture to Burgundy proper. The first vineyards of the region, Côte Saint-Jacques, cover the hills, pressing Joigny towards the river.

Once securely moored, I insist that Shiv leave the kids with me while she goes to explore the town. I've been trying to do this more and more lately so she gets some time on her own and I get to prove that I *can* look after our children after all. For years I have been urging Shiv to stop telling me what

to do with **Noah** and **India**, although now that she's letting go, I feel bereft. It's like driving a car on your own for the first time: even though you've been waiting for the day for ages, you keep looking at the empty passenger seat for your mum or the instructor to reassure you.

Damian literally pushed me out of the boat earlier. In the past it might have worried me, his eagerness to be a capable dad, my knowing that he would never watch them like I do, but now it feels liberating to be the one leaving. For the past two years I have craved time alone, albeit in small doses, playing out endless scenes of 'me time' in my head, egged on by women's magazines.

Now, here I am, no hand-baggage, no wheels and no children, standing on Joigny bridge, a kilometre from *Friendship*, at a complete loss. With no idea of what to do on my own, I march up the hill in search of a decent café, passing a lot of grotty-looking kebab shops on my way.

Joigny is a strange, strange place. The town is chock-a-block with Tudor-style housing (or whatever the French equivalent of that might be). Lots of wooden panelling, exposed stone-work, tiny windows, narrow alleyways, stained-glass panels, wrought-iron balconies and cobbled streets. From a distance (when we moored), it felt like a town that has been bought by Disney and turned into an attraction. Like York on steroids.

Now we're walking around it, I realise the place is dead. It's an absolute ghost town. Shops have been abandoned, the houses are crumbling and streets are empty. It's not as bad as a scene from *28 Days* but it's not far off it.

If this town was in the UK, it would be drowning in second-home owners and Farrow & Ball paint. France is so big though, even a place as beautiful as this can be left to wither because it's too far away from anywhere important.

After dragging Noah and India around the streets I remember (or rather their crying reminds me) that they need feeding. So Noah, India and I are now sitting in a grotty Turkish café. I'm trying to persuade our two sceptical kids

that a kebab is perfectly edible. We're a long way from the Annabel Karmel recipes they were brought up on in cosy, middle-class Queen's Park.

Le Palais du Kebab wasn't my first choice of eating establishment but nowhere else is open and I forgot to prepare something earlier. Normally Shiv never leaves the boat without a bag full of nappies, snacks, water, plastic spoons, beakers and a meal of some sort stowed in small Tupperware tubs.

I, of course, have none of that and am praying India doesn't fill her nappy in the next hour. Otherwise I'm going to have to make a new one out of napkins. This keeps happening to me. Just as I feel I'm getting the hang of being a mum, my lack of suitability for the role leaps to the fore once again. I don't seem to be able to remember the simplest of things and it's quietly driving me mad. It's at times like this when I just want to be in a café on my own.

Cafés. The solace of mums everywhere trying to find themselves. I order a café au lait, twiddle my thumbs and wish I smoked. It would instantly make me feel part of the world of adults, less exposed as a mum trying to fill kid-free time. My desire for a prop is overwhelming. I duck into a tabac, get side-tracked from the cigarettes and grab a copy of *Le Figaro* instead. It might help get my brain in gear.

Later, feeling a little more confident, I'm drawn to a glass-fronted shop, lured by the sight of vast woven baskets of fresh flower heads, bunches of lavender and bottles of golden honey. Before long I am chatting with Antoine, a fresh-faced shopkeeper, tasting fresh pollen and spilling out my inner Shiv to him. Poor bloke.

'Eet must be verry relaxing being on a boat,' he begins innocently, from behind a wooden counter, probably expecting a polite 'oui' back from me.

'Well you see, it isn't what you'd expect. My daily boat life has become almost Victorian; buying food daily as the fridge doesn't preserve things for more than 24 hours. Everything is washed by hand in a basin. Look at my hands.' I show him my dry palms.

'Aha. For zat you need aloe vera. Verry good for ze skein.' What a salesman he is.

'There simply isn't space for us down below so we live outside most of the day, no matter what the weather: rain, wind, cold.'

'Hmmm. You need this pollen. Local. It will ward off hay fever,' he says, adding it to a growing stack of brown paper bags on the counter. I ignore the fact that summer is almost over, as I am having such a cathartic time with Antoine.

'And also this for your circulation?' he asks, handing me a gnarled ginger root. 'What about your husband, your children?'

'Their circulation is okay I think ... Damian is around 24/7 now. We share everything, the space, the chores and the managing of the boat. Instead of watching television we read books and actually talk to each other. Unless Damian is cleaning the boat again. Actually do you have any herbs to ward off cleanliness?'

'Wot iz zat – klenlinezz?' asks Antoine politely.

'Never mind,' I say, continuing my barrage. 'The kids. Well they seem okay with it all. I mean they are sleeping more than ever before. We don't have a car so we walk or cycle everywhere on land. I suppose they are a lot more active. They don't have a lot of toys. In fact our possessions aboard are necessities, not luxuries. The only souvenirs we buy are postcards as they are light and only use wall space.'

I stop to take in air and notice a queue of customers forming. Antoine is looking a little edgy now. Poor guy. He has just had my randomly organised, zip file version of the trip. I feel invigorated. Antoine seems relieved when I wave goodbye and waft back downhill towards *Friendship* clutching my bags of potions.

Quite unexpectedly, glancing inside a kebab shop, I spot Damian's spike of black hair and the rest of my family. My disgust at him force-feeding them kebabs is overtaken by relief flooding over me to connect with what makes me whole again. It's good see that the kids are still breathing. In fact, they look like a very happy, single-parent family on a 'Dad's day out'.

Damian has a lettuce leaf hanging out of his mouth. Noah is punching the air with both hands, throwing his head back with laughter. India is making a tower out of her kebab pieces. I feel like a voyeur with my nose up at the grease-covered window. I don't want to interrupt or to look like I've been trailing them, unable to come up with my own adventure. Eventually Damian notices me, understanding the look on my face that pleads, 'Can I come in now?'

I'm so glad that Shiv happened to catch us at a moment when we were all peaceful and happy. Twenty minutes earlier and she would have found Noah and India almost in tears, too hungry to eat properly, overtired from walking too far and refusing to eat the kebab I was trying to push down their throats. Had she come ten minutes earlier, it would've been *me* she'd have found almost in tears, unable to pacify Noah and India, having tried everything I could think of. Thank God for the 'hang a bit of lettuce from your nose' trick. It's astonishing how desperation can drive creativity.

Replenished by our kebabs, we're tempted to stay in Joigny for longer but in the afternoon a torrential rainstorm breaks so we decide to press on. Even dosed up with Shiv's new medicinal concoctions, there's no fun in walking round a deserted town in the rain so we might as well get some miles under our belt.

I'm at the wheel while Shiv is below with Noah and India, keeping dry. Buckets of conkers, collected earlier, sit next to me. God knows what we are going to do with all of them, but Noah, India and Shiv were insistent they come with us. Next to the conkers is a bunch of mint leaves from Sens. Then there are Shiv's now seriously under-used jogging shoes, an equally untouched yoga mat and her guitar. How am I supposed to steer with all this crap around me? God she's messy.

I'm wet through, absolutely sodden. My head is sticking through the hatch in the roof so that I can get a better view of where we're going. The rain is lashing down and I'm

squinting to see properly. Rainwater is running down my face and dripping off my clothes onto the instrument panel below.

I've been like this for three hours and there's been nothing to see except endless riverbanks lined with woods. There's nothing to do except slowly eat up the miles. There's nothing to listen to except the mind-numbing throb of our noisy old engine.

Then again, I'd rather be up here than in the cabin where poor Shiv has had to keep Noah and India at bay all afternoon. I know that I couldn't do it, trapped in that tiny space with two volatile toddlers.

I return to peering through the rain. All my deepest and darkest misgivings about *Friendship* rise to the surface once again. It's painful (as it has been throughout this trip) for me to quietly acknowledge to myself that she is the wrong kind of boat for us. Although we've had amazing adventures in her, when you really get down to it, *Friendship* just isn't right for a family. She's too small, she's too noisy, the cabin roof is too low, the engine is too smoky and smelly, there's no storage, there aren't enough fixed berths ...

I could probably go on and on (and for that matter so could Shiv), but it has become an unspoken truth between us. We both know that if we were in one of those fibreglass hire boats that I so despise, this journey would be much easier. Neither of us dare say anything out loud though. I suppose Shiv doesn't want to upset me after all my work on *Friendship* and I don't want to voice what deep down I know is the truth but find hard to accept. It was Shiv who proposed we should do this journey in *Friendship* to justify all my years of hard work and sacrifice. We both know that if we openly acknowledge she is the wrong boat, then we are tacitly accepting that I did all that work for nothing.

Rain pounds on the cabin roof, streams down the windows and threatens to squeeze in through any gap it can find. Our home has become a cocoon, wrapped in misted glass with three larvae squirming around inside. Well, actually two squirming larvae and one mother trying to remain calm. Now I know where the seaman's term 'cabin fever' comes from.

In the past few hours, every ounce of imagination I possess has been used to entertain the kids. Six Lego spacecraft adorn the galley, playdough has been rolled into party food for India's teddies and I have read Richard Scarry's book, *Cars and Trucks and Things That Go*, three times, using different accents for each animal. I could be a *Blue Peter* presenter, for goodness' sake.

Now the cabin is beginning to feel damp and cold. Damian turns on the Eberspächer heater for the first time since we left England. After the dust has blown through the pipes, warm soothing air soon blasts into our cocoon, turning everyone sleepy. Perfect. I wrap both kids in duvets (they look like chrysalises now), prop them up together on the starboard bunk and reach for the emergency pack of videos. We brought along my laptop and three DVDs in case of times like this. *Bob the Builder*, *Postman Pat* and *Maisy* have all been well hidden until now.

Damian probably feels sorry for me being cooped up down here, but there's something wonderful about this cosy intensity with the kids. Up there, at the wheel in the sleeting rain, I think Damian has the raw deal, probably cursing the fact that *Friendship* hasn't got a high coach roof, which means in bad weather that you have to stick your head out into the elements to see around you. Rather like driving a car in a rainstorm with your head poking through the sunroof. No amount of waterproofing can keep you dry.

Maisy is mesmerising the chrysalises so I brew mugs of tea, pull on my wellies, raincoat, waterproof trousers and hat to carry up some tea and Galettes Bretonnes biscuits to the outside world where my soldier is on the front line. There is solidarity in being drenched together in the grey autumn monsoon.

Over the side-deck, rain turns the river into a writhing pattern of drops and swirls. It is beautiful being out here. However, there's a sharp wind blowing and Damian's face is braced against it. For the first time on the trip, I see a hint of disappointment in his face. Like that feeling you get the first time a truth creeps into a new love. The moment you realise they have faults too.

Perhaps he is finally admitting to himself that *Friendship* is not the perfect boat for this voyage. I down my tea before my mug fills with rainwater, kiss Damian on the cheek and disappear down below, leaving him with his thoughts. I dare not start that conversation now, rain or sunshine.

I check my watch. It's nearly 6 o'clock. I should pull over and find somewhere to moor. On the outskirts of the next hamlet, I see a rickety old wooden deck next to a restaurant where we can tie up for the night. I've no idea where we are.

I open the doors to go below and am hit by a wall of warmth. Our heater uses diesel to warm up air that is then blown around the cabin via tubes and vents. I hang my wet clothes above the shower tray and close the door. We have put one of the vents in the tiny bathroom to create a kind of airing cupboard so that drying clothes is easier.

Later, kids in bed, Shiv and I squint through the steamed-up cabin windows to a restaurant on the bank. We are like paupers at Christmas, looking into the home of a rich family, watching them decorate a splendid tree. A large group of friends is halfway through a meal. The waiters are scurrying backwards and forwards with bottles of wine and plates of hot food.

'God, it would be nice to be in there right now, wouldn't it?' I salivate.

'Yeah but you look like a drowned cat, we haven't got any clothes that are smart enough and there are two small children sleeping in the bow that we can't leave on their own – remember?'

'Hmmm. Do you think we could go in shifts?' I plead desperately.

'But why? I like our damp, overheated cocoon. Give me our little den any day over some over-smart restaurant.'

The next morning we notice that a hire boat pulled in behind us last night. We didn't even hear them arrive, the rain was so loud on our roof. I wander over to say hello and

realise the boat is manned by the group who were in the restaurant. Three retired couples and a single man from Scotland, who have flown over to celebrate one of their birthdays. They've never been on a boat before and ask me for a few tips on steering and lock handling. I think even Noah knows more about how to handle a boat than they do.

A couple of hours later, porridge eaten and the kids' excess energy burnt off (for now), I put on my waterproofs again. Thank God they are dry. I look at our soggy map and realise that yesterday we unwittingly sailed straight past the turn-off for the Bourgogne canal. In the torrential rain I didn't even notice it. I'm glad. It means we had no chance for last-minute changes of heart.

Just before our second lock of the day, we notice a white fibreglass Connoisseur hire boat weaving about from side to side in the river ahead. It is low and wide, with a huge box cabin on top, like a margarine tub.

'It's the Scots,' says Damian. 'From this morning. Totally clueless. What on earth have they been doing? They left hours before us. They obviously didn't listen to a word I said.'

It's like watching a drunk man go through a doorway. The Scots aim for the lock gate, attempt to pull along one side to tie up but then bounce off the concrete wall, shooting across to the opposite side of the lock. Their timing is all wrong. They're going too fast. They reverse, the stern pulling them out again, and then repeat the whole process, with exactly the same result.

We nudge into the lock behind them as their boat twirls around at right-angles to ours, nose and tail jammed between the lock sides, no lines attaching it to either bank, and lots of 'oching' and 'aahing' from the crew who are hopping about on deck holding ropes.

As I tie off a central spring line to a mooring ring inside the lock, Noah wails, 'Daddy's gone. Daddy's jumped off the boat.'

I swing round. The cockpit is empty. Panic surging in my stomach, I hunt for clues around the bow, search for a hand reaching out of the black-stew lock water. It takes me less than

60 seconds to race around the decks looking for goodness knows what. My heart is doing a drum roll, Noah is crying, India has joined forces from her place on the fridge seat. I feel sick. My hands are shaking. Damian has fallen overboard and I don't have a clue what to do. It is me now – completely in charge. No one is on board to bark orders at me. I'm not used to this. Momentarily I'm paralysed with fear. Then I start talking to myself.

'Okay, we mustn't start the lock mechanism until Damian is found. He is probably clinging to the Scots' boat. I must get Noah and India down below in their netting quickly. Then get everyone searching the murky water. Now, where's the lifesaver ring? On the stern, hemmed in by a baby bath and some vegetable baskets. Bloody hell, it'll take me hours to wrestle that off.'

'Mano . . .' I shout, but the beginning of the 'Man overboard' cry sticks in my throat as I catch sight of Damian's ruffled black hair moving past me at eye height . . . from inside our neighbours' boat.

'Shiv, this is Martine and Andy,' he announces as his head pops up from their cabin, a quizzical look on his face as though to say, 'What's up with the kids?'

Damian had leapt aboard their boat to help when my back was turned to moor. Now he has a long rope in his hands, nimbles around their deck and ties their stern up to the lock bollard. Within moments the Scots are safely turned the right way round and linked to the lock wall, ropes coiled once around bollards.

I should be proud of Damian for acting the hero but that emotion has been overtaken by an urge to bollock him for not telling me he'd jumped ship.

We follow the Scots slowly through the next three locks to Auxerre, feeling like a mother swan with her ugly duckling on the water. Relief at Damian being alive and of me not having to assume total responsibility crashes down over me. It takes hot tea with three sugars to get me functioning again.

Wow, I never expected this. Arriving in Auxerre is almost more impressive than getting to Paris. Rather than chug

through miles of suburban and industrial sprawl to get to the heart of the city it feels as if we've just turned a corner and here it is.

Even more impressive, the whole of Auxerre seems to be on our right-hand side. All I can see are cafés, trees, churches and ancient buildings climbing on top of each other to get to the top of a massive hill.

On the left there is almost nothing – just a park, a play-ground and some low-rise buildings. All of Auxerre is preening itself, waiting for us to stop and turn towards it.

I say there is nothing on the left bank, but actually, there is. Maybe not on the land, but in the water there are hundreds of boats. Boats of all sizes from 100-foot live-aboard *peniche* conversions to plastic hire boats; steel motor cruisers from the 1970s; brightly coloured English narrowboats; snub-nosed Dutch tjalks and even sailing yachts with their masts lashed to the decks. The boats are jumbled together, tied two or even three deep in some places, with flags of every nationality flapping lazily in the afternoon breeze.

I find a tiny 12-metre space and edge in. I would never have attempted this a few months ago but now I handle *Friendship* with the confidence of an old sea dog. Finally I am living up to my boat and look as if I know what I'm doing. Just as well, given the amount of people who are watching us. Even here, *Friendship* stands out.

The four of us, safely on the bank now, gaze at the city before us. We were told that this is the very best way to see Auxerre. Despite the cold, it's bathed in sunlight. It's a picture postcard. The view of the cathedral is supposed to be mag-nificent from here but it takes a while to identify it. There are at least four grand churches spread out in front of us and frankly any one of them could be a cathedral. *That* is how impressive Auxerre is.

Our first evening in Auxerre feels like being back in London with the orange glow of a city preventing night from falling in earnest. However, the light here mostly comes from the floodlit

Saint Etienne Cathedral (they seem to like him around here), like a shepherd awake on the hill, watching its flock.

Auxerre is how I imagine Oxford or Cambridge might look if the cities were pushed upwards after an earthquake. Vast spires and flying buttresses soar skywards like giant organ pipes, holding court from on high.

It's incredible that the place is so intact. As a vital trading point for the Romans and many others (because of its location on the crossroads of the Yonne River and a Roman road linking the Mediterranean to the North Sea), Auxerre was constantly under siege. Over the years, walls and fortifications were added to shore up the ever-growing town. Although it has a cathedral, it lost its city status during the revolution and is now simply called 'Town of Art and History'.

My mum would love this fact. I hear her voice, echoing from my childhood, explaining that 'a city has a cathedral, a town doesn't.'

There's a knock on the door. 'Ferr all yerr healp. We'd niver huv done it without ye,' says Martine, one of the Scots, handing us a bottle of Châteauneuf-du-Pape.

They are hitting the town later, chinos pressed and blazers on, and invite us for a pre-dinner drink aboard their boat.

'Why not,' we say, feeling decidedly under-dressed.

We sprawl in their white plastic, spacious heaven for an hour or so, a weather eye and ear on *Friendship*'s locked cabin doors only metres away.

'Och, look at me hands,' says Mike, the single chap, who, recently bereaved, felt like doing something he'd never done before when he booked this trip. 'Rope burrens.'

'Yes. Your ropes are cheap plastic ones. They're horrible to handle and give you rope burn. You should really wear gloves,' advises Damian, sounding like a master mariner.

'Or Marigolds. They do the trick,' I butt in, remembering too late that Leslie and Margaret never interrupted each other's conversations.

Several glasses of perfectly chilled Chablis later, we somehow learn that the Scots have no effluent storage tanks on board.

Which means that everything flushes straight out into the rivers and canals. Damian is distraught.

'You mean all those trips in the middle of the night with our stinking Porta Potty could have been avoided?' he moans.

He has been carefully disposing of our chemically neutralised effluent at marina toilets or, at worst, down drains. The Scots, however, are effectively skipping that part, sending their sewage straight into the canals. One boat of Scots' waste wouldn't be that bad, but there are hundreds of these hire boats on the canals during the season.

My stomach churns. No wonder the water is brown, not clear, fresh green.

'Right, I'm dumping it over the side from now on,' says Damian.

I raise my eyebrows, which is enough to say 'We've got to show our kids that we care about the planet. We'll carry our excrement with us till we find a proper place to dump it.' Thank the Lord it's Damian's job.

I can't wait to return to the warmth of *Friendship* that evening. Being aboard a 'plastic fantastic' (as wooden boat owners like to call them) has been like flirting with a good-looking, single bloke for an evening, then returning to the comfortable arms of my husband. All at once I appreciate his usually annoying charms anew.

The fact that we can only take six steps across the length of the cabin feels cosy after the leagues of space on the Scots' boat. So what if we can't stretch out, constantly knocking into one another as we move about the boat – well, it feels truly romantic now.

We polish off the Châteauneuf with sausages and mash (again), appreciating *Friendship's* eccentric but lovable ways. The varnished roof slats, cabin sides and chunky doors soak up the soft light and radiate back security and warmth. Much as a big white boat would provide so much more space, we could never trade in *Friendship*. She is one of the family now and I am fond of her, faults and all.

I'm becoming a bit concerned. There must be over a hundred boats here and yet no-one I have spoken to is going down the Nivernais. In fact, most people are shocked that we are even considering it in an old wooden boat, let alone one with two young children on board.

Maybe I'm being paranoid but people appear to take great pleasure in trying to scare us about the Nivernais. The thing is, there must be some truth in what they say because they all focus on the same things:

- There are no shops for miles and miles, so boats often run out of vital supplies.
- If you have an emergency or medical problem you can forget any kind of help as you are out of radio contact and often there's no mobile phone coverage.
- There are very few places to moor that have basic services such as toilets, showers, electricity or even drinking water.
- The canal often runs dry and boats have been known to run aground and lie stranded for over two days before someone comes along and finds them.
- At the end of the canal there's a staircase of locks that has to be completed in a day because there are no rest points. It sounds like it would test the fitness of a marathon runner, let alone an ex-advertising man fast approaching 40 and a mother who still feels ragged after her second child.

The Nivernais is becoming more and more appealing. The more tales we hear, the more intrepid I feel and the more I want to court its dangers. Like fancying the bad boy at school or smoking behind the bike sheds and maybe getting caught, the risk only adds to its allure. The Goody Two-Shoes, Bourgogne, is long forgotten.

The more people who turn up at *Friendship* to give advice, the more I look forward to this less-travelled route. There is something intoxicating about flirting with danger. I don't want to play safe – kids or no kids.

Shiv has just turned up with a bag of food. The kind of food

we never buy. There are pretzels, salted biscuits and bags of boiled sweets.

'A gift from that nice couple on *Final Fling*,' she says, throwing me a sweet.

'Funny gift.'

'Well, they'd heard we were going down the Nivernais and thought we might need the supplies.'

'Bloody hell. This morning we get a bag of extra kids' clothes from the woman on the blue barge and now we're being given food by *Final Fling*. Do you think the Nivernais really is that bad?' I ask, hoping for a reassuring answer.

'No, of course not. Maybe it's just because almost everyone chooses the Bourgogne. By default the Nivernais is the great unknown. The remote, dangerous cousin of the Bourgogne,' says Shiv, clearly loving this.

'Hmmmm. It's making me nervous. I don't want us to be stuck in the middle of nowhere with only a bag of pretzels for company.'

Somehow the word 'remote' brings also the feeling of coldness. 'Remote' and 'hot' don't seem to have the same ring and, appropriately, over the next few nights, temperatures suddenly plummet. We wake one morning to a stone-cold boat, misted windows and dew on the decks. The icy morning dash to the fridge for the milk and to turn on the gas becomes our first negotiation of the day.

'You go,' I plead, rolling back under the duvet.

'No, it's your turn,' urges Damian.

'I'll make the tea. Pleeeease.'

It nearly always works. Damian acquiesces, playing the gentleman.

Gulping steaming hot tea and seeing fog form in the cold of the cabin, I realise how unprepared we are for really icy weather. I have three bikinis, several sarongs and sandals that I thought I'd be living in on this trip. The kids have no winter coats, no thick duvets, nothing really warm. I did pack one emergency pair of trousers each, which they are wearing every day now.

In London I'd imagined we would be following the sun south, so I didn't pack for winter conditions. However, despite the heatwave in Sens, even the capitaine here in Auxerre warns that a cold winter is on the cards.

I feel a shopping trip coming on, even though I hate shopping. I'd rather sit in a café than trawl through racks of clothes. However, shopping for an expedition is different. It makes me feel like an explorer, gathering supplies for the harsh winter ahead.

Shiv's right, we need to go shopping. I can't go through another night like that again. Both Noah and India woke up crying at 3 am because they were so cold – we had to cover them in coats, fleeces and even towels, anything we could find in the cabin to keep them wrapped up and warm. Meanwhile Shiv clung to me all night. I radiate heat constantly while she is always cold to the touch. It meant she felt like she had a huge hot-water bottle in bed, while for me it was like sleeping with a block of ice. Those magic potions she bought in Joigny don't seem to be working, although she now swears by ginger tea throughout the day.

The weather is definitely changing. After the sunshine of Paris, Saint-Mammes and Sens, we're now into the unpredictable temperatures of autumn. If we don't prepare ourselves properly, we're going to suffer on the Nivernais. Time to take advantage of the huge Carrefour that lies just behind the quay.

As soon as winter clothing arrives on board, easterly winds channel through the narrow alleyways of Auxerre, rushing past the timbers that have stood for centuries. We finally accept that winter is on its way – we need to get through the Nivernais before it arrives.

There is one last thing to buy as Damian is testing the engine for the umpteenth time in preparation for our departure. Damian's 40th birthday is in less than two months and I cannot be saved by Amazon or finding something decent in a French village.

I don't think a case of French pâté and some tins of cassoulet will go down too well.

Boats, old stuff and cool stuff – that's what Damian loves, so I nip into a nautical barge shop selling mariner's goods. I buy a large, beige, canvas sailor's smock and a capitaine's deep navy felt hat, which I wrap together in a plastic bag. I know Damian harbours secret fantasies of looking like some bohemian artist on a boat. Perhaps this ensemble will kick-start his forties, although bets are off on the level of cool I've achieved for him. At least, when he has stopped being a sea dog and becomes an old goat, this might remind him of our life-changing trip.

Hiding the present on the boat is nigh on impossible. We both know every nook and cranny there is and Damian's cleaning frenzies are sure to uncover these treats.

Hunting for a suitable hiding spot, I lift up a half-empty water tank that lies under our port seat. I figure this is one place Damian will never need to look. Lifting one end of the slate-grey water sack is like picking up a seal: when I lift one end, the other flops down. After wrestling with the seal for 15 minutes, I finally stash the carrier bag underneath its grey bulk. Safe till 5 November.

CHAPTER 15

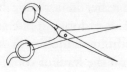

Now we are at the mouth of the Nivernais, I know that I don't want to be anywhere else or with anyone else.

So what if I have no idea how I'm going to earn a living once this is all over? So what if I should have spent my salary on ISAs instead of 32 feet of wood? So what if my children aren't in a nursery but are playing on riverbanks instead? This is exactly what I should be doing with my life.

Damian is lining up *Friendship*'s bow between the two open lock gates. To the left a large metal sign on the bank announces the Nivernais Canal. We are the only boat going through. There's something lonely but lovely about this, like we are running against the crowd.

Already I know that forgoing the Bourgogne in favour of this canal was the right decision. One glance at the lock-keeper drives away any secret doubts I had before. Despite his paunch, he's a sprightly, denimed and bearded octogenarian, who winds the lock's paddles like he has all the time in the world and not a trace of arthritis.

He saunters over to chat with the confident swagger of a teenager. Perhaps it's the effect of the golden home-made honey he sells us in great glass jars while we wait for the water to pour into the lock and lift us our first metre uphill.

'Mais oui. It is mostly students or people like me who man

the Nivernais locks. No-one wants to live out there, so far away from any towns. It can be very lonely at times if you are in the depths of the Morvan,' he says, stroking his beard. Images of dense forests, solitary chimney smoke and *Little Red Riding Hood* territory drift into mind.

'But in the summer many students take placements. They get a cottage to live in. It is a great experience for them. For me, I love meeting people from all over the world.'

The speed of the rushing water eases as, on both sides of the lock doors, the water level equalises. Our lock-keeper almost skips over the narrow bridge to turn the lock paddles. I take the one on my side and we open the gates together. He smiles as I step back on board, his sparkly eyes disappearing into a well of wrinkles, and he waves us off into the unknown.

Despite the stiff wind and the russet leaves falling and swirling down to the water, an overwhelming feeling of spring-time surrounds me. I feel like that woman in the Timotei advert, birds singing in the trees, buds blossoming, and flowers and summer grasses blowing in the breeze. Expectation. That's what it is. The powerful sense that anything could happen. Not because it is summer but because it isn't.

Ahead of us lies 174 watery kilometres. We'll have to manoeuvre safely through 112 locks, all set in place to lift us and the five-tonne *Friendship* up and over an enormous rise in sea level.

So far, so easy. In my imagination this canal was going to be 'Touching the Void on Water', an experience laden with danger, fear and survival. But as we waft out of the first lock and into the gentle countryside I wonder what the fuss was about. The scenery is beautiful and simple. The light is soft and gentle. Even the sun has come out of nowhere and the temperature is warming. The sound is of silence.

Maybe autumn is the best time to be here after all. I don't think I'm trying to post-rationalise things when I say that. Honestly, I think we may have struck gold by accident and we are the only ones here to enjoy it. All of this is ours.

The sun has chased away the morning chills and the day, along with the four of us, is already slow and lazy. India is sleeping through most of it. Noah is mesmerised by the panorama of countryside, trailing his fishing line over the port side. A cream padded cushion on deck provides a comfy spot for me to lie and read. Like lizards on a hot tarmac road, we soak up the unexpected warmth of the sun radiating back from the decks.

The Nivernais, it seems, has quite a history. Various kings, from Henry IV to lots of the Louis's, put energy and money into planning a waterway linking the Morvan valley to Paris, for the sole purpose of bringing firewood to the capital more quickly.

For a short while the impoverished Morvan region became the 'in' place but the age of small, narrow canals was already diminishing and by the 1960s, fewer than sixty boats (of any type) passed along the Nivernais in any given year. The canal had become little more than a backwater and was on the brink of closure. The Nivernais had gone from 'hot' to 'not' overnight.

Pierre-Paul Zivy was the man who saved the Nivernais in the 1970s. I think I would have liked him. He was an Anglophile who marvelled at the strength of the canal holiday industry in the UK. It inspired him to create the first inland hire cruiser fleet in France, which in turn fuelled the renaissance of the country's beleaguered canals. It was because of Zivy's tireless campaigning that the local authorities agreed to restore long sections of the Nivernais and thus it was reborn. For me there is something deeply resonant about travelling in a boat that was rescued from death, along a canal that was rescued from death.

I'm sure we won't meet the modern heavily loaded barges here that we saw all along the Seine. No, this is definitely the Seine's more traditional older sister. Everything is more old-fashioned. For a start, the locks are a mere five metres wide, compared with a whopping eleven on the Seine. Our maximum speed here is eight kilometres per hour, compared with a racy 20 on the Seine. In every respect, meandering through the Nivernais promises to be something quite special. And good for the arm muscles, if there are really 112 locks over 174 kilometres, as the guidebook suggests.

Despite Zivy's heroic rescue, the Nivernais is still quite an unusable canal for most boats. It isn't only the number of locks that puts people off; it's also the fact that the canal is very, very shallow. As Shiv keeps reminding me, in some places it is just 1.4 metres deep. That means even Kylie Minogue could stand on the bottom and her head would stick out of the water.

Luckily *Friendship* has a shallow draft but even so, we'll only have 50 centimetres between the bottom of our hull and the canal bed. That doesn't give us much leeway. I have already calculated there are four things that could screw us:

– A large rock or abandoned bike on the bottom could easily catch the boat and even crack through wood if we hit it at the wrong angle.

– We are going down the canal at the *end* of the summer, which means the level may have dropped significantly. (Incredibly, the water actually evaporates in the heat of July and August.) With all the rain we had earlier in the summer, I hope it won't be a problem.

– We also need to beware of periods of high barometric pressure (whatever that means – I've seen it on the weather reports but I still don't get it). Apparently, at these times, the pressure of the atmosphere pushes down on the water and the level actually drops. (Can you believe that?)

– Unknowing hire boat users often leave locks open or don't close them properly. This means water runs away down the system, creating pockets of very low water between some of the locks. I just hope the Scots from Auxerre haven't come this way. The idea of wading ashore with Noah and India before carrying them five miles to the nearest help fills me with dread.

Despite my initial fears, I look around me at the achingly beautiful countryside and can't believe we are going to have

any problems. The sun is so strong we've had to root out our shorts and T-shirts again. The air is filled with the scents of grasses and hay, the iPod is playing soft chillout tunes and everyone is smiling.

We are on a high. After a few hours, seven locks, no shouting or arguments and the picture postcard villages of Vaux and Champs-sur-Yonne, we pull over at a quay dripping in willow trees. All along the riverside, slopes swathed in fruit trees and vineyards have pressed down to the water's edge. This is the first accessible mooring we have seen for miles. And so for everyone else, it seems. A large, sleek navy blue hotel barge and a tubby plastic hire boat are also moored here. It's quite a shock to have company – we've seen no other boats all day.

The hotel barge must be four times the size of us, with a foredeck bigger than *Friendship*. A dozen day-tripping bikes are lined up, shiny-new, on deck. Soft decadent lighting outlines enormous windows from cabins below. Three well-dressed men and an attractive woman with red hair recline in teak deckchairs, reading and sometimes glancing at us over their books.

Immediately I feel self-conscious. God, I can't remember the last time I bothered looking in that tiny mirror of ours. My feet are bare. My khaki shorts are stained with rope sludge. Thank goodness for my sunglasses. I shall employ the same technique India uses – if she is not looking at us, then she assumes we cannot see her either.

I focus on mooring, which now is a rather simple, relaxed procedure compared with our time in northern France. Damian motors *Friendship* within half a metre of the bank. I step off and locate a huge heavy metal mooring ring, pass a rope through it and loop it back on board at the bow. Then I signal to him and move to the stern where I attach a second line, thrown ashore by Damian. He cuts the engine and it shudders still. Every time we moor like this, stress-free, shout-free, a deep satisfaction warms me. Finally we know what we're doing.

I admire the hotel barge, a converted *peniche*. The long and high slab sides are no longer tarred black. Now they are resplendent in a deep glossy royal blue. The cabin sides shimmer in white and every edge is picked out in crisp crimson. The boat looks like this is its first time in the water, such is the shine of the paint. Then I spot the reason why. Hunched down on the pontoon is a good-looking young bloke, brush in hand, touching up some scratches on the bow.

'God, no wonder she looks so perfect,' I say.

'Yes, I have to do this every day. Make sure she is always gleaming for the guests.'

'Who are they?'

'Mostly rich Americans. They pay enough to be here so we have to make sure this old tub looks the part.'

'Why have you stopped here? Seems like an odd place to bring them. It's in the middle of nowhere. Although I suppose you have no choice, *everywhere* round here is in the middle of nowhere.'

He laughs. 'Aha! Then you're in for a surprise treat. Just up that hill behind you are the Bailly Caves, kilometres of tunnels that are used as a giant wine cellar. All the grapes in the fields that you can see are brought here and turned into Crémant de Bourgogne. Basically champagne in all but name. It's an amazing place, you really should see it. We're taking the guests round it tomorrow morning. We normally have to book months in advance but you never know, it's the autumn now, you might be able to catch the tour this evening if you're lucky.'

'Brilliant. Thanks. We'll go for it.' I turn to run back to *Friendship* but then stop and double back towards the lad who has resumed his painting. I thrust out my hand.

'By the way, my name is Damian. I'm on *Friendship*, the wooden fishing boat at the other end of the pontoon.'

'Oh yes. Lovely boat. We all spotted her earlier. Covered in kit and kids, right?'

'Yeah, that's us.'

'Nice one. You look like you're on a *real* adventure,' he says as he shakes my hand and grins. 'The name's James.'

Damian reappears. Something's up. I can tell by the way he bounces, rather than walks, towards us. Like Tigger. Tigger with hot news. He has barely finished telling me about the caves before we are all whisked uphill towards them.

This is the wonderful thing about not slavishly reading the guidebooks. We follow our instincts and listen to the people we meet. We stop where we want, rather than where we should.

An hour later we are 50 metres underground, enclosed by solid rock walls, the damp and cold wrapping round our lungs and bare legs. The white limestone has been quarried since the 12th century to supply Paris (she really was a greedy diva).

'It must be three degrees in here,' I whisper to Damian, who is pretending to understand the rapid French being rattled off by the tour guide. Deeper and deeper we shuffle into the stone chambers, passing vast damp walls packed with millions of dark glass bottles.

'At least if we get lost we won't die of thirst,' quips Damian.

By the time we emerge from the dark caves clutching our bottle of Bailly-Lapierre Reserve Brut (also known as Crémant de Bourgogne), I have goosebumps and India is asleep (either that or she's died of hypothermia). We shall store this precious bottle of stuff they are not allowed to call champagne, though it tastes just like it, in our bilges for the right moment.

The sun is setting and throwing swathes of pink and orange onto the tree-covered low hills and river below.

'We should crack that bottle tonight. Can't think of a more perfect day,' oozes Damian, giving me a squeeze.

That night as we knock back the fizzy froth, I think about the whole idea of 'saving things for a special occasion'. In London we used to have to wait months for a special occasion. Really nice bottles of wine or the odd bottle of champagne used to sit gathering dust. On this trip, we're giddy with the number of moments that count as 'special'. My head is already

bursting with them and it feels like each week, the bar is raised higher. If it carries on like this, we *will* end up with gout, just from the richness of life.

We crash into our bunk, tipsy and happy. I ponder that at some point, normality will return. Lows will even out these highs. But for now I want to keep riding the wave.

The next morning I wake up with an idea. I realise that I've never really seen *Friendship* out on the open water because I'm always on board. I've never trusted anyone enough to let them take *Friendship* out while I watch from the shore. The time has come for me to loosen the apron strings.

I'm excited but also nervous about leaving Shiv to handle the boat on her own. I hope to God she doesn't prang it. Mind you, she's no longer the nervous, tired and unconfident woman who got off that ferry in Calais. This is a new Shiv.

I saddle up and cycle off with my camera and India. I need a spot to take my pictures and eventually find the place, about a mile down from our mooring. There is a clearing on the bank, next to an enormous field of sunflowers. They are all dying now, their heads grey and drooping downwards. I think they look beautiful. Less clichéd than they were in their yellow clothing of just a month or two ago. Now they look strange, enigmatic and brooding. It's a good look. I spent most of my teenage years trying to achieve it.

I plonk India onto the grass next to me and we wait for *Friendship* to appear.

If I were a psychologist studying Damian, I'd say he has just taken a huge step forward, relinquishing control of *Friendship*. Even if it's for just ten minutes. It's the start of him letting go of his precious baby. Rather like me on my parallel journey with the kids.

Now it is just Noah, *Friendship* and me. What a feeling. Suddenly with only half the people on board she feels twice the size. Noah is crouched on the engine cover driving cars round a pretend track. He's safe. I have no-one else to worry about. No-one to bark orders at me. No-one who might topple off a seat with a scream. So instead of setting off, as agreed with Damian earlier, I relish being left in charge and make just the one mug of tea, carry it out on deck and sip it slowly, surveying the river ahead.

I feel I could almost manage this whole journey on my own now. As I sit, legs over the side, leaning over the safety netting, I realise I have made a pact with *Friendship*. Finally, I begin to understand her. I am accepting her idiosyncrasies, rather like in a marriage. At first you push and pull against the natural rhythm. Slowly, understanding creeps in. And patience. Then, if you stick with it, you soften a little and learn to accept. That's when you begin to really enjoy each other. That's where I am with *Friendship*, and Damian too, I guess.

I start the engine, put her in neutral, loop the stern line through a ring and bring it back on board so I can reach it from the deck. Next I undo the bowline, coil it up and lie it on deck. The boat jiggles with my movements but waits patiently. Then I turn the wheel, nudging the accelerator for a tiny burst of movement. As we edge into the river and move forward, I have to leave the wheel unmanned and clamber out to the stern deck to release the line. A few months ago I would have been petrified of losing control of *Friendship*, but now I know how she will react – slowly. I have plenty of time to coil the line, walk back to the wheel and steer us into the stream. I feel like a child who has just learnt to walk. Independent. I love it.

After a long, long time *Friendship* appears from round a bend upstream and the bright early morning sun bounces off the deep varnish of her hull. She is a blaze of golden light. As the bow turns towards us, I don't see Noah, but I spot Shiv's head popping through the steering hatch.

I can't get over how *Friendship* looks. She's not the vessel I had in my mind's eye when I pictured this trip. The boat in front of me is dripping in crap: massive black fenders hang off every part of the hull and every inch of the decks is covered in prams, bikes, potties, toy boxes ... you name it. If it's brightly coloured and found in Mothercare or Marine-store,

then it's on that bloody deck. 'Kit and kids' is how James described it. He got that right.

Almost reluctantly I take a couple of pictures and then wait for Shiv to come alongside and pick us up from the bank (she handles the manoeuvre perfectly). I climb back aboard somewhat chastened. Now I understand why people look at us they way they do.

'Well, how'd she look?' I ask.

'Hmmmmm. Fully loaded,' answers Damian, without the enthusiasm I had expected.

'Great. Show me, show me.' I am jumping up and down in the cockpit like a kid. My half-hour of responsibility has puffed me up.

'Gosh. It looks like we are off round the world,' I say, scrolling through the tiny digital pictures on his camera.

'Hmmm,' says Damian, coiling up a stray rope.

'Looks like we've been to Africa and back with all that clobber. Fantastic.'

'Hmmm.'

'Okay, you want to steer now? There's a château up ahead, I think.'

'Yeah, and maybe I'll do a little sort-out of the fenders and the stuff on deck when we moor later.'

We revert back to our roles, me plucking India out of the cockpit and up onto the deck, Damian clearing away my empty mug from earlier that I had left by the wheel.

I soon forget how *Friendship* looks as we manoeuvre through the next nine locks to Vincelles, a faded, glorious quayside looking onto tended lawns, gravel paths and neat little houses with blue wooden shutters.

My God, the French just have a way with the colour blue. It doesn't matter what they paint, they always choose the perfect shade. In the last five days I've seen the sun-faded blue of wooden shutters on a rambling old farmhouse; the rich and lustrous blue of a bench in a flower-filled garden; the

chalky blue door of a tiny lock-keeper's cottage; the slate blue clapboard sides of a wooden summerhouse; the deep, dark blue of the window frames on a small, impeccable château; and the washed-out blue of a sign above a quiet bar at the end of a quiet village.

We English think we can capture these blues in a tin of paint from Homebase. But we can't. These blues are at home here.

I can feel France seeping into me now. It's not just the blues, it's the very fact that I even noticed them in the first place. That wouldn't have happened 'before'. The blues are another sign on my 'Road to Damascus'.

Damian is in rhapsodies about the colour blue. He seems to be slowing down at last, becoming more aware of things around him. Blue things, that is.

As he slowly changes gear, so does my relationship with him. It all comes down to trust, I suppose. I realise I trust him more than anyone else in the world. Which is why I'm now sitting on the bank letting him cut my hair. Something no sane London woman would allow an unqualified husband to do. He is snipping and caressing my head in equal measure. Something's definitely changed between us here in Vincelles.

There's no mirror, no cup of coffee, no magazine to flick through but this has to be the best-located salon I've ever been to. In the distance the vineyards of Irancy sparkle in the afternoon sun. Leaves are turning colour and some float on the water beside me. From my canvas stool I can see inches of dark hair drop to the floor, taking with them the years of angst of new motherhood.

Shiv had clung on for too long. Her hair has gone past the point of no return. She finally snapped as we tied up and suddenly exclaimed that she wanted me to cut it. I am stunned that she is resorting to letting me wield the scissors. The hairdresser in Compiègne must have left a deeper psychological scar than I had realised.

However, the request didn't come without strings attached.

In fact, it was accompanied by endless disclaimers about 'Not taking too much off', 'Not getting carried away' and 'Not thinking I'm Trevor Sorbie'. In other words, lots of 'nots'.

I don't see why she's so worried. I've been cutting my own hair now for the last few months (even at the back). Okay, so at first I looked as though I was going through chemotherapy, but I've got the hang of it now and simply look 'surfy'. A look most of the young lads at the agency were paying £75 a time for at the hairdressers in Covent Garden.

I'm actually enjoying letting rip on Shiv's luxurious mass of thick black hair. I know exactly how I want to cut it. I want it to be how it was when I first saw her: a shaggy bob that refused to stay neat with stray wisps falling seductively over her brown eyes. At least that's how I remember it. Gorgeous.

I snip away with a glass of red wine in hand (like Keith Floyd crossed with Sweeney Todd). I say snipping, but 'scything', 'slashing' and 'hacking' might be more appropriate words. Huge lumps of hair now lie all around us and Shiv keeps asking to look in the mirror. I tell her to wait until there's something worth looking at.

Finally I finish. Shiv looks great. Or at least I think so. Younger. Sexier. Cooler. Proudly I give her my small shaving mirror to see what she thinks. She peers into the three-by-two-inch glass and smiles.

CHAPTER 16

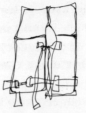

When we get into our bunks that night, we hear another boat pull in behind us. Why do people do that? Everyone on this canal must be trying to 'get away from it all' and yet there is still an overwhelming drive for humans to cling together. Everyone wants to be free, but not too free. We're all like pets that have been let into the wild – most of us don't know what to do with our freedom. But Shiv and I seem to have crossed some unspoken line. Maybe we've gone feral ...

After breakfast I emerge from *Friendship* at exactly the same moment our neighbour pokes his head out. It's obvious we both want to get off quickly so I'm hastily coiling ropes in the dew and mist while he does the same. We end up chatting a little. He's called Wayne, he's fat and he's American. He's flown over for a four-week cruising holiday and this is week two.

Quietly and imperceptibly, we compete with one another to be the first ready. Or maybe it's just me who is competing. Either way, without an assault course of buggies and bikes on deck, he beats me.

Wayne starts his engine first and duly sets off with an ostentatious roar. Just a few minutes later I'm in hot pursuit.

As I follow Wayne I watch him at the wheel of his boat. Moments ago he proudly told me that he has lost more weight on this trip than he has done in three years with his

personal trainer back in Ohio. Considering all he is doing is sitting at the wheel of a motor cruiser all day, I think he should sack his personal trainer.

Crouched in the galley, I'm rifling through drawers looking for the jam when the smell first hits me. It's like burnt toast but there's nothing on the hob. It must be coming from the banks. I jump up and peep through the galley porthole. The banks are deserted – nothing untoward out there.

A mechanical screeching startles me – it's our smoke alarm, which blots out all thought apart from 'There must be a fire on board'. There's no smoke down here, so where on earth is it coming from?

Noah's yelling, 'Mummy, what's that noise? Is it the police?'

India has her hands clamped over her ears and she's crying now.

Ignoring them both, I throw open the cabin doors to see if Damian knows what's going on. Perhaps we have a faulty alarm.

That's when I see it. Behind him. Massive clouds of grey-black smoke bellowing out from the back of the boat. Damian's totally oblivious. It's staggering how single-minded he can be. It's almost like all other senses have been shut down while he is looking forward, trying to make up distance between ourselves and the fat man from Ohio. He's the same with the children. Sometimes they can be screaming his name and he doesn't even hear them.

'Oh bloody hell. It's us. Smoke!' I shriek at Damian.

'What?' Damian asks, confused but with his eyes still locked on forward. He clearly hasn't heard the screech of the alarm.

'Look behind you.' I only just stop myself from adding, 'Dickhead!'

'Oh shit!!' yells Damian.

I nearly have a heart attack when I turn around. I can't believe I haven't noticed the smoke or the alarm. I get such a shock when I see the black fumes enveloping the back of the boat. It's like turning round in the dark and realising the Bogeyman is stood right behind you.

Shiv yells, 'Dame, where's it coming from? Are we on fire?' And then rushes below to grab Noah and India.

At that moment the engine dies.

'Oh shit,' I shout again.

Our momentum carries us forward but we're drifting now and have no control over our direction. The rudder is virtually useless without the propeller forcing water against it.

'Oh shit.'

I go to the back of the boat to look for flames. Nothing. They must be coming from the engine. I go to the engine cover and do the most stupid thing in the world: I lift it off to see what's happening. In a more rational moment, I could have told you that all this does is allow new oxygen to breathe life into the fire and make it even worse.

The moment I lift off the heavy wooden cover, black smoke pours out of the engine box and races up to the sky. I shield my face and flinch, waiting to be burnt. Nothing happens. There are no flames. Just choking, stinking black smoke. I slowly open my eyes and wave away the fumes. I still can't see any flames.

'Oh shit.'

'What is it? What's happened?'

I don't answer Shiv. I'm thinking too much to talk. In times of crisis I can only do one or the other. Desperately I scrabble about on the cockpit floor and start lifting up the floorboards to see where the smoke is coming from.

My frenzy is interrupted by Shiv calling me from the cabin in an icily calm voice.

'Damian, there's water coming over the floorboards in here. About six inches and rising. Let's get the kids off.'

'Oh shit.'

Even in the heat of the moment, I notice how cool Shiv is. I can tell she's stressed out but she's keeping a lid on it. I'm impressed. I, on the other hand, have been reduced to a gibbering wreck with a vocabulary of two words.

My feet splash through rising water as my mind races into automatic emergency mode. Lifejackets. I grab them from the bathroom and grapple them calmly onto Noah and India, fixing the straps as quickly as I can, with slightly trembling fingers. The water is already over my deck shoes.

'This is exciting, eh? Let's put these on and then we are going to get off for a little walk.' I do my best to sound like a hypnotist and induce calm rather than the panic that I'm feeling.

'Are we sinking, Mummy?' asks Noah.

'Of course not! Daddy has to check the engine, that's all.'

'Why is there water on the floor?' he says, pointing to the cabin floor. The floor is floating.

'Hmmm. Maybe there's a little leak. Daddy's going to have a look at it.' It's no good lying to them, they always know.

While Shiv is in the cabin, I carry on ripping up floorboards in the cockpit. It's when I get to the very back of the boat that I get the shock.

A hole has been blown in the silencer on our exhaust system. Through the burnt gash in its side, water is pouring into the boat. Gushing and flooding into our hull.

'Oh shit.'

I turn to tell Shiv what I have found but she is already standing right behind me with Noah and India at her side. They're wrapped in the fluorescent orange of their ocean-going lifejackets. Like me, she's looking at the water surging into the boat and is slightly mesmerised by the sight.

Gallons of water are rushing into the boat through a hole the size of Damian's fist. Instinctively I leap back into the galley and grab a tea towel, thrusting it into Damian's hands. He looks at me, confused.

'It's not for *you*. Shove it in the hole.'

Luckily I have just read *Sea Change*, where a guy sails his boat single-handedly across the Atlantic Ocean. It springs a leak and I remember that he sealed it by pressing a blanket into the hole. My mind is on sinking in the vastness of the Atlantic.

Miraculously the tea towel starts to stem the flow of water. By the time we have lagged the hole with every towel in our kitchen and bathroom, the water coming into the boat is reduced to a manageable rate; little more than a trickle. We've switched on both electric bilge pumps and finally they seem able to pump water out faster than it's coming in. That means we're floating and we're safe. We're going to be okay.

I breathe out for the first time in half an hour. We're all strangely calm and quiet. Then Shiv delivers the killer blow: 'You *did* open the seacock, didn't you?'

'Oh shit.'

In my rush to chase Wayne, I'd forgotten to open the seacock. That means no water was circulating around the cooling system. So it got hotter and hotter until it blew the silencer apart (hence the black smoke). Suddenly the system was no longer watertight and the whole canal started rushing into our boat through the gaping hole.

Stupid, stupid, stupid mistake. Especially because I had been warned about it in Calais by the 'Couple-in-the-know' who had done the same thing.

To stop myself from exploding like our exhaust system, I focus on getting the kids and me off the boat. Damian cannot sort out the engine with their constant questions and I need to cool off. How can he have been so stupid? The seacock. It's elementary. Bloody competitiveness.

Noah and India are swung out and up onto the unkempt grassy bank. I leap off after them, unaware of the nettles stinging my legs. It's only when I look back at *Friendship* from the safety of the bank that it hits me, and I begin laughing, the panic and fury releasing.

'What now?' queries Damian angrily.

'We're not going to sink, are we? It's impossible. We've only 50 centimetres of water under the boat. There'll be a lot of water inside her, but she'll just settle on the mud.'

'Oh shit,' says Damian for the umpteenth time. 'I hadn't thought of that. It would be a complete disaster if that happened.

We'd never get her off again. We have got to keep her afloat or we'll need a crane to lift her off the mud. There are no tides here to help us.'

At last my brain kicks into gear and I analyse the situation:

– We can't use the engine any more because of the exhaust.

– The water leak has been stopped for now, but very soon the towels will be too wet to soak up any more water.

– The bilge pumps are coping at the moment but they will drain the battery unless we can get connected to mains electricity.

'Oh shit.'

I scan the river ahead for signs of anyone who might be able to help us.

Fat chance.

We're on the edge of a small hamlet. It's typically beautiful with maybe just a dozen or so houses crammed along the riverbank and a few others gathered around a small square with a huge tree in the centre. No-one is around. In fact, it's like a ghost town. Maybe they're all asleep.

Even in my state, I realise there isn't going to be anyone here who can sort us out. We couldn't even buy a tin of baked beans in this place, let alone an exhaust silencer for a boat. We're going to have to get the boat to the next big town, Clamecy, just eight kilometres away.

This is where our secret weapon comes in. Thank God for the endless nights I spent poring over boat magazines. It may have killed our sex life in London but at least it might save us now.

The one thing about boat mags is they love a good disaster. And a sure way to get into trouble is to have a motorboat with only one engine. It's like an aeroplane with one engine; if it breaks down, you're buggered. I can't begin to count how many stories I've read about this, so before we left the UK, my spending spree on safety equipment included a brand-new, outboard motor. It looked ridiculous, perched on the back of a boat as big and as heavy as *Friendship* but the man who sold it to me at the boat show promised it was powerful enough to serve as a back-up engine in emergencies.

Well, this is an emergency.

I've never even started the outboard before, let alone steered with it, so I decide not to take any risks. Before we give her a go, we need to be on a good stretch of straight and open water. That means getting *Friendship* past the bizarre obstacle in front of us: an iron road bridge that has to be raised in order to let boats pass under it, just like Tower Bridge in London, except that this bridge is raised by hand.

I size up our options and then prepare the boat with various ropes. I have a plan. Shiv's not going to like it, but it's the only one we've got.

I explain to Shiv that I'm going to tie a long rope around her waist and loop it back to the Samson post on the bow of *Friendship*. I tell her that in the last century before engines were commonplace, wives and children often used to pull barges along the canals from the towpaths. Horses were expensive and this was the only option. These families were known as 'The Dandelion Collectors' because with the rope around their waists, they had to bend right over as they strained and pulled to get the boat moving. As soon as I tell her that last bit, I realise I have made a mistake.

At moments like these I really question my sanity and wonder whether most other women would be so compliant in my situation. Or would they be dabbing dripping mascara, crying, 'No way. I'm calling a taxi from Auxerre. I don't care how much it costs. I'll check into a hotel with the kids and wait for you there.'

I expect Shiv to let rip at me but instead she quite reasonably protests, 'Why don't you pull and I'll sit in the boat and steer?'

'I can't pull because I have to stay on board, trying to steer while at the same time pushing us off the banks with that bloody great oar we've had tied to the roof for the last few

months. It's twenty foot long, for Christ's sake. You couldn't even lift it let alone push us off. Believe me, I've got the hard job here …'

We look like a barge family from the turn of the century. No wonder they all died by 40. I grumble to myself about Damian's 'plan' as I manually hoist the iron road bridge by turning a large metal handle, a rope coiled round my waist.

Noah and India huddle close, looking forlorn, staring at the ground like hungry, homeless kids (who happen to be wearing lifejackets). They really are entering into the spirit of the crisis. We could even earn money if only I had a hat to throw on the ground.

Three cars sit waiting and watching for us to pass under the bridge. It must look quite cruel to see a woman, more donkey than shire horse, pulling a boat. I feel ridiculous. Thank goodness I'll never see any of these people again.

Despite her size, *Friendship* is surprisingly light to pull. I had imagined a couple of sleeping elephants. Deadweight. Instead, once we are moving, she glides along quite easily. It's impossible to stop her, of course. I pull back on the rope and feel my feet being dragged forward, the same sensation as being pulled along a beach by a powerful kite.

Once past the bridge, Damian steers her gently into the bank where I wait with a fender to stop *Friendship*'s sides smashing into the concrete sidings.

Secure once more, on the other side of the bridge I try the outboard motor.

'Bloody thing won't start,' I groan.

'What? But it's brand new. That thing cost a fortune. What do you mean it won't start?' whinges Shiv from the bank.

'I mean, it won't start. That's what I mean,' I snarl through gritted teeth.

'You must be doing something wrong.'

'I am *not* doing anything wrong. It's the bloody outboard. It must have got damaged on the Channel crossing or

something.' I start re-checking all the connections, grumbling
and swearing quietly to myself.

'Dame—'

'Bloody thing.'

'Dame ... listen to me.'

'What?!' I snap.

'The outboard. It's on. It's running.'

'What do you mean?'

'It's running. It's been running the whole time. It's just so
quiet you can't hear it.'

The outboard is no louder than a sewing machine. I can't
believe it. After months of the loud thumping of *Friendship*'s
diesel engine, I can't understand how forward propulsion can
be achieved without deafening everyone.

Back on board, Noah and India sit on the 'fridge' seat, silenced
with Lego and Smarties. At this rate, they are going to grow up
loving disasters. Whenever something dangerous happens, the
sweets come out. They sit like angels, probably wondering if
I have gone mad, ripping open their Smartie boxes quickly in
case I change my mind.

The eight kilometres to Clamecy would take a car travelling
at 30 kilometres an hour just sixteen minutes. Even walking
(without a colossal boat attached to your waist) you could cover
that distance in two hours. For us, however, with a top speed of
two kilometres an hour we have a long morning ahead.

Damian is at the wheel and also operating the outboard controls. My new job is to keep us on course with a back-up steering
system. Another grand plan.

Our giant oar is now being lashed to the back of the boat with
an assortment of ropes and bungee cords. The baby bath, wicker
baskets we were using for fruit and vegetables and the gangplank
have all been flung aside by Damian to make room. These are
strewn now on the foredeck. My new position is perched on the
rear deck, only half a metre in width, oar in hand like a bloke
on a Venetian gondola.

The silence of the outboard is breathtaking. We don't have to shout at each other. Even a whisper can be heard. It's wonderful.

I sigh. 'Do you think we could do the whole journey like this, on the outboard?'

'Are you crazy? It's going to take us a day just to get to Clamecy. If we're lucky,' says Damian.

It's hard to control *Friendship*'s steering with only the outboard on and we are swerving from side to side in a gentle S-shape, but luckily the canal isn't busy. We only have to pull over once to let the hotel barge pass us.

'All okay?' yells James as they plough past at a steady four knots, pushing a tiny wake against our hull, sending us wobbling into the long grass and mud of the bankside.

'Sure,' I shout. 'Just a little engine problem.' There's no way I'm going to admit my seacock cock-up to this young buck.

'Need help? Can we tow you?' asks James.

'Ummmmm. No, don't worry, we're okay.' I hesitate as the well-dressed American chick wafts past on deck. I try desperately not to look like a dizzy old fool.

The passing barge has left Damian all in a fluster. I swear I smell the American woman's musky perfume drift down to me and I make a mental note to be more feminine. Quite tricky at the moment though, given I'm grappling with a giant oar, sweating nerves and adrenalin through my stained T-shirt.

James shouts down to me helpfully, 'Careful up ahead. You need to keep to the left or the current will suck you into the weir on the right. Remember, keep to the LEFT. Okay?' He gives us the thumbs-up sign.

Seething inside, I smile at James. I knew Damian would never, ever ask him for help. If I were in charge I would have played the damsel in distress, no problem, no embarrassment, no shame.

The obvious danger of the impending weir pushes aside all other thoughts. *Friendship*'s and my family's safety is in my hands.

Can you believe it? We haven't seen a weir for weeks and weeks. Now that we're without an engine, one rears its ugly

head. I wonder if James means a weir that's more like a fast-running stream or one of those big buggers that looks like a mini waterfall.

In front of us, the navy blue of James's hotel barge is our beacon. If I simply do what she does, we should be okay. We see her slew to the side and then correct herself before gliding into the lock ahead. Even from here we can see her fighting the pull of the weir. I glance over at Damian. He looks back at me. He's seen it too.

The kids chew on their Smarties. I pull out two more boxes from my pocket and throw them each one, unable to leave my perch and the giant oar.

'I love you, Mummy,' says Noah.

Within moments it's upon us. The rush and panic of water pouring over the weir is terrifying. It sounds like Niagara Falls just off to the right, but I can't see anything. Except, that is, for leaves, sticks and other debris on the surface being sucked over the edge.

'Keep us to the left, Shiv,' urges Damian, quietly and firmly. At least he's not yelling at me.

My whole body leaning against the giant oar, I force the paddle against its will, feeling the pressure of the water juddering against the wood below the surface. Damian is thrusting the old steering wheel into a locked position and gently nudging the outboard controls. If he puts on too much power, we'll scream off in the wrong direction. Too little and we won't push against the current.

We seem to slow down and almost stop. Then all of a sudden we slew off to the right, towards the sucking weir. Water, brightness, gushing, rushing, tumbling.

'Shiv! Push! We're going the wrong way,' screams Damian.

'I AM pushing!' I yell back. I force my whole eight and a half stone against the oar, willing it to win against the infinite power of the water. In my head I play over what to do if we roll over the precipice. Grab both kids and jump off to port, away from the boat and the weir. Then swim to the side. Damian can fend for himself. My heart is pounding so loudly it's masking the sound of the water.

It's no use. We are slipping towards the weir and I'm unable to correct it. Damian slams the outboard into full speed ahead and abandons the wheel. He jumps across the cockpit, slams into me and forces his weight against the oar as well. It lurches another foot and we twist around, away from danger.

'Yes!' he yells triumphantly as he hurls himself back to the accelerator, which is still on full steam ahead.

Too late.

A wrench of scraping metal and stone shrieks through the air and cuts our triumph down to size. *Friendship*'s bow has just smashed head first into the left side of the lock, then bounced along the metal gates and finally thumped into the stone sides and overhanging bushes.

The gates are closed of course because the hotel barge is in there. As we languish against the bank, it majestically rises above us. James looks back quizzically.

'That's the trouble with having no brakes,' yells Damian, even now trying to save face.

James clearly can't hear Damian. Instead he sees a bloke who has crashed into the side of a lock and is now grinning inanely while sticking his thumbs in the air. He gives us a friendly wave; he really is well brought up. I'm not sure I will be able to look James in the eye again. He is way too cool to think this is acceptable boating behaviour.

While Shiv moons at James I leap onto the bank, steadying myself by hanging onto straggling branches.

I walk slowly, edging towards the part of *Friendship* that hit the wall: the very front of the boat, where all the clinker planks of iroko wood meet in a beautifully raked, long and slender point.

It's like watching a scary movie. I squint my eyes, ready to shut them tight as soon as I see anything horrible. I feel hollow inside. This is like waiting to hear if you've passed your driving test after you've just side-swiped a Mini doing your

three-point-turn. You just *know* that the news will be bad but you can't help hoping for a miracle. My stomach is doing somersaults. As I get closer I can't see the point of impact. It must be on the other side. I creep round, prepared for the worst ...

Nothing. No scratches. No marks. Nothing.

I don't get it. We hit that wall like a Volvo in a safety test. There should be smashed wood everywhere. I can't work it out and then I see our anchor. It's still in its mounting bracket, protruding 30 centimetres from the front of the boat but it's completely bent out of shape. The metal has been forced in four different directions at once. It looks like it hit the wall almost dead-on. We couldn't have aimed to do that in a month of trying. The anchor has taken all the shock and absorbed all the impact. It saved *Friendship*. I lean forward and kiss it.

Damian looks like the Pope landed off the plane, kissing the tarmac. Except it's not tarmac, it's an anchor. Must be some strange response to our near brush with death.

Relief is coursing through my veins too. My mouth is dry, my shoulders yet to return to their normal position. I'm so shocked that we're all alive, all in one piece. Jumping down from the back deck I snuggle in between Noah and India and squeeze them both to my side.

'Mummy loves you so much, you know. More than the universe times infinity,' I gush, kissing their heads.

'Can we have another box of Smarties?' says Noah.

'Marteez,' echoes India.

After the weir and lock, being on the open river again feels easy. I manage to get the steering more under control and we glide silently to Clamecy. It would be a beautiful way to arrive were it not for the fact that the water level in the bottom of the boat is beginning to rise again. The towels we lagged around the hole in the silencer are now sodden and the water seems to be seeping through them at a much faster

rate than before. The bilge pumps are going flat out but they can't keep up. In other words, we're slowly sinking.

We have two options. Keep going and hope that we can get to a safe mooring before we fill up with water. Or stop, remove the towels and find something else to wrap around the hole (maybe a sleeping bag or a quilt? But I don't know how effective they would be).

The big problem with stopping is that as soon as I loosen the towels, the water will gush in and I don't know how quickly we'll be able to re-seal the hole. If we're too slow, there will simply be too much water in the boat for our pumps to cope.

I decide we should press on. It's only a few more kilometres to Clamecy.

While we limp along, more and more water pours into our bilges. After an hour, I wonder whether we have done the right thing. *Friendship* seems to be moving more slowly than ever. Just as I start thinking about Plan B, Shiv spots a long row of grey stone buildings and a bridge. Clamecy is in sight.

At the very same moment we hear a shout from the banks: 'Bonjour *Friendship* . . .'

CHAPTER 17

'It's Jean Yves,' I utter slightly hysterically, grinning like a mad-woman from my position at the oar. The tanned, eloquent, languid teacher we met 500 kilometres north in Watten stands firm on the bank, his arms outstretched waving.

Jean Yves looks like an angel standing with his arms in the air. What's he doing here? I half wonder if he has been fol-lowing us. Or maybe he's been trying to find us because of something that happened at Watten? Nothing seems to make sense but who cares. He's here and he can help us.

Abandoning my oar, I skip along the side-deck and throw Jean Yves the bowline so that he can pull us the last few metres along the stone walls into Clamecy Lock. Then we'll be in the safety of a cul-de-sac marina.

Damian stows away our giant oar and whispers loudly, 'I wonder why he's here? And how on earth did he know it was us?'

'Well he'd have to be blind to miss the baby bath and clobber on the deck, two kids, the bike seats on the roof and the general air of gypsy about us.'

Damian looks wounded. The word gypsy was perhaps just a little too much for his sensibilities after the drama of this morning. Damian has the same reaction to criticism of *Friendship*

232

as I do to any negative comments about the kids.

I turn back to watch Jean Yves as he slowly hauls us into the marina lock. This manoeuvre, essentially a U-turn, would have been a nightmare with the giant oar getting in the way and only an outboard for power. Jean Yves' appearance is perfectly timed.

What could have taken us hours is sorted within minutes, as Jean Yves and I haul *Friendship* to the far bank of the little marina at Clamecy. Before long the bilge pumps are on auto-drive and the gash in the exhaust has been re-lagged, although this time we had to make do with one of my fleeces and two of Shiv's tops as all the towels had been used.

The key thing is that we're in a marina. This gives us access to shore power so the bilge pumps won't run the batteries flat. All we have to do is keep an eye on the leak and ensure we have a good supply of dry cloth on hand. Even that will be easier once we have found the town's launderette.

I look at my watch. It's getting late so we won't be able to make a start on finding a new exhaust until tomorrow but at least we are out of danger now.

I feel my whole body sag with relief. I was more uptight than I'd realised. I watch the kids play in the cabin with their Sticklebricks, oblivious to what's been happening around them, and my mind races through how many different ways we could have killed them today. I push the images out of my head and give them a big 'Daddy hug'.

With the appearance of our cavalry, Jean Yves, I can switch off from red alert. That same feeling I get whenever I arrive back at my parents' house surges through me. It's home. I can toss my bag in the hall, rifle through the fridge, perch on the yellow stool and simply be myself.

There are no yellow stools here but we shake out green canvas chairs on the stone quayside and offer Jean a warm beer (without any engine the fridge has been heating everything up, not just us). It turns out that Jean Yves was returning to his Brittany home from his winter boat base in Baye (just upriver) when he spotted us in difficulty on the canal.

Shiv is giddy. That evening all she talks about is the 'wonderful', 'amazing', 'charming', 'clever', 'cultured' and 'kind' Jean Yves. Obviously this is getting on my nerves but it will be worse if I let her know it. Then we'd end up in a petty argument about me being jealous, which is true of course, but I would have to deny it. Perhaps the most annoying thing of all is that Jean Yves *is* absolutely wonderful. He is a true gentleman and frankly we'd be lost without him at the moment.

The next day Damian is like a mother with a sick child. He cannot possibly leave *Friendship* till she's well again. I put on the kettle and then knuckle down to my mission, which is to empty the boat and lay our disaster-sodden things on deck or on the quayside to dry in the autumn sun.

The on-board flood mostly affected our food supplies (much of which were loaded in the bilges or in low cupboards), some of the kids' drawings and lots of our clothes. All the towels, tea towels and most of my clothes need washing. But that isn't all . . .

The disaster-water squeezed its way into my hiding place for Damian's birthday present. It has washed the black dye from the new captain's hat into a hippie tie-dyed swirl all over the front of the smock. His very expensive fleece-lined smock.

With Damian's keen sense of design, I cannot imagine him believing that it's supposed to be there. He'll never wear this now. It looks like something I've found in a bin.

'There's good news and bad news,' I tell him when he peeks his head up from the engine. 'The good news is nothing's really damaged apart from one thing. The bad news is that the one thing is your fortieth birthday present. Here. You might as well have it now.'

I hand him the soggy captain's hat and artist's smock. He holds up the non-designer fleece against his chest. He looks at it, smiles and then grimaces. 'Guess I should find a launderette?' Noah immediately commandeers the hat and runs off with it screeching with laughter. Damian chases him round the marina before giving up to tackle the wet towels and our dirty clothes. It'll be another week of no knickers for us all unless we get to the launderette.

In like a bullet at number one. That's how the launderette at Clamecy stacks up in the top ten chart I've been compiling since Calais. There are various criteria which I use to decide chart positions: their proximity to the boat, availability of machines, capacity of drums, options to buy washing powder, seating, price, smell and décor.

The previous number one had been a very clean launderette at Sens and it had ruled the roost for weeks. However, the launderette at Clamecy has simply blown it away. Not only is it empty, warm and cheap but it's also situated right next to a great bar. This means I can shove three washes in the massive machines and then pop next door for a beer and read my book while I wait for them to finish. I'm currently wading through a biography of King Juan Carlos of Spain (just in case we head for Spain once we reach the Med). The other option when we hit the sea is to turn left and go to Italy so I've lined up *The Godfather* to read next.

I ponder these destinations as I sit in the funky French bar next to the launderette, sipping a cold Kronenburg 1664 and pretending not to be looking at the pure-faced and stylish young girls in the corner. Even as I approach 40, I still look at the same girls I would've looked at when I was 18.

My mind wanders and I imagine what it would be like going through France on a boat on my own. My head fills with fantasies of women in every port and whisky every night. Truth is, though, I'm just not like that. I'm too pathetically romantic. I'd probably end up heartbroken in Lyon, drinking turpentine and writing poetry about a pretty waitress who dumped me for a truffle farmer.

The alarm on my watch beeps and brings me back to earth.

Forty minutes have slipped by already and the washing will be dry.

A little later I walk past the young girls in the bar balancing a huge blue IKEA bag of dry, neatly folded and fresh-smelling washing on the saddle of my bike. They don't even look up but little can match the excitement on board *Friendship* when I return with a bag of clean clothes.

Best of all, doing the washing is normally a crap job so when I get back to the boat I get a modicum of sympathy from Shiv. She's even moved enough to make me a cup of tea. I don't tell her about the bar. I'll keep the launderette and its adjacent pleasures a little secret for now. Hope she doesn't smell the beer on my breath.

Over the next few days in Clamecy, Jean appears, magic-like, around ten in the morning in pressed trousers. Like a 'day fairy' he then disappears around sunset. At his insistence, he runs endless errands for us. Marine directories are brought from goodness knows where. Phone calls are made. Chandlers are visited. Even the capitainerie must have been charmed as they give us a reduction in harbour fees.

Despite Jean Yves' best efforts, we can't find anyone who knows how to find the part for the silencer that we need. I'm getting panicky when finally I have a brainwave and call Simon, the boat mechanic from Sens. Although it's weeks since we were there, it's only a couple of hours' drive north, so if he can locate the part he should be able to deliver it too. Ten minutes later, I put the phone down and leap in the air. We'll have the new exhaust in three days. All we have to do now is wait and keep the bilge pumps running.

While Dame is at the launderette once again, I enjoy some time off from boat chores and bask on deck in the late autumn sunshine, closing my eyes just enough to watch the toings and froings of *La Belle Epoque*, the hotel barge with James aboard. When Damian trudges back an hour later feeling tired and looking for sympathy, I decide that I am going to have to do at least one trip to the launderette while we are here. It is unfair to leave him to do all our washing. Poor bloke.

I've been rumbled. It couldn't have lasted forever but I had hoped it might have gone on for a *bit* longer. Unusually for me, I've been insisting on doing the washing while we've been in Clamecy, but for a change, today Shiv took it up there and saw the wine bar. My secret sanctuary is no longer a secret.

The oddest thing about Shiv's visit to the launderette was that she came back with a telephone number. And a man's telephone number at that. She tells me he is Italian and he runs the launderette. What is it with her and launderette owners? Last time she did this, she was discussing frilly knickers with some bloke in Cambrai.

Shiv tells me that he used to be a mechanic and he's offered to help fit the new exhaust system when it arrives tomorrow. The only thing I can think is: why? Why would a bloke who runs a launderette want to take time off to help me fit an exhaust? It sounds way too dodgy. There's no way I'm ringing him. I'm a man. I can do it myself. I don't need help, especially from a launderette owner in need of friends.

The next morning I preside, like mother hen, over Noah and India on the quayside. We have a wonderful mooring spot facing the canal and woodland, uninterrupted by other holiday boaters, most of whom have returned to their centrally heated homes for the winter.

India totters dangerously close to the canal edge but veers away again. She is absorbed in making 'stew' with water, sand and leaves foraged from the quayside, and practising her growing vocabulary. For some reason the word 'oar' has crept into her top ten words as well as 'up', 'down', 'buggy' and 'water' – all of which she shouts out at intervals to me during her stew-making. Luckily she didn't latch on to 'Oh shit' from our disaster day.

While watching the kids I spot Ferretti, the man from the launderette, out of the corner of my eye. Dressed in casual trousers and a faux leather blouson, he saunters up to Damian on the quayside, cowboy-style. Uh-oh. Better make myself scarce.

A fat Italian man with a big moustache and a leather waist-coat has just turned up on the quay. It turns out he is not from a Village People tribute band but is in fact the owner of the launderette and is 'here to help'. He eyes up the recently arrived exhaust silencer on the foredeck and climbs on board without being invited. I don't know whether to feel offended, grateful or emasculated. Probably a bit of all three in truth but I swallow my pride, get out some spanners and two cold beers.

All I see of Damian is his backside as he 'uumms' and 'aaahs' in the bilges of the boat with a torch. The scene has all the drama of giving birth but with more grunting and groaning. Ferretti and Damian have already spent two hours fitting the new exhaust box, fiddling with spanners, cursing pipes, and requesting more and more beer.

As I watch them converse in three languages, I think about how kind people are to us. Whether this treatment is offered to all boaters, or whether we look particularly needy, we shall never know. But the kindnesses of the people along the canals shall stay with me forever. It's quite humbling to be offered such help and time for nothing more than a chat or a beer in return. Our years of city, eye-for-an-eye living, are being replaced quickly by another much gentler force.

Four hours, four cups of tea and six beers is all it takes to repair *Friendship*. Oh, and the help of Noah, of course, with his screwdriver in one hand and a spanner in the other, bashing everything around him that is below two feet high. When, finally, Ferretti and I fire up the engine we all cheer. Noah and India wave their hands in the air without quite understanding what's going on while Shiv, Ferretti and I all hug and dance a little jig around the cockpit. We're back on track and the next bit of the journey awaits.

Clamecy disappears as we chug into the narrowing waterway early the next morning. No mist today so the orange glow of decadence twinkles from *La Belle Epoque*'s portholes as we glide past. That's the last we shall see of them and of James, as their cruise takes them from Auxerre to Clamecy, then back again.

'We are the *real* adventurers. That's what James called us,' says Damian proudly, a man again now that he is at the wheel with a working engine and a hot mug of tea in his hand.

I love him when he's like this. An outdoor man, stubble growing into a beard, scruffy shorts and a cheeky grin. Gone are the lines and furrows of winning new business at the agency. I know we'll have to return to work at some point, although Damian proclaims to everyone we meet that he has retired at 39 years of age. But for now I'm revelling in this sense of freedom, our ability to literally go with the flow (or against it in this case).

I'm feeling better about life. Having fixed the engine somehow, I've reasserted my manhood. Even Shiv can sense it. After months of changing nappies and looking after the children, it's energising to feel like a bloke again. Yeah, yeah, I know it's horribly old-fashioned and sexist but I can't help it. I feel a great sense of achievement at getting *Friendship* sorted. I've 'provided' for my family. I've given us our home and our freedom back (which is just as well considering I was the idiot who took it away in the first place by racing 'Fat Wayne' from Ohio).

With Damian at the wheel I soak up the views. If Constable were French I'm sure he would have lived and painted here. Beech trees, vast fields splintered by clusters of bushes and decorated with cream-coloured cows lazily chewing the cud. Not that Damian has noticed any of this. He's been very attentive to the engine since we left Clamecy. We are both wary in case deeper damage was done that won't show till further down the Nivernais. A new sign hangs next to the ignition switch. It loudly proclaims 'SEACOCK!' Goodness knows what my friends in Queen's Park would think if they saw it.

As afternoon drifts into evening, we pull over at a very unassuming mooring. Nothing more than a bit of grass and a power point at the end of a long string of trees. With nothing better to do on board, we load Noah and India onto the bikes and set off to investigate the village at the top of the nearby hill.

Half an hour later we find ourselves in Tannay, standing in a dimly lit cellar, admiring barrels of wine and chatting to Maurice, a remarkable man who is determined to make these wines famous. Yet again, fate seems to be steering us towards fascinating characters, the kind of people who make me love the world.

Maurice used to work in advertising but ten years ago, he left to help launch this small winery. He is a man on a mission; determined to fuse traditional wine values with cutting-edge technology. I like his approach; he wants to support the growers who normally get abused by the corporate giants. He insists on organic farming methods and he wants to innovate with different grapes. He's schizophrenic like me; traditional and experimental. Capitalist and socialist. Bastard and benefactor.

Inevitably I am completely beguiled by his passion and we end up buying a whole box of different wines. We can't hope to carry them back to *Friendship* on our bikes so he promises to drive home via the canal and drop them off tonight.

Maurice is true to his word (of course) so now Shiv and I are drinking wine in the dark cockpit, wrapped up in warm fleeces. The air is still and our oil lantern casts a dim glow over the varnished wood. We're quaffing a new Chardonnay, 'produced in the Loire style'. To be honest, I can't tell the difference but I don't really care. This is just fantastic. Everything we touch turns to gold at the moment. Everything we do is a treat. Everything we see appears unique and special. If we were American sportsmen we'd be 'in the groove'. I think again about Maurice and his new life after a career in advertising. I wonder how hard it is to grow grapes ...

For once, our morning is not military-style. After breakfast, Damian stretches out on the recently vacated kids' bunks and within minutes is snoring.

I set the kids up in the cabin with playdough and plastic cutters. They are in heaven patting and pressing pretend sausages for a teddy's tea party. This should occupy them for a while now, maybe even half an hour. Until they begin to jostle over colours or India eats the stuff through boredom. Thirty minutes. Just long enough to recharge my batteries.

I nip up on deck with my book and turn my face to catch the surprisingly warm morning rays, checking through the hatches every now and then on India and Noah. Their chitter-chatter wafts up to me, breaking the stillness of the air. This is one of my private little pleasures, hearing them interpret the world when I'm not there.

I wish, oh how I wish, my dad could have seen the kids here, on the trip. Being so free. I wish he could have seen me and Damian in our new, unharassed way of being.

If Shiv's dad *had* come to visit us, one thing that he would *not* have approved of is Chitry-les-Mines. Not the town itself, which is perfectly pretty, but the way in which Shiv and I react to its name. You see, it's pronounced 'Shitry' and we can't say it without breaking into adolescent giggles. I'm sure I wasn't this juvenile when I left England. Is it because I've been with Shiv for too long or is this what I'm *really* like underneath my polished advertising skin? Either way, Shiv's Chaucer-loving, Shakespeare-quoting father would have been appalled. We can't help it though and 'Shitry' crops up frequently in our conversation, not simply because it makes us laugh, but also because it lies at the bottom of the infamous 'Nivernais Staircase', which we face tomorrow (cue the sound of horror music).

The Staircase is a heart-attack-inducing climb through 16 locks up a long and steep hill. It's called The Staircase because upon entering each lock you can see the ones ahead, rising into the woods. Between some there is as little as 200 metres.

There is no rest, no let-up. The rules are simple: once you enter The Staircase, you have to go all the way to the top. No-one is allowed to stop or moor overnight. It's one long, relentless haul and it lasts all day.

Drizzle, a grey smudged sky and grumpy children kick off our day on The Staircase. It's going to be a tough one, especially as Noah and India are both running a fever.

Through the driver's hatch I can see lock after lock rising sharply, cutting through dense woodland. True to its name, these 16 locks are going to raise us up what looks like a mountain.

Damian prepares the boat, and checks the seacock for the tenth time. We get going as soon as we can.

In a way it's great that Noah and India are ill. (Only fathers can say things like this.) They'll both be a bit quieter and more subdued – just what we need on a day when they are going to be boat-bound.

The fact that Shiv has resorted to the DVDs is a sure sign of how serious today's going to be. Usually they only come out when all else fails. It's almost a point of principle for us. Some would call it stubborn pride but I think if we have to stick our children in front of a screen on a trip like this, then we're doing something wrong.

Lock One – Sardy 16 (I love the way each one has a name). A white holiday boat packed with Swiss people is ahead of us and it's rewarding to see that in their case the Swiss genes for accuracy seem to have mutated into something more hectic.

One chap, clad top-to-toe in black and wearing open sandals, tries to hang onto the mooring bollard with his hands, simultaneously pushing the boat away from under him with his feet. We watch agog, as his body moves slowly from the upright to near horizontal position. It's like watching McEnroe play – secretly we are waiting for an eruption. So although we know it's bad sport, it would be so funny to see the guy splosh into the lock, cartoon-like, rope still in hand.

Damian's better side wins him over and after lashing us up to a bollard, he levers himself onto the top of the lock by clambering onto *Friendship*'s coach roof and runs over to the hapless crew in front of us.

I enjoy watching Damian at moments like this. He's an experiment in reinvention, and the results unfold before me. He's a lot kinder than he used to be, jumping up to help. I used to feel that the advertising world had got its roots entwined so deep it had made him overly harsh and cynical, taking the piss even out of the innocent and unsuspecting. Now, it's as if he is returning slowly to the inner him, the blood of the cut-throat advertising world slowly seeping out of him. I love this warmer, kinder version.

It's just a couple of locks after the Swiss debacle when India starts crying. Her temperature is up and she's feeling miserable. Noah is just as bad, but unlike her he is entranced by the DVD. I worry that this is what happens when they don't watch much TV – they overdose whenever the opportunity presents itself. At this rate all our middle-class struggling against the 'goggle box' will backfire on us and he'll turn into a reality TV star.

We've already completed three locks. Lining up for Doyen 13, we know there's no going back now, so we decide we're going to have to take turns to stay below and keep an eye on the children. That means whoever is left at the wheel is going to have to take *Friendship* through the locks *on their own*. Neither of us have ever done this before but we don't have any other option.

Taking a boat into a lock alone is a massively complex process. It's a bit like entering a car park and trying to stop at the tollbooth to collect your ticket using only one hand and without being able to apply your brakes. It has disaster written all over it.

Maybe it's because we know we *have* to make it work that Shiv and I both master the technique of steering alone through the locks at almost the first attempt. Or maybe it's because we're actually pretty good at this boat-handling lark

now. With so many locks close together, we each get a rhythm going and make it look easy. For me this is a symbol of just how far we have come as a couple. Handling a boat like this isn't only down to experience and confidence, it's also about being calm and trusting one another completely.

I know that as I rush from the wheel to the bow and back again, grabbing ropes and steering with one hand through the window of the wheelhouse, that I look like a real expert. I can almost *feel* the admiring stares of the wizened old lockkeepers. The Swiss can barely believe it. They have five people running around their decks and are *still* making a hash of it.

However, my glory is nothing compared to Shiv's. When it's my turn to sit below making barges out of Sticklebricks with Noah and India, I'm sure I can hear the cheering and applause that greets her every move. I can't think of many more surprising and sexier things than the sight of a beautiful woman handling a beautiful boat in a beautiful place. Add the twisted romance of the warm rain and I'm a happy man. God I'm lucky to have found a woman who wants to do this with me. I'm even luckier to have found one who does more than just put up with me and my dreams. She's actually made this dream her own.

I thought that this trip was going to be about discovering who my children were. In fact, I'm also learning who I am and to my surprise, who Shiv is. I thought we had a pretty good relationship in the UK. Sure, we had the usual niggles and gripes but we were happy. When I look back at it now though, I realise how much of our conversation, our personalities and our energy was being overwhelmed by the sheer effort of getting through each day. Years of babies crying in the night, clients screaming and colleagues arguing had sucked us dry of any sparkle.

Shiv is a different woman now. Thankfully, she is the woman I wanted all along. She seems to have found herself. This new world of water, wood, lamplight and bare feet has poured deep into her soul. I'm not far behind her but then again, I've got bigger personality deficiencies to deal with.

After three hours we are still on The Staircase. Nothing will move now till the lock-keepers have had their lunch. I wonder if that is why the next lock is called Demain 5.

After a bowl of hot beans and crusty baguette aboard, the kids are snuggled below for sleep and Damian and I enjoy the peace and space of the cockpit to ourselves.

We invent a game as water fills the Demain 5 lock. 'Okay. What are my top five annoying habits?' Damian kicks off contentiously.

'Hmm. You really want to know? Here goes. Talking really loudly all the time, even first thing in the morning; changing the topic just when I am getting into it; planning everything. And cleaning. Oh and putting away all my stuff so I can never find it.'

'Cleaning?'

'Yep, your obsession with yellow sponges and Cif. Oh, and one more, that damned white vest.'

'What?' laughs Damian. 'I thought that looked quite cool.' A year ago a conversation like this could have led into an argument. But now we have fun with it. 'My turn now,' he says. 'Hmmmm. Let's see ...'

I unloop the one rope holding us to the bank from the centre of the boat and we motor out slowly. No need for fenders now. Damian steers the boat perfectly, pride focusing his concentration.

Damian launches into his list. 'Okay, number one, you always want me to turn down the music. Two, you never tidy up. Three, you use fifty words when four will do. Four, did I say that you never tidy up? And five, wearing socks in bed on cold winter nights.'

'First record bought?' Damian changes the topic before I can argue about his list. He loves bringing things back to music.

'Ummm. Easy. "Sexual Healing" by Marvin Gaye,' I say with confidence. 'Played it non-stop for weeks. Still know the lyrics.'

'What? That's far too cool for you!'

'Is it? Anyway, you knew that already,' I laugh. Somehow it

feels like we are having those conversations we had when we first met.

I'm sure we covered all this stuff before we decided to get married, but it has been filed at the back of my memory, along with those other rarely used snippets. You need time to dig these out. Watching water fill a lock offers perfect, bite-sized moments of slowness. Being half-Irish I could waffle on like this all day, but Damian prefers shorter, to-the-point, bullet-point conversations, finished off with a conclusion. When we leave each lock it provides the perfect ad-break to our lateral conversations and he can succumb once more to the sound of the engine and his own thoughts.

'Okay, mine. It was "Sweet Dreams" by The Eurythmics.' He pauses, then adds, 'Just think, James from the hotel barge was probably in his cot when I bought that.'

My turn for a swift topic change I think as we line up for La Roche 4.

Our game dwindles into laughter and then we imperceptibly slide into silence. Not an awkward 'What do we talk about now?' kind of silence but a comfortable calm.

My attention turns to the lock-keepers and their funny little cottages. They're only just big enough to contain one or two rooms but each one bursts with a different personality. One is surrounded by flowers of every colour; another has hand-carved wooden sculptures all over the garden; two are selling home-made honey; another is littered with old scooters and Renault 4s.

By the time we pass the last of the cottages and arrive at the peak of The Staircase, it's late afternoon. The drizzle has stopped and the sun's making a late showing as if to celebrate our arrival.

'Moon Safari' by Air yawns out from the on-deck speakers, yellow leaves slowly spiral down in the breeze, the sun highlights speckles of water on the deck. The high banks and the white bark of the trees crane down from above.

Having worked our way slowly and methodically through Patereau 3, Crain 2 and Port Brule 1 (who gave them these names?), we are now on our own. No-one to be seen behind or in front. The Swiss, having regained their Swiss composure, have raced ahead. The canal has narrowed to a mere few metres across, so shallow we can clearly see rocks on the bottom. Walls crumble and weep mini waterfalls into the canal. Moss and moisture drip and echo while trees rustle gently above. It seems the branches are reaching out to each other from both sides to unite and hold this magical waterway in secret.

Three stone tunnels are coming up, each one longer than the next. No lights. Noah and India have got bored being down below and have both wandered up to the cockpit in pyjamas and fleeces. India hangs onto my knees and sucks her thumb as we enter the darkness of Breuilles, 212 metres long, so we see the end even as we enter.

As we break into the light at the end of the first tunnel, it feels as if we've passed into another plane of existence. This is probably the most beautiful place I will ever go to by boat. We're at the bottom of a steep valley that's been cut into the rock. Ivy covers the near-vertical banks and trees block out the sun above us. The canal itself is little more than a stream. It no longer looks like a waterway. Instead it shines like a silvery path beckoning us to follow its lead. We're alone in an enchanted garden. I turn off the music and we ghost along the water in reverential silence.

As suddenly as it appeared, the magical world we have entered is swallowed by the darkness of another tunnel.

By the third tunnel, Collancelle, 758 metres long, we are all relaxed with the dark.

'Wooh, wooooooohhhhh,' cries Damian, pretending to be a ghost.

'Waaaaaaaahhhhhhhhhhhhhh,' joins in India and I take her in my arms and cuddle her.

'We are going to be in here forever,' says Noah in wonder.

Moments later we emerge into the marina at Baye and our secret paradise has gone. We're back in reality with its pontoons, boats, sheds and cranes. We moor up quietly. Even the kids don't say anything. It's as if we all know we've lost something.

It's a feeling that we can't shake off. In fact, the next few days pass by in a blur. It's as if I'm in that strange state of half sleep, the time between being deep in a dream and waking up, when part of me is still clinging to sleep while the rest of me is being pulled awake by the outside world.

The Nivernais was that dream – mysterious and beguiling. But it wasn't just the canal, it was Shiv and the kids too. Somehow we reached a higher state of being on those waters. Deep down inside I know that this is what I have been striving for. I don't believe I've ever been so at ease with my life.

I think about the end of this adventure. It *has* to finish at some point and we will return to 'normality'. I realise that it's not the places we've been to or the people we've met that I want to cherish. It's this feeling of inner peace; of happiness with who I am and who I love. I need to hang onto this; to remember it and continually strive to return to it.

CHAPTER 18

Getting up 'The Staircase' is a watershed both geographically and emotionally. Our dreamtime was left behind in the last tunnel. We all felt it.

Now the practical task of 'heading south' is our focus, skirting the edges of the remote Morvan National Park, only famous because Mitterrand came from there.

Descending from Baye, after the natural high we have experienced, the world seems somehow less bright, less alluring, like coming down after a drug. The Nivernais is definitely one I'll take again. Although we are still technically in it, I'm pretty sure we've had the best bits. I really cannot believe all the fuss people made in Auxerre about us taking this route. I'd recommend it to everyone. Well, actually I wouldn't – think I'd like to keep it rather secret so it doesn't lose its magic.

I'm getting morose as we descend. Soon the canals will give way to the fearsome Rhone, which will speed us to the Mediterranean before we know it. And then what? I have no idea but I know that going 'home' is the most likely option. Back to work, back to Queen's Park, back to a version of my old life and maybe even a version of the old me.

The weeks run in slow motion on the last stretch of the Nivernais. Slow, autumn sun warms us through our fleeces until sevenish each night. Lock-keepers amble languidly from one lock gate to the next. They use half-dead mopeds to trundle comically between locks, having to man great stretches of canal here, linking up with each other via radio. They always seem to know who's coming and whether a boat is still to pass by that day. They've all heard about the 'beautiful wooden boat with the young family' so we're greeted like friends as we are passed from one lock-keeper to the next.

We have to follow a drunken route through oddly named towns like Dompierre-sur-Besbre, Coulanges and Digoin that circle us back northwards, as if magnetically drawn to the heavily saturated wine regions of Côte de Beaune and Côte de Nuits.

Lethargy has gripped us both. We sail past the uninspiring town of Decize with not more than a cursory glance at the hilltop spire. We're both in similar, listless moods, made worse by the grey rain that has followed us since just after Baye. It's like we've finished a great book. It's difficult to give the next one our full attention.

I wake up in Digoin frustrated. Frustrated with my self-pity and moodiness. This is no way to pass the time. So what if the Nivernais is over? Have I turned into one of those people I so disliked at the beginning of this trip? Those that hate the less glamorous canals and talk only of the Bourgogne, Nivernais or Midi? Surely if I open my eyes I will discover equivalent beauty here too?

I focus on choosing an interesting place for us to spend Noah's third birthday. It's the day after tomorrow and I want to make sure we celebrate it properly. If he ever asks, I want to be able to tell him that he had a cake, presents, running water and a clean Porta Potty.

As I look for the Navicarte, I happen to glance down at our dashboard and the various dials. They are always the same; the oil pressure, the speed, the revs, the water tempera—

Hang on. The water temperature looks high. I'm sure it wasn't like that before. I look at it closely – it's definitely different. But I can't remember what it is normally. Months of looking at that gauge and I have never consciously

registered the numbers, just the fact that it was the 'same as usual'.

I grab our ship's log. This is supposed to be our bible. In it, we should note every detail of the boat, the journey and the engine. It's virtually empty; another casualty of the decision to reject my 'old ways' and be less uptight about life. My last entry reads: 'Lovely sunny day. Decide to wander round Sens market and buy some cheeses.' Briefly I think back to that day and remember how warm it was. I look at the temperature gauge again. It's definitely hot. We're overheating. Oh bloody hell.

All my Zen-like calm of the Nivernais evaporates with the heat of the water in our radiator. I'm not sure what we should do. Predictably we are in the middle of nowhere; 360 degrees of hills, fields of grapes and woodland. We're going to have to edge our way to the next town and hope nothing awful happens on the way. I look at the chart, we're about ten kilometres from Montceau-les-Mines. I guess that's where we are going to be celebrating Noah's birthday.

Secretly I wonder whether the overheating is something to do with me. A few kilometres back I motored too close to the banks while distracted by the triple-towered basilica of Paray-le-Monial, rising up behind the town. It's here that a nun allegedly saw several visions of Christ, with his heart exposed. Now it's a place of international pilgrimage.

Anyhow, while distracted by holy things, I sent the front of the boat squishing into soft mud. We've done it a couple of times before and it's nothing serious but instead of waiting for Dame to heave us off the bottom with the giant oar, I revved heavy-handedly into reverse. Although we did get off the mud, I wonder if some gunk has been sucked up into the cooling system and is now blocking it. I keep quiet about it. No point spoiling the calmness between Damian and I.

My fears are forgotten as we approach Montceau-les-Mines. Instead I feel regal as we motor into the town and our arrival is marked by the raising of the road bridge. This is the closest I'll ever come to a red carpet entrance. A bell rings continuously like an alarm but no-one is running. The barriers go down across both sides of the street to stop the cars. The Pont Levant begins to rise slowly like a giraffe raising its head from a waterhole; two of them, side by side. Painted lurid pink and blue, they are almost cartoon-like.

People stare from their cars. Kids hang over the lime-green metal railings and cheer. The lift-bridge operator comes out of his booth and waves. This can't be for us alone? There must be someone important following us in their cruiser. I glance behind. No-one. The canal's empty. Once again I wish I was wearing lipstick as I catch a photographer leaning over from the port side and snapping away. Do they all know something we don't?

'Dame, have I got knickers on my head or something?'

'What?' snaps Damian, too absorbed by the temperature gauge to indulge in frivolities.

We head for a pontoon that reaches into the water from the long canal bank. There are only a couple of other boats here. I guess winter is approaching after all. Normally, I'd be itching to jump off and explore but my mind, body and spirit are absorbed by the overheating problem. It's as if *Friendship* is also coming down from the high of the Nivernais; as if she senses a change and is doing her best to delay it.

Damian ties up and then immediately lifts off the engine cover to inspect the radiator for the umpteenth time. I offer to pop the kettle on to make us a cup of tea before we explore our new home.

'Tea? Are you joking?' roars Damian from the engine. It's not just *Friendship* who is running over 100 degrees. Damian, too, is losing his cool. When tea is declined, I know it must be serious.

Months ago, around Calais, Damian's tea comment would have escalated into a row. Now it washes over me. Better, in fact, it acts as a warning sign for me to give him space with his engine. I can read him so well now. Perhaps because we have had so much time in close quarters, I'm beginning to really get to grips with the man to whom I pledged myself till death do us part.

When Shiv sets off for the market, I decide to run the engine again to see if I can work out why she is overheating. I motor up and down the canal between the lock at one end of the town and the lifting bridge at the other.

All along the bank, market stalls are competing for trade. The shouting of the traders and the chitter-chatter of old women shopping carries across the water as if transmitted by radio. Even with *Friendship*'s engine thumping away, I can hear who is selling the cheapest Brie and who claims to have the freshest tomatoes.

Strangely, even after an hour, the temperature gauge doesn't rise above its normal position. At first I feel enormous relief that whatever the problem was, it has sorted itself out. But after a while I get suspicious. How is it possible that one moment she's about to boil over and the next, she is running cool again? I want to believe *Friendship*'s all right, but something inside won't allow me. It's too weird. Still, I can't cure something if all the symptoms have disappeared. Maybe it's fate telling me to forget about the boat until after Noah's birthday. I'm happy to acquiesce; the only thing I should be focusing on right now is my son's big day.

Being away from the overheating problem, wandering past shop-fronts at snail's pace, I am reminded of my absolute pleasure and joy in just 'being', not 'doing'. We stop and stare into windows, take a detour to clamber up church steps, pass by prominent statues to pick a flower. I notice things now that would've been blotted out before.

No matter how much Damian has slowed down, I've slowed down even more, which means we *still* move at different speeds.

But finally I've found a way to replenish my need to 'be' with his need for 'action' – time away. It's a solution so simple I cannot believe it's taken me almost four years of marriage and several months on a boat to work it out.

The intensity of the trip, the close quarters, the living on top of each other; all these things have been pushing Damian and me in ways we never expected. I think the hardest thing has been living with him 24/7. It's very difficult to remain desperately in love with someone when they are no further than ten feet away at all times. You never get the opportunity to miss them, to look at their features from afar, to remember them fondly in their absence.

Finally, though, I've found a new way with Damian. I've learnt to grab pockets of time for myself, which was near impossible when we lived in London. Through snatching those times alone, I'm starting to appreciate Damian again. He's a very intense and almost hidden person under the surface frivolity. I'm not sure I even realised that before France. Seeing him pushed, tired and stretched is revealing his insecurities. He is fiercely loyal – to us, to the boat. He is also scarily self-reliant. Unlike me, who, I have realised, needs the bump, grind and hum of others peppered by utter solitude. Perhaps this is a journey of discovery for both of us.

We cross back to the market and join the sway of stalls touting plump plums and juicy peaches, table linen and terracotta wine jugs. Fresh bread is sold by weight; huge hunks are carved off a loaf and plonked on scales. There's a queue a mile long so I figure it must be good. More importantly, getting the bread will kill time. Now is not a good time to return 'home'; kids and faulty engines do not make for a happy husband.

The next morning Noah is awake at 6 am. This is the first birthday he's properly been aware of and he's bursting with anticipation, eager to enjoy it.

I make us all a breakfast of jam rolls, with milk in Tommee Tippee beakers for the kids and tea for Shiv and I. We sit on top of our narrow bed in the cabin and Noah rips into his small selection of presents.

Our little boy is all grown up – three years old today. I know everyone says it, but I can hardly believe that the time has passed so quickly. It reminds me of what used to be my

biggest fear about having kids: they're like a clock that won't go away, constantly reminding you just how quickly time is disappearing.

I remember that before I became a father, one year pretty much rolled into the next. Time seemed to be slower. I never took much notice of my birthdays, while Christmas was just another holiday. Year in, year out, I always felt about the same age – 28 to be exact. In my head I hadn't really moved on from that number; I reckoned I wasn't so young that I was still stupid, but neither was I so old that my life had stopped giving me options. So 28 felt right, even when I was actually 35.

Then Noah and India arrived in my life and the big clock began ticking.

Three years ... I remember that bursting, falling-in-love feeling when Noah was born, along with the absolute utter exhaustion of physically delivering him into this world. The explosion of our life that occurred with his birth has settled, with pieces slowly falling, one by one, to the floor to make a new jigsaw. I squeeze my love onto him as he sits cross-legged on the bed, only to be shrugged off with, 'Mummy, can I have ice-cream today?'

'Of course you can. I promise.'

Shiv and I are determined to make today special but soon understand that we don't need to do much to make it memorable for Noah. A cycle ride around the park, a walk up to the fountains in the town square and ice-cream are all he wants out of life. Oh, the joys of being three.

Later, shrieking and whirling like seagulls over a fishing boat, India and Noah run semi-naked in and out of the fountains that grace the front of the Hôtel de Ville. The promise of ice-cream is the only bribe that tears them away from the water. Thankfully Damian's mid-life crisis has a boundary and he keeps his clothes on.

All we want is ice-cream. A couple of simple *crème de glaces*. No chance. Montceau-bloody-les-Mines doesn't do ice-cream. Not one shop, not one café we've been into sells it. Not even tubs of Häagen-Dazs. We've been searching for an hour and still haven't found any. The more restaurants that say no, the more determined we become. It has become a point of principle for Shiv. A matter of morality even. She promised Noah ice-cream for his birthday and so he's going to get ice-cream.

'What is wrong with this town? Don't they have any toddlers?' I rant at the fourth restaurant owner who has declared, coldly, 'Non, Madame, nous n'avons pas de glaces maintenant. 'C'est l'hiver.'

Winter or not, I have promised ice-cream, so if I have to knock on doors to get some I will.

By eight o'clock I am happy to forgo any principles I had of refusing to support American big-gun chains and almost run towards the lurid red neon light of an American diner across the canal. The Buffalo Grill, we have been told, serves ice-cream.

'Quatre glaces de neopolitan s'il vous plait?' I ask our cowboy-hatted waitress, once we are settled into the leather dinette cubbyholes.

'C'est tout?' asks our waitress, agog.

'Et un bouteille de vin rouge,' I add, just to complete the story of the strange English family ordering ice-cream and wine for dinner on a wintry October night.

The day after Noah's ice-cream-fest passes slowly and easily. We like this funny little town and decide that maybe we should stay longer. The locks won't close for another few weeks and we have only a short distance to travel before we join the big rivers of the Saône and Rhone. Why rush? Let's make the most of the canals and being able to moor right in the centre of towns like this.

The day is typical of our new life: we go for a walk, we have a long morning coffee, we play Pooh-sticks on the bridge, we

chase pigeons and we feed ducks. In the evening I cook my speciality, spaghetti bolognese (the kids prefer my bolognese to Shiv's, which is a minor victory for me). Even in the galley I'm starting to hold my own, although I suspect the success of my bolognese is down to my secret ingredient – lashings of cheap red wine. I haven't told Shiv about this but everyone seems to eat up and the kids always sleep well afterwards.

We eat together at the end of the pontoon. Noah and India are at a tiny fold-up table, while Shiv and I sit on the wall next to them, swinging our legs and watching people chatter in the bar across the road. There is something very rewarding about having our dining room outside. After dinner, I bathe Noah and India and then read a few pages of *Maisy* before tucking them into bed. There is no shouting, no frustration and nothing is forgotten.

I can do this now. Just as Shiv can handle *Friendship*. By osmosis we have learnt from each other and become one. A kind of androgynous 'Mum-Dad' figure.

With the kids in bed, Damian and I curl up and read in different corners of the cabin. The evening omelette and frites from the bar across the road have been cleared away. The noise of the quay has died. Almost imperceptibly *Friendship* tilts to one side. It's the weight of someone on the side-deck. 'Someone's getting on board!' I whisper and stiffen, relying on Damian to make a move.

'Bonjour!' yells Damian as gruffly as he can.

'Bonsoir, Monsieur, Madame. 'C'est moi, Philippe,' cheeps a voice we recognise as our new friend, the lift-bridge operator.

We sigh with relief and pad out to the cockpit. Philippe is already on board, decked out from head to toe in black leather. But there's someone else too – a woman.

For a moment I think he's going to ask us to join them in something suspicious. French men are strange beings: mistresses, eel fishing, moustaches.

Instead he shyly introduces his daughter. 'Cecile. She is seventeen. She really would love to see ze boat.'

'Of course, of course.' I motion her on, feeling guilty of doubting Philippe's best intentions.

I feel worse when Cecile presents us with a gift. A small terracotta *pichet* – a jug, hand-made, for wine. The spout has been pinched between two fingers when the clay was compliant.

'This ez what ze restaurants use. You can put a vin ordinaire in 'ere, and leave it for a while. Ze flavour improves so much, becoz of ze oxijenne, you know.'

Immediately we christen the *pichet* by filling it with wine and the four of us sit around the engine on our canvas chairs, chatting about life on the canals and in Montceau-les-Mines.

'Only today we were saying how much we liked it here,' Damian tells Philippe. 'In fact we think we might stay here a bit longer. Maybe even a week or two.'

'But 'aven't you erd?'

'Erd . . . heard what?' I ask

'Zey are going to close zis part of ze canal early zis year.'

'Sacre bleu,' exclaims Damian, sounding like Peter Sellers in a *Pink Panther* film.

Philippe continues, 'Oui. Ze canal is low on water. They cannot lose any more, so it must close for repair works.'

'How many more weeks have we got?' I ask.

Philippe looks at me and shrugs his shoulders. 'I do not know. Maybe twenty days?'

'Twenty days? Is that all? We'd better get out of here.'

CHAPTER 19

Kids still asleep, sun only just over the yardarm and already I'm jittery. It's 30 minutes since we left Montceau-les-Mines and we've started overheating again. All that engine testing with no problems at all and now this. I can't bloody believe it.

We're going to have to sort out the cooling system before we go any further, especially as we're getting closer and closer to the dreaded Rhone, a river so big and fast that some people reckon it's as dangerous as crossing the Channel.

We look at the Navicarte and agree to try for Saint-Léger. It's not that far and the guidebook says there is a hire boat centre there. Maybe they have a mechanic or a chandler we can talk to.

We spend the rest of the morning turning the engine off in the locks to keep it cool and travelling as slowly as we can to keep down the revs. It makes the day very slow and frustrating, but at least I'm not shouting at anyone. Obviously I'm grumpy and short-tempered, but not in a homicidal way, which is what I would've been like in my London incarnation. Instead I'm trying to exude a steely calm (like blokes do in action movies). I think I'm managing to pull it off quite well.

Damian must be worried as he is deathly silent. Not in his usual, distracted, 'not-listening-to-me-but-busy-compiling-a-top-ten-list' way, but in a more concentrated form of silence. That bothers me.

We limp past Montchanin, a tile-making town and one of the many places, no doubt, that prospered because of the coal in this area. Various hints at industry are covered over by dense woodland until we reach the summit of the Canal du Centre, about 300 metres above sea level. From here a series of locks will take us on a rapid descent down the valley of the Dheune.

I notice that the first lock, almost cruelly, is called Ecluse 1, Méditerranée. A sharp reminder that if we don't get this over-heating thing fixed, we may not reach our goal, the Med.

As we limp into Saint-Léger, both of us slightly preoccupied, thank goodness we see signs of prettiness rather than industry. It might just be the perfect antidote to the heat and repressed worry on board. A low stone bridge ahead drips flower baskets in pinks and purples. Peeping through the semicircle under the bridge is a luxury barge, a bit like *A Belle Epoque*. To our right lies a basin with moorings that face a wide grassy verge. Wooden decking leads down to the water. One space, the size of *Friendship*, invites us in. This is exactly what we need.

'Come on. Let's go check out the village. Maybe someone at the boathouse can help,' I suggest cheerily, doing what I always do in these situations – seek help from someone qualified.

'Why don't you go? I'll stay here and see what I can figure out on my own,' answers Damian, doing what he always does, even in a possibly trip-ending crisis like this: close in on himself and try to come to a solution alone.

I've been studying my *Guide to Diesel Engine Mechanics* for the last hour. (No, not a book full of men in garages; the title refers to the engines themselves.)

From what I can work out, we either have a blocked cooling system or there's something caught around the propeller. Both are possible on the canals; the cooling system could have sucked up a bit of rubbish, mud or even a condom (God forbid) while the prop could have snagged on anything from a branch to a plastic shopping bag.

The solutions appear to be simple but out of my reach. If the cooling system is blocked, we'll need to 'back flush' it and that's not something I have the tools or knowledge to handle. If there is something caught round the propeller, we'll either have to haul the boat out of the water *or* we could get a diver to go down and have a look.

Money. That's the problem. This might cost us a small fortune and we have already raided our meagre emergency fund for the batteries in Sens and the new exhaust silencer at Clamecy.

There is only one way I can think of to keep down the prohibitive costs of hiring a diver: I'll go under the boat myself. At least it'll sort out whether there's something round the propeller or not.

The charming canalside restaurant, Au P'tit Kir, has just come alive. It's on the other side of the bridge from where we are moored and it looks like a good place to begin my search for help.

Five old men in slacks and brown button-through cardigans gesticulate and 'ooh' and 'aah' about our problem. One of them leafs through the French yellow pages looking for a *plongeur*, a diver who will look under the boat.

This exceptional French hospitality erupted into play as soon as I quietly mentioned to one of the old men over my coffee that we were on a boat, were overheating and needed help.

'Mais oui. Gaby. Ici. Il peut vous aider,' said another, pointing to a rugged-looking chap who I notice is missing the ring finger on his left hand. A svelte lady dodges their arms and hysterics in her attempts to set tables for lunch. Clearly these guys are a permanent fixture in the bar area.

Their gallantry is overwhelming. One chap suggests we telephone 18, for emergencies, to call the *pompieurs* (fire brigade) out. It's an emergency to do with water after all, he pragmatically suggests.

Another swears he knows a diver in Saint-Jean-de-Losne, only 80 kilometres away. On and on they haggle, each determined to help me – this older-than-damsel in distress with two kids in tow.

'Thank goodness,' I sigh, as I catch sight of Damian entering the café.

I've walked into a maelstrom of activity. Our engine emergency is the highlight of the year for these bored men. The place goes into overdrive when I proclaim my intentions to dive under the boat myself. It's only then that I realise the potential folly of my plan.

'You are med. You Inglis, you are all vraiment med. Do you know how cold eet will be?'

'Oh, I'll be fine,' I retort, trying to sound confident but knowing that it will be bloody freezing. Especially as I have no wetsuit. And it's nigh-on winter.

'And ze water will be black. You won't see a thing.'

'It can't be that bad. And anyway all I'm looking for under there is a bag or a tree branch. If I swim close enough I should be able to see that.' More bravado. I don't have a mask or snorkel. There isn't even a pair of swimming goggles on board. I pray I'm right and that it's not too dark down there.

'And what about all the sheets?'

'Sheets?'

'Yes, ze sheets from all ze hire boats. You will be surrounded by sheets. Ugh.'

It's only then that my mental image of white fluffy cotton sheets is replaced by something much more hideous. Suddenly I remember the Scots at Auxerre who pumped all their effluent directly into the canal. I make a quick mental calculation of the number of hire boats around here and the amount of sewage they are chucking overboard. I then allow for the fact that the canal has no current or tide, so nothing gets washed away. It just sits there and then slowly sinks to the bottom.

I go quiet.

'Well you are a brave man. It ees good to see someone who does not give up. I like zat. We all like zat.' The little

group of Frenchmen who are sat around the bar all laugh and one of them hands me a beer.

'Bon chance mon ami,' he declares and everyone laughs again.

I've only ever heard that phrase in war films. It sounds cool and makes me feel brave. I raise the glass of beer triumphantly and announce that I will make my dive after lunch – no point hanging around.

The hour for Damian's dive arrives. Foolish it may be, but I'm tickled by the idea of him plunging into the depths. Once again I cannot dispel my deep-seated need for an action man, brave and fearless. Ready to swim in 'sheet' to save his family.

'Have you had a tetanus jab?' I ask.

'What?'

'Well, you know if you get infected by something terrible down there in the murk . . .' I trail off.

'This isn't Africa,' Damian snaps. He's nervous. I shouldn't have mentioned murk and disease just before he dives.

Damian strips down to his boxers, and does what he always does these days – sucks in his stomach. Either he is keeping up the pretence of having a solid six-pack or it's so cold that his deep intake of breath was involuntary. It's probably the cold as the rest of us are decked out in fleeces.

I stand by with a towel draped over one arm, my camera poised and a stopwatch to time him for posterity. And also in case he is down there too long I'll know when to get help.

Noah and India don't understand what's going on. We've spent the last few months telling them not to go near the water and now they see Daddy getting ready to jump in.

Even more weird – Mummy is watching, taking pictures and generally laughing at everything Daddy does, which includes shivering in his underpants, moaning about his expanding belly and whining about poo in the water.

Shiv laughs and says, 'Come on, get on with it.' She can tell I'm stalling. 'Don't worry, Noah and Indy,' she says. 'Look.

Daddy is diving under *Friendship* – maybe he'll bring back some treasure.'

I lower myself, feet first, into the water as slowly as I can. It's unbearably cold but I know this is nothing compared to how it'll feel when the icy liquid reaches my balls. I tense as the water rises up my thighs and then actually yelp out in shock at the dreaded moment. I hover for a while, hanging by my arms, my brain unable to force my body to keep going. Finally I realise that the only way to do this is to plunge in the rest of the way. I let go and drop off the edge of the quay.

I don't get very far.

Before the black water has even reached my neck, my feet hit the bottom of the canal. I say, hit, but this is the wrong word. They actually slowly sink into a slimy, thick mud. I can feel it squeezing its way in between my toes.

Of course, my first reaction is that this isn't mud. In my mind, I'm standing in the accumulated human excrement of over a century of canal users. If I could leap out of the water I would but the mud is sucking me to the spot.

Slowly, very slowly, I wade round to the back of *Friendship* with what feels like sewage up to my shoulders. The boat seems huge from this level. I grope around under the water-line trying to find the propeller and realise it's quite far forward and pretty deep down. There are going to be no easy options here. I won't be able to reach it without diving under.

There are moments when I am unboundingly pleased to be a woman. And this is one of them. Damian's clearly trying to look unfazed, his Yorkshire roots helping him to be stoic, but I can see he's psyching himself up for when his head dives into the blackness. I'm sure he'll be okay, though. Damian's always okay. It's hard to worry about him; to me he seems so indestructible.

As my head dips underwater, it is pierced with pain. The cold seems to bore its way into my brain. I open my eyes but I can hardly see a thing – just a brown blur with lots of bits in it. I try not to think too hard about the bits.

I can't swim freely in the confined space between the bottom of the boat and the canal floor so my hands are above my head and I'm using them to push myself under the bottom of *Friendship*. The hull is covered in barnacles and I can feel them cutting into my flesh. Already it feels like I have been under for ages and I'm nowhere nearer to even finding the propeller, let alone seeing if there is anything caught around it.

It's no use – I'm running out of breath. I jerk back and crash my head against the hull. I lunge up again and splutter to the surface, spitting out brown water that has the texture of thin minestrone soup.

'Eeeuurgh,' says Shiv as she snaps away with the camera.

Noah, eagle-eyed as ever, spots where the barnacles have cut my hands.

'Oh no, Daddy is bleeding,' he shouts and immediately starts crying. India joins in, not quite sure why, but fully aware that this is a moment of family melodrama.

I realise I was better off underwater and plunge down again. This time everything happens much quicker. I'm less terrified and more determined to get this over and done with.

I reach out into the dirty water in front of me, like a blind man groping for something to hold. My hand hits a flat piece of metal. The rudder. I grab hold of it and trace it back until I find the propeller. I've got it.

I can't let go now. I've got to hold my breath for a bit longer. Not easy for a bloke fast approaching 40 with a paunch. I slowly walk my hands around each blade of the propeller and then reach behind it to feel the prop shaft. There's nothing there. No branches, no bags, not even a lousy condom. The propeller is fine. I keep groping about, my lungs on the edge of bursting. Nothing.

I push back up to the surface and suck in huge gulps of air. Phew, I'm still alive, I think. I grab the side of the quay and clamber out of the water. I'm suddenly shaking and feel very weak. Shiv wraps me in a towel and shouts out 'Hip-hip-

hooray for Daddy.' Noah and India join in but very quickly descend into laughter at the sight of Daddy in soggy underpants, covered in slimy poo.

Damian stinks, so hugging him is done with caution, making sure the towel is wedged between our bodies. He looks quite pale under the slime and there is blood on his arm. I daren't tell him he was only under for 15 and then 22 seconds. It probably felt like hours to him.

He is shaking, probably with relief that he has escaped the 'sheets', and I hand him a mug of tea strengthened with the dregs of our Lagavulin whisky.

Now I've confirmed it isn't the prop that's causing the overheating, I don't know whether I'm relieved or disappointed. Half of me is glad that there's nothing jamming it and that we didn't waste our money on a professional diver. The other half of me is gutted that I've been swimming about in a cesspit for nothing.

'At least we know the prop is okay. We should celebrate and eat out tonight. You know, just on the off-chance you've caught some deadly disease and only have days to live,' I say and wink at Damian.

'Let's go to Au P'tit Kir. Then maybe we should call that mechanic in Montceau-les-Mines that Philippe told us about – Monsieur Laroche.'

That evening we move the boat to the other side of the low bridge and moor right outside Au P'tit Kir. The kids are in bed and the baby monitor is turned on. While Shiv gets ready for our meal I sit in the open cockpit with a glass of wine. The sun slowly splashes to the ground in an explosion of pinks and reds. If I saw this sky in a painting I would dismiss it as artificial chocolate-boxy crap. To see it for real, I just want to grab my camera.

I don't. Instead I muse on how important it was for me to

dive under the boat today. I hadn't consciously understood it at the time, but now I realise it was another act of reasserting my manhood. It was like fixing the exhaust at Clamecy, except this was a much more extreme way of reminding myself (and maybe even Shiv too) that I'm more than a surrogate mum.

I hadn't realised that I would go through this kind of identity crisis once I left work. I should have seen it coming though. After all, it happens to women all the time once they have children. I've spent so much time and energy over the last few months trying to be like Shiv (and mostly failing) that it was good to do something on my own terms again. To be a man, instead of a new man. Maybe the pendulum had swung too far the other way but today the balance has been restored.

After a hot shower with no time restraints (Damian has relaxed about this now as we hook up to water taps whenever we can), we step out, relishing the excitement of dining ashore.

Only moments away from *Friendship*, determined to eat outside, we huddle under a gas umbrella heater, wash down Oeufs Meurette with a dry local white wine and laugh and talk the night away. Whenever Damian reverts to being a real bloke, I race back towards him again. I guess, for all the equality we sought at the beginning of the journey, it's still *him* I want to dive under the boat, to lock up at night and to ward off danger.

We wake with fuzzy heads.

'Christ, that food last night was absolutely unbelievable and the wine ... the wine was ... exceptional,' I proclaim to Shiv as I clean the engine area in preparation for the arrival of the mechanic. I scan through my mental list of Top Ten Meals for a point of comparison. Funnily enough, the roast pork baguettes from Sainte-Mammes were a recent hot entry in the lunchtime chart but I can't think of any *dinners* that match the one from last night. Maybe that meal at Nobu in London with John and Louise three years ago?

Our memories of great meals gone by are disturbed by the awkward sound of an ungainly white van scrunching noisily over the cobbles on the quayside nearby. The marina is on a quiet lane, off the main village, so any noise feels rude. The van wheezes to a stop. I almost expect the four hubcaps to pop off and the body of the van to collapse in a heap once the engine is cut. Monsieur Laroche has arrived. Reinforcements have arrived.

Damian's excitement is palpable. That's something I will never, ever understand: men's ability to get worked up about mechanical objects. Damian has spent all morning cleaning the area around the engine, I assume to show off the dull, greasy metal at its 'best'.

Rather than get annoyed about the male courtship routine that's about to ensue as two adults prance around the engine, I make plans to sort out the washing.

Now that I'm a 'man' again I have decided I should help Monsieur Laroche with the engine so here I am, dressed in my brand-new 'workman's overalls'. I bought them at B&Q before we left and they've only been worn once (back in Clamecy). There's hardly a mark on the deep blue cotton and the creases are still sharp on the legs. It's when Monsieur Laroche steps out of his van that I first feel like an idiot. Far from making me look like someone who wants to help and 'get stuck in' I look like someone going to a fancy-dress party in Hampstead. Monsieur Laroche's overalls are covered in oil and his pockets are bulging with tins of tobacco and spanners. He's already won the dance and we haven't even lifted off the engine cover.

I can't back out now though, so for the next two hours I doggedly follow Monsieur Laroche's every move (he never reveals his first name so I must always refer to him as my elder and superior). Maybe it was deliberate on his part.

I pass Monsieur Laroche a stream of my shiny new sockets, screwdrivers and wrenches while at the same time giving Noah the ones we don't need so that he can have a go at 'fixing the boat' too. Already he's covered in oil and engine

grease. He's loving this. It's like Lego on a massive scale. In between these two workers covered in dirt and grime, I stand immaculate, like a meek nurse between two surgeons.

While the men fix things, India and I do some making of our own. We need a washing-line and a row of trees is perfectly placed on the narrow strip of grass adjacent to the quayside. Stringing a length of blue nylon between two of them we stand back and admire our work. There simply is not enough room aboard to dry clothes with the engine debacle. Ducking and diving under lingerie is only going to add to the stress.

As I peg Damian's less than white wicking underpants to the line I become aware of someone behind me. 'Uh-oh!' I whisper to India.

'Uh-oh!' echoes India, handing me a bright red pair of my knickers. (Which law of the universe comes into play to provide an onlooker at the same time as I'm hanging out my knickers? Why didn't they appear as I flapped out the creases of a pillowcase?)

'Bonjour,' announces a brightly spoken woman, wearing that conservative uniform of middle-age: a woollen tartan skirt with a neat round-neck cardigan.

'Bonjour Madame,' I reply, breaking from the line to give her my full attention, hiding my knickers behind my back, feeling rather coy all of a sudden.

'Bojorrr,' echoes India.

'Vous êtes d'ou?' she queries.

'Angleterre, Madame.' I proceed to give her a potted version of our trip, stressing the ages of the children to gain the maximum sympathy vote, just in case she is thinking of denouncing us to the local police officer for hanging our washing in a public place.

'Moi, j'habite ici. Just là. Dans la maison grande. Venez avec moi. Vous pouvez "ang out your washing" dans le jardin.' It's more a statement than an offer.

Usually I would have declined, rationalising that the sun in her garden will be the same sun on the line here by the quayside, but a niggle inside suggests I follow. Perhaps the conservative country folk of Saint-Léger will be distraught at our family's underwear flapping in the wind.

'Merci, Madame,' I comply and follow her across the lane through vast black metal double gates and around the side of a grand stone house to a back garden. Rabbits and guinea pigs are penned in a chicken-wire run, nibbling on chicory leaves. I duck under laden apple and plum trees as we march on to the end of a scruffy lawn.

'Ici,' she announces. We are invited to retrieve our washing whenever we like, she says, using the side gate. Then she disappears.

'How strange,' I say to India, as I peg out our large and smalls in a stranger's garden in the middle of France.

'Stainge,' echoes India, passing me a pink peg.

'Monsieur Laroche has taken away the radiator. It's going to take a few days to sort out but he says we'll get it back in plenty of time to reach the end of the canals before they close.'

'So what's wrong with it?'

'It was blocked. One of our filters had a whopping great hole in it so we've been sucking up bits of leaves, mud and debris from the canal into our engine. That's why we were overheating.'

'Fascinating,' says Shiv, her lack of interest in the details abundantly clear, but there's also something else. I think she's quietly pleased that we've been delayed, relieved that the end of the canals has been staved off for just a little bit longer.

Of course, I'm not very interested in engine parts – well, about as interested as I am in the gruesome details of someone's operation. It's only the top-line diagnosis that I want. The punchline. In this case, we have extra time here, waiting for a spare part. Hooray!

I like Saint-Léger-sur-Dheune. Once again I find myself wondering if we could set up a life here. I could become best friends with the lady that runs Au P'tit Kir and invite Madame

Tartan-Skirt over for tea and cakes. Damian could argue football and politics with the old guys at the bar.

Given that *Friendship* is doing her level best to ensure we stay here for a little longer, we get to know the locals at Au P'tit Kir as well as the wine list. Shiv finds out, mortified, that 'Madame Tartan-Skirt' is actually the mayor's wife; I discover that 'missing-fingered Gabby' is the town's under-taker and we soon realise that everyone in the village has heard of the beautiful 'bateaux de bois' with the mad diver, the woman with the washing and the two children who can't swim.

I've almost forgotten that we have to leave Saint-Léger when one day I'm surprised by a familiar voice and a face peeping out of a neat, sky-blue Citroën 2CV. It's Philippe, the swing-bridge operator from Montceau-les-Mines.

'Ah, bonjour!' he cries.

Before Damian can respond, I tug his shirt and screech under my breath, 'Why is he here? Did you pay the mooring fees at Montceau-les-Mines?'

'Of course!' he replies indignantly.

Philippe and his daughter get out of the car and explain.

'We were worried about you,' he begins. 'We av bin driving along ze canal, all ze way to Chalon-sur-Saône and back. We 'ad to tell you about the locks. Zey are closing zem early – in just four days' time. If you do not get to Chalon by then you will be stuck 'ere until the spring.'

Philippe's news comes as a shock. Suddenly we are thrust back into the world of time pressures and deadlines. The strange thing is, there's nothing we can do about it. Our fate is in the hands of Monsieur Laroche and I'm quite happy with that. If we are meant to stay here we will, and if he returns within the next three days then we carry on. I marvel at how much I have changed. There's hope for me yet.

The very next morning, a familiar, rusting, white van

arrives on the quay. It's Monsieur Laroche. Fate has made her decision.

Within an hour, the newly cleaned and flushed water system is bolted back onto the side of the engine. We start her up and the sound of 70 horsepower rampages through the morning air. I love that sound. I absolutely bloody love it. I know I've whinged about the noise on this trip but at times like this, there is nothing more satisfying than the noise of our big engine thumping away and warding off all evil.

It's sad saying goodbye yet again. I'm getting weary of constantly moving, of making new friends and then leaving them. Maybe it's a sign. Perhaps I'm ready to stop travelling and put roots down somewhere. But where?

I have no idea, but of one thing I'm quite certain: I don't want our adventure to end at the Med. I don't know what I *do* want, though, so I'd better keep quiet about this. Things will become clear, I'm sure of that.

I think both of us might be ready to have a 'home' again. At the start of this journey, the fact that we never stayed in one place for very long was a symbol of our freedom. But now it makes everything very fragile and short-lived. There's something going on in our hearts. Something's changing. Maybe the end of the canal system is affecting me more than I thought. Even though there are miles of huge rivers ahead, perhaps I know that this journey is nearly over.

I go quiet again and bury myself in the noise of the engine.

Down, down, we descend. Each lock on the Canal du Centre lowers us 2.56, 2.71, 2.89 metres and so on. All too quickly we arrive at the last lock in the chain. This is it. The end. We are about to leave the canals for the last time. From here on, we'll be travelling on rivers until we reach the sea.

I clamber off *Friendship* onto a wide leaf-strewn, grassy verge. Ahead lies the monstrous concrete frame of the lock. We have seen nothing like it since the one near Fontinettes in northern

France. Up on the bridge of the lock, we can just see a man in a control room.

'Well, I guess this is the end of the gorgeous little locks, lock-keepers' cottages and us doing everything ourselves. Look at that. There are traffic lights that guide you in. The whole thing is automated,' says Damian morosely.

Ten minutes later, *Friendship* is inside the cavernous lock. In my mind it becomes a colossal edifice to mark the end of one life and the beginning of the next. Goodbye canals, I think to myself, as we slowly drop with the falling water level.

When these enormous lock doors open, we'll be beginning a new journey. From a cartographic point of view we are halfway down France, but our mental, emotional and spiritual journey has gone much further than the physical one.

The man in the control room waves at us to check we are ready. In truth, I don't know if we are. We've got so used to the canals. They feel comfortable and easy now. But, rather like the kids, just as we reach the point where we understand them, they change and enter a new phase. Always keeping us on our toes.

A harsh scraping, grinding screech bounces off the lock walls as the doors open. It's like spring blotting out winter. The sharp blue of the sky, the dull green of the grass and the still shine of the water ahead grows bigger and bigger in our view. The black hole of the last lock in the central canals closes and delivers us out gently into our new world.

CHAPTER 20

There's no easing into our new existence. The Saône is nothing like the straight and narrow canals we've grown accustomed to for the last few months. It's wide and sweeping. I look ahead at the way it curves around the long bend to the left. This is a huge, mature river and it's the first of two that will take us all the way to the sea. The second is the Rhone, which we'll pick up at Lyon. That's when the race to the Med will really kick in. Its fast currents will literally pick up *Friendship* and carry us to the sea.

We're still over 400 kilometres from the coast but the whole time-distance continuum that we have been used to for so long is about to be overturned. Whereas short distances have taken months on the canals, now we'll be able to travel for hundreds of kilometres in just a few days. Even as I think about this, I realise that Chalon is almost upon us and before I can take breath, we reach the outskirts of the city.

On first appearances, Chalon-sur-Saône ticks all the boxes. The gently flowing Saône River flows past majestic 17th-century stone buildings lined up along the bank, like a crowd watching a boat race. It has a rich history and therefore, I presume, a soul. It's not simply a collection of buildings waiting to be restored by foreigners.

Because of its geographical position, it has always shouldered responsibility. Julius Caesar chose it as a food store in the Gallic Wars; it was once capital of the kingdom of Burgundy; in the early 20th century torpedoes, destroyers and submarines were made here and transported down to the Mediterranean on shallow-draft vessels.

Its link with the Mediterranean is unmistakable. Step on here at Chalon-sur-Saône and the moving river travelator will speed you south to the sun.

Perhaps that's why so many boats are moored here, adjacent to an island, Ile St Laurent, which is linked to the town by a tree-lined walkway.

The marina is packed. Wide-bottomed sailing boats rub fenders with sparkling white cruisers, most covered over, seemingly lying in wait till spring. There is a large clubhouse but not much going on. There's no-one washing down decks, loading bags aboard or chatting to neighbours. The whole place is quiet, almost deserted. Although the boat names make it appear quite international, there's not the buzz that I was expecting after the sleepy marinas of the canals.

I should love Chalon-sur-Saône. If it were a man it'd be my perfect partner: tall, dark, handsome, rugged, well-read, smart, funny. I should fall hopelessly in love. But the first time we go out, something puts me off irrevocably. Damian answers his mobile during dinner without even a nodded apology to me, and talks loudly for the next ten minutes, leaving me feeling like an accessory. I cross that line from 'Wow!' to 'Not with a barge-pole'.

Chalon makes me cross that line too. The tiny thing that happens is a bunch of kids, probably freshly teenaged, launching rocks at three female swans from their vantage point on the foredeck of a glitzy, 40-foot, gleaming white motor yacht.

Moored only a few boats down from them, Noah and India can see the whole sorry scene. Damian shouts at the teenagers to stop but gets insults hurled back. Furious, he marches along the pontoon and tells them off again. They sneer at him, like he's an old guy, approaching 40, but at least they desist and slope off below decks to sulk and grumble.

All of a sudden I want to leave this place. Whatever glories its streets hold, the memories will always be marred by these kids. I don't care about the historical streets of Chalon, the churches, streets and museums. That's the thing, now. We can afford to act on impulse because we know there is an endless list of places that will take Chalon's place. Our months in France have made us more choosy.

'I hope this isn't a sign of things to come. Maybe now we're off the canals, life is different. We're like the little kids from nursery arriving at big school and being in a state of shock,' I say to Damian.

Damian's hardly listening. He's agitated about the teenagers. 'I hope those bloody kids don't do anything stupid to *Friendship* during the night.'

We are suddenly behaving very middle-aged.

I'm feeling low. All the magic of the canals seems to have deserted us. I'm like a country boy who finds himself in a city for the first time. In fact, I'm reminded of the day I went to London to start work in advertising. It was only the third time I'd ever been there. I stared across a small stretch of park opposite Embankment Tube Station. It was rammed with people lying in the sun and making the most of the one bit of grass in the area. I looked at them in disbelief. Having just left the Yorkshire Dales I found it hard to comprehend that this sliver of grass could ever be regarded as something special.

I feel similarly about Chalon and the Saône. I'm sure if I had simply turned up here on an aeroplane I would have liked the place. But I've been spoilt. I've seen the very best of France's waterways and people. In comparison, this place feels cold, hard and heartless.

'Look, I've got an idea,' I say, desperate to cheer Damian up as we lie entwined together in bed after a day wandering the Gap, Benetton and Starbucks-lined streets of Chalon.

'Go on. Hit me with it,' he sighs, curling his hand round the back of my neck.

'It's a bit radical.'

'Good. I need a bit of radical right now,' he says, propping himself up on his shoulder, more intrigued.

'How about this. Instead of going along at our usual pace, why don't we just whizz down the Saône. Pass Lyon. The books say Lyon is a pretty dangerous place for boats anyway. So why not head on as fast as we can to somewhere special like Avignon? Imagine being in the depths of Provence for your fortieth . . .'

Damian is silent for a few moments. Maybe even as long as a minute and then smiles. 'You know what? That sounds great.' I'm stunned by his response. His usual devil's advocate stance has dissolved. I must remember to use this pre-sleep time to get him to make more big decisions.

'How long do you think it will take us?' he asks.

'Well, it's a few hundred kilometres away but we've got a river current with us now. That adds a couple of knots to our boat speed. Then there are fewer locks to slow us down. And also, the locks don't close at lunchtime. They stay open from seven in the morning till six at night. So we could really make headway. I reckon we could be in Provence in about ten days.'

'Wow,' exhales Damian. I can feel the tension in his body ebb away as he wriggles back into his pillow. 'Wow. Provence. In just over a week. Mmmmm.'

Almost immediately Damian drifts off into a blissful sleep of relief, I imagine, now that he has some plan that can take root.

I stay awake, listening to boaters' steps on the pontoon, returning from nights out. For me, a big factor in heading south fast is my desire to celebrate Damian's 40th birthday somewhere memorable, a place that does justice to our journey and captures all that is good about it. A swan-stoning, cold-hearted marina in Chalon or an anonymous berth in industrial Lyon simply wouldn't do.

Damian has never liked birthdays much but they are important to me. They were always a highlight in the year when I was a kid. It was a day when everyone stopped arguing and made me feel special. That's what I want for Damian. That's why we have to head south.

The next morning I wake up even more excited about Shiv's plan. The more I think about it, the less radical it seems; there isn't that much to see on the Saône or Rhone anyway. Not to mention the fact that they're dangerous rivers, especially for kids. There certainly aren't many places where we can moor up and safely leave the boat for a while and the chances of finding playgrounds on the banks or parks where we can picnic are almost zero.

No, let's not even *try* to make the most of these massive, industrial rivers. Let's just bomb to Provence. Shiv's right, it would be a great place to celebrate my birthday. I think I'd wake up on my 40th a happier man if I knew I was blinking in the light that the Impressionists fell in love with rather than the greyness of Lyon (or even London for that matter).

Over croissants in the cockpit, we excitedly read about the towns in Provence and come down to two options for my birthday: medieval Avignon, or Arles, the town featured in so many of Van Gogh's paintings.

The river seems to be on our side as an extra knot of current pushes us downstream, rapidly putting distance between us and the stoners of Chalon.

It's quite addictive, this new-found speed of over six knots combined with the openness and freedom of the river. The river winds left, then right, then left again. Gone are the strict concrete sides of the canals with kilometre markers. Instead bright red and white buoys show us where the deepest part of the river is. This is also the bit that flows the fastest, so to maximise our speed we stick inside the buoyed channel. There's a downside to this strategy though. This is also where the 'big boy' boats are.

'Holy cow, look at that thing coming towards us,' I shout to Shiv, who is building a farmyard on the foredeck with Noah and India.

'What are you looking— oh my God,' says Shiv as she suddenly clocks the leviathan of a boat heading straight at us.

'That isn't a barge, it's a bloody oil tanker,' I croak, while at the same time spinning the wheel hard over to get us as close to the bank as possible.

The boat we can see is a green and white slab-sided monster. It must be empty because it shoots vertically out of the water: squat, square and malevolent. It's the kind of boat that you see in films, crossing the oceans, laden with containers. You do *not* expect to see them on a river in the middle of France.

The closer it gets, the bigger it gets. As she comes alongside I understand what it must be like sitting in a Smart car when an articulated truck passes you at speed on a motorway. At the point where I can no longer fit the whole of the steel hull within my field of vision, *Friendship* is rocked from side to side by the tanker's enormous bow wave. Noah and India's farm is knocked to the floor but they barely notice; even they are gawping at the wall of metal that's blocking the sun as it steams past.

'Christ. We better be ready for more of those. A boat like that will smash *Friendship* into splinters if we don't get out of its way quick enough.'

Shiv hasn't heard me. She's already down below with the kids dusting off the lifejackets again. A big bow wave could easily throw India overboard. She still weighs only ten kilos.

After the lack of watercraft on the Nivernais, it's a thrill to see huge barges, laden with cargo, sunk low in the water with menacing names like *Mustang, Diligente* and *Por Dios* (the smallest ones load around 350 tonnes, so even those are gigantic). The barges ply up and down, like whales, tooting to each other and fitting snugly into the vast locks. We're certainly not going to get in their way and defer, like small fish, to their path.

It seems that the Saône, slicing vertically through France and joining forces with the Rhone further down, has always been an important trading route as it races out to the sea. Passenger-carrying steamers used to paddle from Chalon to Lyon. Professional fishermen, floating washhouses, dredgers and even floating mills all made a living on the river at one time. The Saône seems to have been a cross between a road and a high street. In fact, it's probably quieter now than it's ever been.

In only three hours we travel 30 kilometres and that includes passing through a massive lock. The distances we're now covering are shocking. It's as if we have mastered the art of teleportation.

I keep losing my page in the Navicarte guide because I'm so used to one page-worth of travel lasting hours. Now we're flicking through the book at speed. Provence is no longer a dream, it's going to happen now.

I'm incredibly excited, but in all the talk about my birthday I had failed to notice something else: Avignon and Arles are just 50 kilometres from the sea. I look at the map in front of me and stare at the tiny space between the two points. It's probably no more than three or four days' travel time. Frightening. The end of this voyage could be no more than a fortnight away. In Saint-Léger I thought I wanted to settle down again, but now that the end approaches I realise I want to keep travelling.

'Shiv, what are we going to do?' I ask plaintively

'What do you mean?' she replies anxiously, recognising the sadness in my voice.

'After we get to the Med. What are we going to do? Where are we going to go? What's next for us?'

'What if we kept going? How much longer before it gets too cold for us to travel, do you think?' I ask.

'Most boats seem to have wintered already. Loads of people peeled off at places like Chalon and Mâcon to moor up and fly home for the winter. But I can't imagine parking up and going back now, can you?' Damian asks rhetorically.

'What would we go back to anyway?' It has occurred to me that for all our vague ideas at the start of this journey, we had not really thought about what would happen next.

'I've no idea what we'd go back to. It's strange. This is one of the few times in my life when I don't know what to do next.'

Shiv smiles. She's loving this.

Poor Damian. He's suffering. Despite all of his new laid-backness, he still needs a plan of sorts.

'Maybe we go back to England,' I almost whisper. 'The agency would have you back like a shot, as long as you shave your beard off. We could move out of London, like our friends, and you could commute in.'

'You aren't serious are you?' he asks incredulously, thankfully giving me the right answer.

'Not really,' I reply sheepishly.

'I tell you, if there is one thing I do know, it's that I can't possibly go back to advertising. Not after this release from a life of suits, deadlines and shaves. This is a one-way ticket. I realise that now. And that's exactly my problem.'

Around us, broad meadows dotted with Charolais cows provide a peaceful backdrop to the inner turmoil on board. They intensify my feeling of freedom. Like a kid in my tree house, once the sun sets I don't want to pack away my toys and return to the big house.

'What about we keep going? We could winter up somewhere and then carry on next spring like everyone else. The kids are so happy now. And we have really got to grips with life on board. I love it. Being so free from all the constraints of a house. If this doesn't lead to something new, then I am not sure there was a point to it all.'

'What about your friends and family?' queries Damian. 'Aren't you still missing them?'

'Well they are still there. The real friends have kept in touch.'

'Mummy. Up. Up. Ngrhy,' interrupts India. I lift her from their den onto my lap and wipe her nose. She's hungry and is streaming with a cold. Noah joins us, he wants dinner too.

This conversation's going to have to go on hold but with Damian's impending 40th and us screaming towards the Mediterranean, it's not going to be the last on the subject. I carry

India down below, Noah clomping down the steps behind me and leave Damian at the wheel, staring ahead and steering on auto-pilot while his mind races.

To be or not to be, that is the question. Now that we have found how to be ourselves (our true selves), do we want to give that up and return to the rat race? I feel torn between two entirely different lives. It's no use pretending we can simply transport the way we live on the boat to a house in the UK. It wouldn't work and we both know it. The magic, the self-awareness, the peace and closeness all come from being on an adventure together and cut off from the rest of the world. But it's a gilded cage and we can't live in it forever.

Whether we like it or not, reality is already forcing its way into our consciousness; I also have to earn a living at some point – our savings won't last forever. And what about schooling for Noah? We don't want him and India to become social outcasts, unable to connect with other children because they never meet anyone under the age of 70. And no matter what Shiv says about friends, I know that a snatched mobile phone call is no replacement for drunken dinner parties, lazy afternoons chatting in the park or weekends away with her mates.

There are so many questions. I'm left feeling that there are no answers. When we left London, people talked about us 'living the dream' but we forgot that at some point we would have to wake up.

That night we moor against the quay in Tournus, which, in the dying light of the day, looks like a charming if tired town. Honey-beige buildings line up behind a string of plane trees, showing off the last of the day's winter sun. Only a few hardy fishermen are setting up their tackle, flasks plonked beside them, canvas chairs unfolded and heavy waxed coats wrapped over jeans to keep out the cold.

It's freezing at night now. Our cabin becomes a feast of duvets, heaters and hot chocolate at bed-time, falling short of hot-water bottles (I have Damian instead).

I stretch my legs out on the cabin seat, thick socks on, sipping a glass of Mâcon, and map out how fast we can get to Avignon and Arles. They are roughly 250 kilometres away, with 11 locks in between, so I reckon in five days we could be somewhere fitting for Damian's birthday.

The one thing Damian hates planning is a party. He's always shied away from them, scared no-one will turn up. Since we are 1,000 kilometres from anyone he knows (except for Professor Jean Yves, perhaps), he can be sure of that this year.

Nevertheless, I've noticed that he's not as uptight about his 40th as I was expecting. Since leaving the central canals and with his birthday the next target on his horizon, I have been steeling myself for a crisis to erupt but there have been no signs of it so far, just a lot of shrugging when I try to pin down what he would like to do.

So, I have settled it. No party. Just the four of us. We shall wake up on *Friendship*, tear through presents, then stay overnight in a local hotel somewhere in the centre of Avignon. The luxury of a big bed that we don't have to build – well, I cannot think of anything more memorable.

It's odd but the closer it gets, the less anxious I become. Turning 40 was a huge milestone for me before this adventure. In fact, it was one of the things that drove me to believe the time was right to abandon my career and throw caution to the wind. I wonder if without the impetus of my 40th, I would have been like most other blokes I know: talking about what they are going to do 'one day' but never actually making it happen. Men are great at three- or five-year plans. We always say things like, 'In five years I'll be doing this ... or that ... or the other' but it always turns out to be a *rolling* plan. The five-year countdown never actually starts. There's always an excuse.

I look at Shiv poring over the maps and think about that

conversation last year in our living room in London, the one where she suggested we take *Friendship* through the canals. Between us, that night we cast all excuses aside and it made perfect sense to leave our home, friends, family, job and security. I realise now that we hadn't a clue what we were letting ourselves in for but the point is, we did it. We made the break. If I die tomorrow, I'll know I wasn't a man who kept making excuses. Maybe that's why I'm approaching 40 with a sense of calm. I know I won't wake up on the day and fret about what I'm doing with my life.

When it comes to captaining *Friendship*, I'm quite cocky now when I take the wheel. She is as much my boat as Damian's now. So when I volunteer to steer her out one morning before the kids are awake, Damian is not surprised.

That quiet time of the day, when only bin collectors are at work, when the birds still rustle in the trees, is my favourite. No radio, no music, no-one asking me for anything. Stillness, time to think. My dad used to say: 'Only fools fill their space with constant noise – radios, music, chatter. The wise use the silence.' I'm not quite sure I'm using it well enough but I sure am enjoying it.

According to the fishermen, Tournus has various old churches and antique shops and is worth a look. The trouble is, we're no longer charmed simply by old churches. We lust after something altogether more magnificent. Damian's birthday now demands that each stopping place is considered as a suitable '40th party venue'. So we won't hang around for Tournus.

I pull on my fleece-lined jacket to barricade me from the sharp morning cut of cold. Thick swathes of mist hug the water. I can only just make out some of the arches of the bridge through which we are headed. An angelic light diffused through the cotton-wool mist provides an eerie scene. Two fishermen, hunched motionless on canvas chairs, fishing lines in the water, look over and nod to me.

'Mais, il ne faut pas aller maintenant. C'est trop invisible,' one of them says.

Foolishly, drawn by the silence of the mist, I ignore their

advice, throw our ropes on board, start the engine and turn the wheel away from the quay. I'm sure the mist will clear within minutes. Damian's still in bed down below.

But the mist doesn't clear. It gets thicker with every turn of our motor. Enveloping the bridge and merging left and right banks, I cannot see anything but white cloud. I drop the engine to idle, turn on the mast lights and strain my ears to listen. I'm worried a huge barge may appear out of the mist. We would splinter like balsawood.

The words of my old sailing instructor echo in my head: 'Knowing when to turn back is the most important skill to learn.'

I look behind me. I can't see the quay. Suddenly aware of the stupid risk I've taken, I spin the wheel around 180 degrees. I motor as slowly as I can, feeling my way back to where I think the quay is. The fishermen come into focus as I putter past. They look up, smile and nod approvingly. I shall wait here, tied onto the quay with one central line only until the mist clears. Damian, thank goodness, hasn't appeared on deck.

The days are racing by now. It feels so different from the canals. After Tournus and Trévoux, today we are going to pass through Lyon, France's second city. It's their equivalent of Birmingham and the two are probably very similar: ugly, grim, industrial cities with a chip on their shoulders about the capital.

I have so many memories of Lyon. It was always a staging post of enormous significance on my family's annual pilgrimage to Spain for our summer holidays. Once we got to Lyon, we knew we had broken the back of the journey. I remember being squashed into the back of a different banger each year: once a Triumph 2.5, another year it was a Renault Fuego, once a Sunbeam Alpine and even a Hillman Imp. Every year we used to wheeze our way towards this massive metropolis along the very roads that I can see from the boat now.

Hills, fields, woodland and all things gentle and pleasant have been our view for kilometre after kilometre as we weave through the Burgundian and Bourbonnais regions. We have skirted, yet not seen, the celebrated villages of Pouilly, Fuisse and other Mâconnais vineyards, all kept hidden by the densely wooded river banks. It's almost winter now, so I imagine there are no longer clusters of visitors in the local restaurants, sipping whites and tasting the local speciality, *pochouse* (freshwater fish stewed in white wine and garlic).

Tell-tale signs of a city start to pepper the countryside: pylons, industrial block buildings and clusters of houseboats replace the acres of vineyards and wine villages. Wooded cliffs press the Saône into a narrower course. Grand houses of 19th-century-old Lyon merchants perch on the slopes.

We pass under several bridges and at times it feels that the river and road converge, cars rushing north above us, drivers' eyes straight ahead. We are sucked towards the centre of Lyon city where rows of hotels and conservative buildings poke their noses upwards. No-one notices us, steadily following the vein of life towards our own new life. We're like ticks on the back of a rhinoceros.

I shouldn't be this nervy but I can't help myself. Every single guidebook we've read has gone out of its way to warn boaters of the perils of mooring in Lyon. They make it sound as desirable as a package holiday to Iraq. Vandals and burglars top the list of threats but I get the impression that most people in the city will have a pop at a boat if they see one tied up.

Arriving here has been similar to our arrival into Paris, but without the romantic connotations. Lyon is a huge city, with something like half a million people beavering away. It's a visual overload of tall Renaissance Italianate buildings, bridge after bridge, grand building after grand building.

All along the river now, we're flanked on both sides by steep, high-sided stone banks, with shops, streets and life held away from us. We pass wide, open quays, but they are empty. It's so tempting to simply tie up and stay for the night in this over-the-top metropolitan setting.

However, as all our boat books warn of unsavoury types, we decide to stop somewhere while it is daytime, just for a few hours.

A street market's canvas awnings just peep over the stone walls of the quay. That will be perfect. We pull in and tie up to gigantic metal mooring rings. An hour or two here will be all we need to explore the market.

Despite the countless times I've travelled through Lyon, I've never actually set foot on its streets. It seems much nicer than I thought it would be but maybe that's why it's dangerous. It lulls you into a false sense of security. With this in mind I dare not let *Friendship* out of my sight. While Shiv walks around an outdoor market to stock up on essential provisions, I sit at a café and crane my neck over the high river wall to get a glimpse of our boat moored below. I'm ready to jump up at any moment to protect her.

Lost in the bustle above Quai Saint Antoine, where *Friendship* lies, I stop at each trestle-tabled, ramshackle stall, drinking in the smells, sounds and sights of a French institution – the market.

Odd-shaped bulbous brown Haute Loire *ceps*, or mushrooms, are laid out on a table like jewellery, each one showing off its particular markings – 25 euros per kilo.

Moon-shaped sections of bright orange pumpkin, bunches of crispy red radish, heads of lettuce in every shade of green. Old women stroll, wicker baskets slung nonchalantly on their arms, poking, prodding, smelling the wares.

In the end I carry back a lunch I hope we can all eat: roasted quails, juicy ripe tomatoes and a hunk of flour-coated bread.

Stuffed with food, we head out of the city and almost immediately join the Rhone, the 800-kilometre-long river that sweeps through France towards the Mediterranean. Its source is a glacier in Switzerland; it then cuts through Lake Geneva before ripping France in half and charging into the sea. It's so ferocious that in the past, most boats travelled with a cross adorned with religious symbols as protection against the perils of the journey.

The Rhone is part of the folklore of the French canal and river system. Everyone talks about the terrifying river and its ability to sweep boats aside with its speed and power. In the spring when it floods, they say small boats simply can't go up the Rhone. The current is so strong it actually pushes them backwards. Luckily we are travelling south, *with* the current as it heads towards the sea, but even so, we have to keep our wits about us. If the Nivernais was a country lane, then the Saône was an A road and this is the M25. Everything is bigger, faster and scarier.

The Rhone. It's hard not to be beguiled by a river that has such a reputation, so many stories about it, so many tragedies linked to it.

It's wide. Wider than anything we have navigated so far. Wider than a football pitch, says Damian. And fast, goodness it's fast.

We're travelling at about eight knots now, faster than ever before, with between one and two knots coming from the river itself. It's exciting. I love this 'speed'.

Green steeply farmed hills, smudges of brown rock and tight clusters of houses almost fly past now, as do the super-barges. Two at a time they come towards us, tied together top-to-toe, loaded with crates, like ferries.

It feels like the whole hull is vibrating. For a while I wonder if the old girl will take it. Will the planks shake apart and the screws pop out? It's been known to happen with old boats, more often than I dare think about right now. The one thing that gives me solace is the knowledge that I was obsessive to the point of being anal-retentive when I rebuilt *Friendship*. Everything was done properly. No short cuts were taken. For the first time in 12 years, I don't feel bad about all the money I have sunk into this vessel. I should relax and simply enjoy

the fact that we are zooming down one of the great rivers of Europe. We're going to be in Provence in no time.

It's impossible to find spontaneous mooring spots on the Rhone – there are none. It's all trees, reeds or shallows. We have to aim for a specific mooring place each day and make sure we're not still on the river when it gets dark – now around sixish.

Kilometre posts along the banks, some overgrown by foliage, urge us on. They are counting us down to the Med. Lyon is the starting block, reading 0 kilometres. We have reached Valence (109) in only two days.

Valence is supposed to be the gateway to Provence and I have a strange sensation when we enter the marina here. It's like a woman who has just had Botox. You know there's something different, that she looks better than she has for years, but you just cannot work out what it is. A haircut? New clothes? An expensive lipstick? That's what I am trying to do as I scrunch my eyes in wonder, wishing I could find my sunglasses.

Valence is glazed with a new light – it feels spiritual somehow. Then I remember – it's the Mediterranean light that painters and artists have been drawn to for years. Its sharp blue skies have been blown clear by the mistral winds. Everything looks in sharp focus. It's as if we've crossed some imaginary line between Lyon and Valence.

The sound of halyards cracking, wind whistling and the shushing of willow tree branches fills the air. We are at the doorway to the south. Wild mint and rosemary scents are rushed to us from the surrounding scrubland. No fully dressed trees fill the hills beyond. It's warm, the air mild and soft.

At last I can sense what we've been aiming for since London. There are more sail boats in the marina, with names like *Jocaste of Sète* lying next to *Majesté* from the Hamble. A meeting of the two souls.

I can almost taste the salt of the Mediterranean on my lips.

CHAPTER 21

'It's a record! That's the fastest and the furthest we've travelled in a day.'

One hundred and twenty-five kilometres in two days and we are on the outskirts of Avignon. The excitement is palpable in all of us. I want to drink in every detail for when Damian reminisces about his 40th in years to come.

A sliver of gold glints from a statue, poking high above the dark green trees on the left bank. Then it disappears. A line of *peniches* appears on the right bank, followed by a church spire, a castle tower with straight sides and trees growing out of derelict roofs. Between us an impenetrable green wall of foliage hugs the bank.

Two long cruising ships are berthed opposite, with the names *Mistral* and *Van Gogh* blazed along their hulls. That settles it. We've definitely arrived in Provence. I feel good about this place. Avignon will be perfect for Damian's birthday.

We putter past the high walls of this ancient city towards the famous bridge. Well, I say famous but I'd never heard about it before and certainly didn't know the 'Sur-le-Pont d'Avignon' song. Nevertheless, Shiv is excited and insists this will be a landmark on our trip.

Having seen thousands of bridges lately, I'm preparing myself for something damn spectacular in order to make this

one stand out. The Pont d'Avignon lives up to my expectations but in the most unexpected of ways. Wonderful curves of hand-carved stone stretch halfway across the wide river and then abruptly stop in a mass of crumbling rock. Its beauty lies in the fact that half of it has fallen down. Like *Venus de Milo*, it's the fact that it's broken that makes it so striking.

We curl around the shattered limb of the bridge. The broken bridge of Saint Benezet has stood like this since floods washed away the other arches in the 17th century. It's terrifying to imagine water forcing apart the massive stone blocks.

Now all we need to find is the perfectly located marina by the bridge. I check the guide again. Sure enough there is a marina marked. I check the right bank. Then the left. Perhaps the book got it wrong. There's nothing here. But this is where we are to wake up on Damian's 40th birthday!

A small group of people on the bridge gather to watch us. The varnished wood must look beautiful from up there, glinting in the low winter sun. We can't see anything that looks remotely like a marina so tie up to a high wall and call out to a neighbouring boater, who tells us the pontoons were all washed away by terrible flooding of the river last spring.

Our mooring lines stretch for metres high above us and only just reach two iron rings that are so far apart they must be for the huge cruising ships we have seen. It's a little precarious, but other boats must do the same. At least there's an electricity point and water tap two metres above my head.

It'll be fine for Damian and me to clamber up the vertical quay wall but I'm not quite sure how we're going to manage with the kids, buggies and our usual paraphernalia. I picture us tumbling off the quay, after Damian's celebration dinner, the whole family squashed flat between a stone quay wall and *Friendship*'s wooden hull.

Putting aside my fears, I'm a jumble of excitement at what lies behind the threatening stone walls of Avignon on our left. Not only do I have to have to track down a decent present, I'm hoping that this city has the right feeling for 'the birthday' – an event that has taken on the importance of a World Cup final.

Passing through the solid 14th-century ramparts is like entering another age. Thirty-nine massive towers interrupt the medieval wall that still surrounds the city. The wall is pierced only by enormous, giant-sized gates. We stare up at the smoothed stone hollows where a chain would have been used over centuries to lower and raise the wooden doors.

Moments later we arrive in a vast open courtyard and are astounded to see the imposing Palais des Papes. This immense gothic palace is a world heritage site and effectively was the Vatican between the 14th and 15th centuries. Seven popes lived here and with them came the riches that made Avignon a European centre for commerce and culture.

Despite its name, the Palais des Papes can't decide whether it's a palace or a castle. The popes wanted a building that was magnificent enough to impress but also strong enough to withstand attack. The result is a sprawling building, rich in crenellations, spires, arrow slits, turrets and enormous gateways. On the inside, the stone walls are bare. The gold, silver and tapestries have long been stripped away but the rooms are cavernous, reminding me of what 'spacious' really means. We see fireplaces that are as big as *Friendship*, discover sumptuous chambers and enormous halls that are as deep as the lock onto the Saône and we find aged wooden panels that are almost as well restored as the beams in our cabin.

It's not only the Palais that impresses. It seems that every corner of Avignon is utterly beautiful. The whole town strives to fulfil every French stereotype; there are beautiful buildings, ivy-covered stone walls, dappled light filtering through tree-lined streets, wooden shutters, stylish men and sophisticated women, cobbled streets, verdant parks, carefully preserved archaeological ruins, boutiques, antique shops, brasseries and the ever-present ancient city walls.

It's all too much. After a decadent meal of a fish I've never heard of (shad-fish), we attempt a stroll up the high street. Noah and India are wide-awake and dumbstruck, as we are, by the shining glass-fronted shops blasting out their messages to buy, mannequins clothed in the latest winter woollens, people racing by in streams.

I'm a rabbit in the headlights – slightly frozen out of action. What I want to do is to run fast, through the alleyways, out of the gates and back to the safety and solitude of *Friendship*. It's a feeling that surprises me. After so many years of London living I should be able to summon that 'city ability' to deal with hordes of people.

Being in Avignon I've realised that we aren't normal any more. To most people this would be a French paradise but I can't cope with it. Being here is like gorging a Black Forest gateau after not eating for a fortnight; it's too much, too rich, too much of a shock to the system. I'm out of my depth and the population of Avignon is less than 100,000 people. It's *half* the size of Luton. That's scary.

Rifling through the books and charts when we are safely back on *Friendship*, I decide that Arles sounds more like our kind of place for a celebration. More quirky than grand, closer to the sea and with a romantic past linked to artists and gypsies. If this was my 40th birthday, I'd want to be somewhere intimate and cosy, bohemian rather than mainstream. Arles will deliver the goods, I'm sure of it. Now I just have to sell it to Damian, who has been looking forward to Avignon for so long now.

'You know, I think Arles might top Avignon as the place for your birthday,' I begin gently. 'Van Gogh is immortalised there, you know.'

'Really? Okay. When shall we leave?' Damian asks.

'We could be there in less than a day, so how about tomorrow morning?'

'Sounds excellent,' he says.

That was easy.

I'm glad that Shiv has decided to gamble on Arles. I know

she's putting herself under pressure to make my birthday special. I think this is partly because she loves birthdays and partly because most men we know have had a little 'wobble' on their 40th.

Motoring gently towards Arles through the pale, cool morning air, the mist hovers a metre above the river. We are travelling down the Petit Rhône, an offshoot of the Grand Rhône.

I clutch a mug of tea and enjoy it standing on the side-deck while the kids are asleep down below. A cormorant silently crosses our bow, its wing tip breaking the perfect sheet of water.

As I contemplate the strength and fragility of the river (and of us), a pang of loss wells up in me. Soon we'll reach the Med and our bubble of calm and beauty will burst.

Arles feels like a great decision. It will be smaller, quieter and more intimate. There are no defensive walls here to keep us out. We arrive late in the afternoon and moor on the far side of the river, opposite the heart of the town but connected by an old stone bridge. The ancient buildings, spires and terracotta rooftops face us as we bed down for the night. From here, Arles looks more Italian than French. This vista could be the opening shot from Merchant Ivory's *Room with a View*.

It's only later, as we are tucked up in bed reading about Arles, that I realise this very mooring is almost exactly where Van Gogh painted *Starry Night on the Rhone* 107 years earlier. At the time he was trying to illustrate a dream. Apparently, stars and dreams were powerfully interrelated for Van Gogh. A year earlier he had written to his brother Theo that: 'The sight of stars always makes me dream, as simply as the black dots on a map representing towns and villages make me dream.' I know what he means about the dots on a map, only in my case they would be harbours on a nautical chart.

From our bunk it's not only the stars that we can see twinkling at us across the heavy blackness of the Rhône but also the lights of Arles itself. The cluster of low stone buildings is dissolving into the night. This is perfectly romantic, hearing the slap of the river reminding us we are on a boat, feeling the gentle movement lulling us to sleep.

As we set off to explore the town the next morning, I'm full of excited anticipation. This is where Van Gogh painted his famous sunflowers, his crooked bedroom and his yellow chair with pipe. This is where he lived with Gauguin, where he was hospitalised for madness and where he cut off his ear.

I decide that with my birthday being so soon, I have the right to indulge myself. That means dragging Shiv, Noah and India around the Van Gogh sights. Luckily I'm able to do this without causing too many problems. For a start, we discover that the house Vincent lived in from 1888 to 1889 is very close to the public launderette. Then we find that the hospital where he was locked up for insanity after cutting off his ear is just over the river from our mooring and has a criss-cross of paths and gardens which the kids think is a giant maze. Finally we find that the famous yellow café on the edge of a central square is still functioning as a restaurant so we resolve to return later for a drink. By the end of the day I can see that everything is fitting into place – Arles is perfect.

'Mummy?' whispers Noah loudly later that night from behind the forepeak doors so that we can both hear him.

'Yes.'

'Don't tell Daddy about the paints. It's a surprise.'

I wake up on my birthday with Shiv's body wrapped around me. I lie there for a moment with everyone else asleep. The ropes are creaking as *Friendship*, almost imperceptibly, drifts from side to side at her mooring. So this is the big day ...

I look around me at *Friendship* in the half-light that seeps into the cabin through the gaps around the door. There is still a brass plaque on one wall commemorating her original launch 38 years ago. So this boat is a mere 18 months younger

than I am. If we'd been at school together she'd have been in the year below me. I'd probably have fancied her.

I can't believe that *Friendship* is younger than me. It's vaguely depressing. I've always thought of her as being very old. Then again, I used to think that once you hit 40 you *were* old. You become a shell of what you were, especially if you're a man. From then on, all you can do is carefully manage slow decline: career, body, health, energy levels, hairline, sex drive, income, attractiveness, sense of adventure; you name it, I used to believe they all fell apart after you hit 40.

But in the last few months I've talked to more people in their sixties, seventies and eighties than I have ever done. They've been truly inspiring; full of conversation, rich in experiences and still driven by dreams. All I had seen in London and especially in advertising was that turning 40 was like hanging a neon sign above your head proclaiming that you were on the way out. I wish I had known more people in the UK who were older, but how would I meet them and why would they want to meet me?

Just as I start getting deep and philosophical about the nature of age, Shiv opens her eyes and wriggles sexily under the covers. Half an hour later we're disturbed by the sound of Noah clambering out of bed. Then India wakes up and after some whispering, they both start shouting 'Birthday, birthday'. The day has begun.

Breakfast is in bed: croissants and jam, with tea. Outside we can hear the cold winter wind but on board, the Eberspächer heater is blowing warm air around the cabin and keeping us cosy. My presents arrive thick and fast – appearing out of strange places all over the boat: drawings from Noah and India come from behind their Richard Scarry books; a beautiful, typically French, hand-painted weathervane (three foot high no less) pops out from under the floorboards in the galley; a bottle of eau de vie is in the sleeping-bag locker and a magnificent wooden box of oil paints, brushes and palette knives is pulled from under the spare water tank.

I put my arms around Noah and India but then get over-

whelmed by the moment and start crying. Noah and India are confused and start crying too. Then Shiv joins in and the four of us lie on the bed in a massive hug, all crying and then all laughing at the absurdity of it.

Is crying a sign that Damian is kicking off a real crisis after all? It's so hard to know with him. He is such a European when it comes to his emotions; no problem weeping if the occasion merits it. And sometimes even if it doesn't.

I wonder what I'll be like when I reach my 40th next year – will it be such a big deal? Ageing has never bothered me. When I am seriously old, with false teeth, wrinkled skin and white hair, as long as I have my faculties I hope to be singing down the streets and being rude to people. Forty is not old – not if I live till my nineties.

I tap the side of my empty mug. 'Ladies and gentlemen,' I say, 'I have an announcement to make.

'Today, after breakfast we are going to lock up *Friendship* and walk into Arles, where there is a bijou little hotel with a suite waiting for us to collect the keys.'

'What???' says Damian, and I can see more tears welling up. I hope he's pleased and not depressed about leaving *Friendship*.

'Yes, one night in a hotel. Sheer luxury and probably a bath! Happy birthday.'

Damian locks the cabin doors, putting our valuable binoculars, Swiss Army knife and hand-held GPS down below out of sight. The trouble with a boat like ours is that it screams for attention. Any Arles yobs would have a field day here. Simply clambering under the green canvas awning they could make away with our treasures that cannot fit below: my out-of-tune guitar, purple yoga mat, smelly jogging shoes and a bucket of conkers.

We march off over the bridge, glancing back to look at our boat. I surprise myself that I feel a touch of guilt at leaving *Friendship*. Like we have betrayed her. Nevertheless, I intend to check into the hotel at 10.30 on the dot to get our money's worth.

I can't believe Shiv has booked a hotel. What a treat. I've never been this excited about staying in a hotel. With my work, I slept in some amazing places, in cities as far-flung as Tokyo, New York, Barcelona, Milan, Auckland and Los Angeles. I know that none of those hotels will match this one. When you have been using a Porta Potty for as long as we have, the idea of a hotel with a flushing toilet takes on an extra-special significance.

The four of us march through town, undistracted by the shops selling toy bulls, Van Gogh postcards and packets of Provençal lavender. We are like hounds that have caught a sniff of the prey – a hotel with fresh cotton sheets and a full-sized bath.

'There it is!' I yell as we round a corner, the curve of the amphitheatre on our left. We race in to the reception area, kicking each other under the counter and giggling as the woman talks us through emergency procedures.

Wow. A hotel. A real hotel with real beds, full headroom, carpets, flushing toilets and a bath. The luxury of these every-day things is intoxicating.

Once in our room we go crazy. It's Noah who starts it. He is the first to jump on the bed but it doesn't take long before we are all bouncing up and down on the huge double mattress, swiping each other with the feather pillows. Just as suddenly as it starts, we stop and start running in a train around our two connecting rooms switching on all the lights, turning on all the taps in the bathrooms, flushing the toilets and opening the windows. There's an endless supply of everything and there is so much space it feels obscene.

After nearly destroying our hotel room we embark on a day of hedonism in the beautiful old streets of Arles. Bearing in mind that hedonism is relatively easy to achieve for us:

– Mid-morning coffees outside a café. In winter sun that fills the main square, we watch people buzz in and out of the old buildings, cafés and shops around us. The town is vibrant with life but not overpowering. Arles is that perfect size;

enough people, shops and business to keep you interested and stimulated, but not so many that you feel anonymous or steam-rollered.

– Late morning wandering around the outdoor market, breathing in the scent of perfumed soaps, lavender and Provençal herbs. There are no tourists here; this isn't a theatre set designed to wring maximum money out of American visitors. The locals here *really do* buy honey in jars with handwritten labels, cheeses from the local farmer and dried flowers to hang in their kitchens.

– A lunch of moules mariniere and frites, sitting outside again opposite the market. The street is lined with restaurants. We chose this one for its proximity to 'child-minding facilities'. On one side a band of buskers is playing music on pan pipes, while on the other, bull fighting is being shown on TV behind the bar.

– After a long lunch everyone is ready for a sleep. The excitement of the day has exhausted all four of us. It's back to the hotel for siestas.

– A slow afternoon is passed wandering around the Roman amphitheatre. It's beautifully preserved and is still used today for the occasional bullfight. There used to be seating for 20,000 people; nowadays numbers have been printed on the back of rows of wooden seats as they sweep around the central stage in a wide circle. I find number 40 and take a photograph. I can add it to my collection of 'found images' to use in birthday cards.

– Late afternoon drinks are in the yellow café. It's the one featured in Van Gogh's 1888 picture, *Café Terrace at Night*. It's easy to imagine the great artist staggering in, smelling of sweat and oil paint, with a prostitute on one arm and an unrecognised masterpiece under the other.

– Early evening is bath-time for the kids. What a treat. Noah and India luxuriate in the warm, deep, soapy water. We can't even remember the last time they had enough space to stretch their legs in a bath.

– Dinner is at a restaurant. The hotel has a babysitting

service, so Shiv and I can grab some precious time alone together. It's as much fun having a full-length mirror, bathing and getting 'dressed up' for the first time in months, as it is going out. Ironically we choose to eat on a barge in the river. We have all the posh restaurants of the town to choose from and we return to the river. The water is deep within our blood now – we'll never shake off this connection. So we dine in a huge *peniche* that's been converted into a stylish restaurant with a live band playing gentle music and a waitress who makes us feel special.

– Finally, at the end of our marathon of excess, Shiv and I sit on our small hotel balcony and look over the amphitheatre of Arles drinking from my new bottle of eau de vie. Above us the sky is jet black and pierced with the very same stars that inspired Van Gogh.

'Happy?' Shiv asks.

'Yeah, I'm happy. Very happy.'

CHAPTER 22

The next day, Damian hasn't killed himself or broken into pieces. He's woken up aged 40 feeling exactly the same as he did yesterday – only cleaner.

The gallons of water we've used in the hotel, not to mention every sliver of soap and every drop of bath foam, have cleansed any thoughts of old age.

In fact, we have 'excessed' in all areas in a very non-rock star way: flicking channels on the wall-mounted television, using all the towels provided and rolling about on every square inch of the double bed.

I'm sure *Friendship* would understand.

Now, we are back on board and moving again, travelling along a purpose-built channel linking the 'Grand' to the 'Petit' Rhone. It's rather narrow, windy and desolate. Only 57 kilometres from the sea, birthday over, we have to face the fact that we're nearing the end of this leg of our journey, the calm before the storm. Reaching the Med will be when the tumultuousness of decision-making returns. The monotonous scenery focuses our concentration on what lies ahead.

'Du-doo-du-doo-du-doo-dudey-doo,' I shout to Shiv over the roar of the engine.

She is at the wheel and turns to me looking utterly

confused. 'Umh ... The Doobie Brothers?' she says, raising an eyebrow.

'No! It's the tune they play on *Countdown* when the clock is about to run out. It felt appropriate. The further we travel, the closer we are to making a choice. Time is ticking away.'

'Yep. Wish we just had to rearrange a few letters. Just think, where we decide to go once we arrive at the Med might affect the rest of our lives.'

'I think if you won *Countdown* it might affect the rest of your life too, but I take your point.'

'Okay then, Carol. So what have we got to play with?' challenges Shiv.

'Well, the way I see it, we have four choices.'

'Four?? Are you serious? Do you always have to look at everything from every single angle?'

'You know I do and you should think yourself lucky. When I woke up I had about eight options to choose from.'

'Thank the Lord for small mercies,' chides Shiv playfully as she rolls her eyes. I know she's curious because she immediately asks, 'What are they?'

'Okay. Option One – we get to Sète and leave the boat there for the ...'

'Winter? Hmm. And go back to England. Then what?' interrupts Shiv.

'Then we return next summer to bring *Friendship* back *up* the canals.'

'I don't think we'd do that in a summer. Anyway we wouldn't want to after taking so much time on the way down,' she says.

'I know. We'd have to make it an annual event – something we do each summer for the next few years: we'd make a holiday of bringing *Friendship* ever closer to the UK.'

'Hmmm,' says Shiv more quietly.

This apparently non-committal, guttural sound is something all of Shiv's family do. It can be translated back into everyday English as: 'There is absolutely no bloody way we are doing that.'

I'm glad she feels this way. Going back to the UK is the last thing I want to do. I move on. 'Option Two is to get to Sète and turn left.'

'Left . . . towards Italy?' enquires Shiv.

'Exactly.'

'Mmmm.'

The 'Mmmm' in Shiv-speak is very different to the 'Hmmm'. This is much more positive and at times can even be taken as a sign of excitement.

'I wonder if we could get *Friendship* into Venice?' she asks.

'We could actually. We could moor right next to Saint Mark's Square.'

'Wow. I like the sound of Option Two. What's Option Three? No, don't tell me – turning right. To Spain. Yep?'

'Precisely. The Pyrenees, flamenco, paellas, paradors, tapas and bullfights. One big melting pot of energy and passion.'

Another 'Mmmmm' from Shiv. This one slightly longer than the first but I'm dancing on pinheads trying to read anything into this. The key thing is that both Options Two and Three might be goers, which is good because they're my favourites too.

'Then there is Option Four,' I continue, determined to be fair and not to be swayed off course.

'Which is?'

'Winter somewhere on the coast and then decide what to do in the spring.'

'I like that idea too,' says Shiv keenly. 'We did miss out on a Parisian winter, didn't we. Wonder what a Provençale one is like. I can't imagine they get snow here, so close to the Med, so it'd probably be quite mild. I think this is my favourite. It means we have longer to decide which way to go and in the meantime we get a winter on board. Sounds cosy.'

'I know what you mean. It sounds great and we're not ruling out any options in the meantime. Which is exactly the approach to decision-making that Rudy told us to pursue when we talked to him in Paris. Remember?'

'Gosh Paris ... it seems so long ago.'

We are racing down the river now at seven knots. It feels like we are literally gliding – bushes, trees, and more trees fly past. The kilometre markers, where they are not swallowed by foliage, count our progress towards the Mediterranean: K265, K266, K267 ... There is not a soul around. No birdsong. No sounds, even from the river. Just the engine, thumping away like a panicked heartbeat.

Thump, thump ...

Thump, thump ...

Thump, thu ... ur ... ur ... ur ...

The engine whinnies like a foal and then ... silence.

This has never happened before. Oh God. I wrench the engine key backwards and forwards. Silence.

The current grabs our stern and swings us round sideways. Beam on, we are being pushed swiftly downstream towards a blind bend in the river, closer and closer into the overhanging tree branches on the left bank.

'Oh shit!' we both say simultaneously.

Shiv and I kick into action. Still drifting towards the bank, we are a blur of efficiency and calm as we jump into our now-familiar roles with the giant oar and outboard motor. Within minutes of losing engine power, we're back on course. All our emergency back-up systems are in place and working.

I check our charts and see the next place where we can stop is Saint-Gilles. Saint-Gilles sounds like a popular marina and as luck would have it, there is a mechanic based there. Perfect.

We almost silently waft into Saint-Gilles on the outboard. It's a strange place. The canal ends abruptly in a dead end. There is no through route so this arm of the canal is purely for boats to moor up.

Once a throbbing seaport visited by ships from all over the Med, now Saint-Gilles is a quiet place with a big history involving saints, a king, an albino deer and a church. Also, close by, according to legend, is where Mary Magdalen and Mary, mother of Jesus, disembarked from a boat after the crucifixion. Every May cowboys from the Camargue and gypsies from all over Europe gather to celebrate this event.

I'm sure no-one is celebrating now as we scan the watery cul-de-sac. There are hundreds of small boats and hire cruisers tied up but not one space free. We pull over against a dirty stone quay, where several warehouse buildings with corrugated roofs are firmly closed for lunch. It's as if a nuclear bomb has gone off – no people, no slinking dogs, just stillness, like midday in high summer. Except that it's November, early winter.

Damian is hunting for clues under the engine cover when, out of nowhere, a man appears: short, dumpy and annoyed, like he has been disturbed from a great meal. It's the capitaine. 'No, no, no. You cannot stay 'ere. This is an emergency pontoon. We are all full for ze winter,' he says, waving his hands and head.

He's not listening when I explain our circumstances. I guess he wants to get back to lunch. Emergency measures are called for.

Ducking below deck I rouse a sleepy India and Noah and bring them into the cockpit, which is already awash with tools and ripped-up floorboards.

'Monsieur. We have two small children. Please. Just one night,' I plead.

On cue India begins to cry. Perfect.

'Zut. D'accord. One night only, but there is no electricity 'ere. The marina is fully booked for the winter. All along the coast, marinas are full. I don't know where you will go next.' I feel like Mary looking for an inn and right now a stable looks good.

The capitaine waddles away.

'One night' … With these unsettling words hanging in the air like a bad smell, Damian doubles his attempts at playing mechanic: engine manual open, tools scattered everywhere, steam almost emanating from his ears.

'Oh bollocks. I don't know what's wrong with it. The bloody thing definitely won't start. Christ knows if there's really a mechanic here. The place is a bloody ghost town.'

There's not much I can help with now so I heave both kids onto the quay and we play together. Sometimes during the trip I have felt a little bit guilty about trawling Noah and India through morgue-like towns, freezing cold caves and endless waiting (locks filling, locks emptying, engines needing repair) and wondered whether they would have been happier at the local park, in the sandpit or at a nursery with little friends.

Just as I'm putting the finishing touches to a den we've made from an abandoned oil drum, another man appears from the end of the quay: a large white doctor's coat straining to contain an enormous belly. He drags his shoes along the concrete. Shlum, shlum, as he approaches.

'Bonjour. Je suis Monsieur Lange,' he growls in the direction of Damian.

'Who?' Damian looks at me as if *I* should know. Clearly I have no idea.

Monsieur Lange rolls his sleeves up, clambers on board without invitation and starts poking over the engine, his grey beard bobbing up and down. From where I sit on the quay, I cannot make out if I'm looking at his face or the back of his head – both sides are covered in fuzzy, matted hair.

Damian doesn't resist, just slaps tools into Monsieur Lange's fat palms as he requests them. If he is a guardian angel then God sure has a sense of humour.

'Mais oui. You need a new, 'ow you say, injection pompe,' says Monsieur Lange.

'A fuel injection pump? You're kidding me,' says Damian.

'Mais non. I niver joke about zees things. Ze engines are serious objets. Ze lock-keeper at ze Saint-Gilles lock, 'e called me and told me you 'ad a problem, to look for a jolie wooden bateau going verry slowly.'

Now that's what I call service.

A fuel injection pump is a small part (about 20 centimetres long) that is bolted onto the side of the engine. Its job is to regulate the supply of fuel into the cylinders. The most important thing about the fuel injection pump is that it has

to squirt exactly the *right* amount of fuel at exactly the *right* time. Sounds simple enough until you realise that we're talking about injecting just five-millionths of a gallon of fuel in a time frame of only 1/100 of a second. In other words, there is no margin for error.

But error we have. In fact, so much error there's no way the engine can be started without a new pump. I can't believe we have broken down again. It feels as if *Friendship* is on her last legs, like an old woman who keeps picking up new illnesses and injuries because she is too weak to fight them off.

I feel sad when I think about *Friendship* like a dying old woman and in remorse for having such bad thoughts, I bend over to kiss the engine cover. I know it's stupid but I've always done that with my favourite inanimate objects. Be they cars, boats, books or bicycles, I talk to them, caress them and kiss them. It's no surprise that I've always had an emotional relationship with *Friendship*. As I look at her old engine, I'm reminded of a song lyric by the band, James: 'So we keep putting our trust in things that rust. And then we feel the pain of loss.' Yes, that just about sums it up for me.

There's no point in moping though. The only thing to do now is throw money at the problem (again). Once Monsieur Lange has gone, I hunt through my pile of boat engine books and find a catalogue from an engine supplies company in Lancing, near Brighton. They specialise in old parts and after a quick telephone call, they agree to courier a new injection pump for a 1967 Thorneycroft diesel engine to our tiny village on the south coast of France. It's going to take three days to get here.

I look up and down the quay at Saint-Gilles. It's stuffed full of boats that have been wrapped in plastic covers for the winter – white fibreglass and blue tarpaulins as far as I can see in both directions. No-one will be back here until the warm weather returns. The whole place has been abandoned by humans. It's vaguely depressing to be stranded here like this. I look at our chart. Aigues-Mortes is only a few kilometres away.

I call over to Shiv, who is crouched on the bank constructing a castle with Noah and India. They're wrapped up in fleeces and hats, their coats left in a pile on the ground next to them. Making towns out of mud is hard work. 'Shiv, I've got an idea.'

She looks up and laughs. 'Uh-oh.'

'As we can't stay here, why don't we take *Friendship* to Aigues-Mortes and wait there for the fuel pump to arrive?'

'On the outboard?' she checks.

'Yes, why not? We're pretty good at handling her with the oar now and anyway it's not very far.'

'Okay. What's at Aigues-Mortes?'

'I don't know, but there's got to be more there than in this god-forsaken place.' I pick up one of our guidebooks and read aloud: '"Aigues-Mortes is a picturesque, medieval city standing proudly in an area of marshes, sand and water. It's surrounded by astonishingly well-preserved walls that have kept out all modern development. As such the town retains a special aura."'

Shiv looks up and down the dead quay and at the industrial buildings behind her and then smiles in approval.

While I replace floorboards, shove piles of tools in lockers and clean up the grease to make the cockpit safe again, Shiv cooks up a comforting bacon and broccoli pasta. It works now; finally there is no friction about who does what job. We both tend towards what we do best. Instead of an under-cooked, shoddy meal and a messy boat, we are ship-shape and stoked with a hot meal when we leave Saint-Gilles.

Shiv handles the oar as if this is how we have travelled all the way through France. There is no shouting, no panic and no frustration. Instead, without the relentless thump of our diesel engine, we chat excitedly about what Aigues-Mortes might be like. The thrill of arriving at a new place still accompanies us everywhere we go. Months of travelling haven't weakened its pull.

The Canal du Rhone à Sète will carry us all the way to Aigues-Mortes and then, hopefully, one day soon, out into the

Mediterranean Sea. The canal narrows steadily, but we have our steering down to a fine art now, so we move almost in a straight line – the S-shaped wobbles have gone.

The canal is lined with tall grasses. Behind are fields, some empty, some overgrown, and beyond them are the out-of-town shopping warehouses that mark the edge of most towns in Europe. Now that we're getting closer there's also a line of houseboats. I guess property in a medieval city in the south of France must be expensive so there are more boats outside Aigues-Mortes than most places. They are as ramshackle and as rough as everywhere else though; large plastic windows have been screwed into slab-sided iron hulls, extra rooms made out of plywood have been built on the decks and every-where there are dead pot plants, benches, faded sun awnings, rusting BBQs and spare orange gas bottles.

Aigues-Mortes stands firm on the lonely, windswept salt marshes of the Rhone delta. A gigantic tower ahead of us rises majestically out of the flats, drawing us near, an anachronism in the uneventful and retiring countryside.

Rounding a corner, immediately by a bridge, we pop into the marina, which is really a continuation of the canal, but wider. Boats line both sides, all moored stern to the quay – a nod to the sea.

'Look, there's a spot. Quick.'

Damian helps me slam the giant oar over to starboard to turn us into the bank, then leaps back and cuts the outboard engine so we drift in beautifully, fenders stopping us scraping the stone.

It's a spectacular mooring. We are dwarfed on our left by the overpowering sight of the Tour de Constance, a 13th-century round keep, with seven-metre-thick walls, which was used as a prison for centuries, and sat apart from the walled city of Aigues-Mortes. Across from us on the other side of the marina lie two barges, sitting high in the water, named *Morgenster* and *Carla* – names that fit with their masculine beauty.

As the sun turns the pale walls a soft rosy pink we wrap up

warm in coats, hats and scarves, and traipse into town to explore. The city is square, enclosed on all sides by beige ten-metre-high stone ramparts. Like in Avignon, towers and gates provided entry and defence to the city. We enter now where King Louis IX, noblemen, crusaders and peasants would all have thronged.

Inside is a neatly kept criss-cross of cobbled and paved lanes vibrant with shops, restaurants and art galleries.

'This is great. We can easily kill a few days here waiting for the new pump.'

After just a couple of days in Aigues-Mortes, we've both been seduced by its beauty. We were extremely lucky to get a slot on the visitors' moorings here. We're only allowed to stay three weeks but we should be off long before then, especially as the new fuel pump has arrived early. I tumble out of the cabin this morning to be greeted by what looked like Chewbacca's older brother. It's only when my eyes adjust to the light that I realise under all the white hair is the face of Monsieur Lange.

As usual he doesn't say much. He simply holds aloft a brown cardboard box covered in stickers from the UK and motions to the engine. After my last experiences with a boat mechanic, I decide not to don my crisp blue overalls. I don't believe that Monsieur Lange would appreciate me getting in his way and also, it's bloody freezing. My breath looks like steam and that's all it takes to persuade me a far better use of my time would be to put the kettle on.

While Monsieur Lange (another mechanic who refuses to divulge his first name) grunts, bangs and crashes about in the cockpit, I get Noah and India dressed. The temperature has been dropping steadily day by day and now they are wearing long johns and vests. Noah thinks it's hilarious that he is allowed to wear 'two pairs of trousers' at once.

For my part I have started wearing jeans for the first time since we left the UK. When I put them on, I'm taken back to my childhood and the feeling of wearing school trousers again in September after a summer of trunks and shorts. Now, like then, they feel horribly unnatural, but I suppose they'll keep me warm and at least I will no longer look like a tourist. I've realised that the only people who wear shorts in France outside of the months of July and August are foreigners.

We pile out of the boat past Monsieur Lange, who signals that the engine should be running again by the time we get back. We head for the central square to indulge in our morning coffee. Even though it's cold, there's still sunshine and we're so used to being in the fresh air that we sit outside. It's too claustrophobic being cooped up in a café. I've brought along a couple of toy cars, so while Shiv orders, I set up a little game for Noah and India, turning the lines between the cobbles into roads and the cobbles themselves into houses. It should keep them occupied long enough for us to switch off and enjoy our caffeine hit.

I can barely wait to get back to *Friendship*. It's not that I want to go anywhere just yet; I simply need to know that we can if we want to. I hate her being disabled like this. We half-run back to the mooring but even as we round the corner of the city walls, I can see that all is not well. Monsieur Lange is sat on a bollard, buried in an oil-covered engine manual. As we get closer, he looks up and shakes his head. Oh great.

It turns out that the new fuel injection pump is on the engine but it won't work. The timing is out. I consult my own manual to find out what this means and discover that engines depend on everything happening at exactly the right time. To ensure this is the case, there are three large cogs inside the engine that have to be lined up precisely. If just one tooth of one of those cogs is out of synch, the engine won't run.

Monsieur Lange explains that to get the cogs to line up, engines have a small inspection chamber (effectively a three-centimetre hole in the bottom of the engine). You look up this inspection hole and set the cogs at the right angle using a numbered dial.

Fine, I think, let's use the inspection hole. Except we can't – that's where the problem lies. The hole is right at the bottom of the engine, deep in the bilges and impossible to get to. It turns out that it's in the only *inaccessible* place in the whole damned boat.

This is one hell of a design fault. It means Monsieur Lange can't line up the cogs and therefore can't get the engine to work. I won't believe there isn't a way around it, but a firm 'Non' is all that Monsieur Lange will say on the subject. He's actually affronted that I'm questioning his inventiveness.

We both fall silent. What about a *miroir*? I suggest after five minutes. It took me that long to find the word 'mirror' in the French-English dictionary, and having found it, the translation was hardly worth the effort. I mimic using a mirror like an upside-down periscope, indicating that we might see up the inspection hole in the reflection.

Monsieur Lange looks at me with disdain and gruffly says 'Non' again. It turns out he's already tried that idea but the inspection hole is too difficult to get at and anyway, there's no way of getting enough light into the bilges to see anything in the mirror.

Silence again. I hate the silences. They mean that our illustrious mechanic doesn't know what to do. Eventually he says he will return tomorrow with a friend. The only solution he can think of is to keep turning each of the three cogs until they magically line up. Even he admits it will be very hit and miss but hopefully at some point they'll all clunk into place. It sounds like a crazy plan to me, akin to hoping you can find the right combination on a safe if you keep turning the dial for long enough.

Surely there is another way? I ask again.

There is. If we remove the engine from the boat with a crane, the inspection hole will be totally accessible and the cogs can be lined up in ten minutes. The downside, of course, is that this will cost a small fortune. Correction – a large fortune.

My stomach goes hollow. I tell Monsieur Lange we'll look into the crane option but would rather avoid having to lift

the engine out. So I urge him to return with his safe-cracking friend in the morning.

It's been ages. It feels like an interminable dentist-waiting-room wait, for days on end, hoping our engine will soon roar back into life.

Monsieur Lange has returned three times now and meddled for hours, a cloud of potent brandy and sweat surrounding his doctor's coat, but the creeping feeling of hopelessness is hard to shake.

Without a working engine we feel slightly incomplete as a family. Like one of us is ill. At least Aigues-Mortes is a beautiful place to be stuck. If we had stayed in Saint-Gilles I'm sure the sense of malaise would have spread. I just hope Aigues-Mortes, meaning 'dead waters', doesn't jinx us with a 'dead engine'.

In fact, Aigues-Mortes turns out to be just the tonic we need. Joining its bustle every day, we meander up and down each road in that same listless way I used to 'do' each aisle of the supermarket.

Tiny narrow shops burst with muslin bags of lavender, horse-hair bags, prettily packaged boxes of Camargue salt, cowboy hats and stuffed flamingos, white horses and black bulls (toys that have India grabbing and grouching that she cannot take them all back to the boat).

Honey crêpes and coffee kick off most of our rambles. Then at lunchtime we are drawn back to the piazza, flanked by restaurants on two sides, a church and a tourist office on the other. Locals and late-season tourists turn their faces into the winter sun, chat and while away long lunches. Although it's not the season, we cannot resist ordering moules-frites again, aware that soon we'll leave France behind. At least we hope it will be soon.

Monsieur Lange is losing heart. Recently he has failed to turn up twice and then when he *did* arrive it was with a different 'assistant' each time. These men are all supposed to be 'pompe specialistes' (experts who can fix any problem) but they never return. As each one bites the dust, I become more

and more sceptical about our chances of repairing *Friendship*. The back end of the engine is in pieces and oil is smeared on every surface of the boat. Monsieur Lange works for hours at a time but at the end of each session, he shrugs his shoulders and tells me the cogs are still not lined up. He can't even tell if one is in the right place as he will only know when all three cogs are in their correct positions. It *really* is just like a combination lock. This job is going to last forever. I can see that we are going to have to crane out the engine, otherwise the cost of Monsieur Lange's time alone is going to cripple us.

Most tea-times Damian is usually left on board scratching his head, leafing through manuals and waiting for bad news from various men in overalls. I take the kids for a wander around the boats in the marina and hope for an invite aboard and a cup of tea.

Lots of boats seem to have wintered here, owners returning next spring. But there is a lively community of live-aboards too and all of them are friendly. We get on best with Chris and Celia, who are housed in a Bristol tugboat and are a long-term live-aboard couple. They have been cruising Europe for years, spending seasons in Ireland, Greece and Spain amongst other places. I wonder if I will be like Celia one day, pictures of our grandchildren on our barge-fridge, moving countries with the seasons. Hopefully we'll have a barge with a decent engine and a thumping great fuel injector attached.

This morning Chris came over to take a look at the engine with me. Having spent the last few decades living on boats he's become a pretty good, self-taught mechanic. We grovel around the bilges on our hands and knees for about 20 minutes. Chris then gets up, wipes his hands and grabs his tea. I anxiously await his verdict.

'Damian,' he opens solemnly, 'I have to be honest with you, I don't think you'll ever get the cogs to line up by guesswork.'

'But ... Monsieur Lange ...'

'I know what he said, but he's clutching at straws. Believe me, as a fellow boater and someone who knows what he's talking about, it's not going to happen. You're wasting your money,' says Chris.

'Surely it's just a matter of time? If we keep going, eventually we'll get the cogs in the right place?'

'Damian, it's not that easy. The actual beginning point of fuel injection must be timed to an accuracy of better than 0.00006 seconds. You'll be here forever if you try to guess it.'

'So what should I do?' I ask desperately.

'You're going to have to get the engine lifted out and repair it that way. But before you do it, you should think about what happens after that. You've said this isn't the first time you've had engine problems and I'm not surprised. This old lump is nearly forty years old. It's bound to break down on a long journey like this. And who's to know what will go wrong next? You could fix the fuel injection pump and then for all you know, the big end could go next month. Are you ready for that, with kids on board?'

'But I had the engine serviced before we left,' I plead, clearly in a state of denial.

'I'm sure you did, but you've got to remember how old this boat is. If she were a car she'd be a Ford Anglia. You wouldn't dream of driving across Europe with all your family in an Anglia, would you? You know you'd be asking for trouble. That's how you should see this boat. Frankly it's amazing you've got this far. What you must think about now is whether you keep throwing good money after bad. If this was a Ford Anglia you'd have called the AA by now, put her on a tow truck and have had her taken home. I don't mean to put a downer on things but perhaps that's what you should do with *Friendship*. There are haulage firms all along the coast that could put her on a trailer and have her back in Walton-on-the-Naze in three days' time.'

'Really?' I say in astonishment. I don't know why I'm so surprised. I know boats are carried across Europe on trailers all the time. I suppose that I find it hard to grasp that it's taken us months and months to get here by water and yet by road, we could be home by the end of this week.

Chris continues, 'Believe me, I don't want to crush your hopes and dreams. I'm simply trying to be objective, Damian. No mechanic is going to tell you the truth because they just want your money. As your friend I'm telling you that even if you fix the pump, it's highly likely something else will go wrong. Maybe it's best to get the boat towed home rather than throwing your money away and risking your lives, because once you hit the sea, the last thing you'll want is more engine problems with the kids aboard.'

I know that Chris is only trying to help and his brutal honesty is merely the result of seeing hundreds of boaters in similar situations over the years. Nevertheless it hurts. Mostly because I know he's right. We can't continue to patch up *Friendship* on an almost monthly basis. Who knows if something more calamitous might break at some point? It's almost okay on the canals because we can drift into the bank, but at sea? It would be suicide. If there is one thing I know, you never take chances with the sea.

It's only when Chris has returned to his boat that I can sit down and take stock of the situation. I feel beaten, upset and depressed. What the hell do we do? We're going to have to make some big decisions because we can't stay on this mooring for much longer but I can't stand the idea of giving up now, so close to the end.

Shiv returns from the market with Noah and India to find me feeling sorry for myself, sat on the foredeck looking into the cold, black water.

'Don't jump. It's not that bad,' she calls out.

'It *is* that bad, Shiv. I think this might be the end of our adventure.'

CHAPTER 23

Is this really the end of the trip, just when we can smell the salt in the air? The pull of the Mediterranean is all the more strong now I know we might not make it.

All night I have lain, frozen stiff, staring at the ceiling struts, going over what Chris told Damian. It goes against the grain to give up. Every problem is solvable. Damian and I have always found a way through things. By three in the morning, that terrible hour when problems quadruple in size, I almost accept that we will be going back to England, with or without *Friendship*.

Now, in the sharp early morning frost, I have crept out on deck in my thermals and jacket with a solitary cup of tea. I feel a lot more positive. Instead of searching constantly in my head for a solution, I will focus on the small everyday things – playing with the kids, cups of tea with Celia and which crêpe I have yet to try. Whenever I have done that in the past, things work themselves out. A greater force lines things up when I stop pressing and pushing for an answer.

I will leave things to fate.

The sun, almost cruelly, lights up the wooden varnish on the coach roof, momentarily bringing *Friendship* back to life. I watch with envy as a battered old motor cruiser puffs black gunk from its exhaust, reverses out of its mooring and putters off down the other arm of the canal, the Grau, out to sea no doubt for a bit of fishing.

If only it were us coiling our ropes, pushing off from the quay and heading noisily away.

Damian pokes his head out from the steering hatch, yawns and rubs his eyes. I can see he's had a torrid night too.

'What're you doing out here? It's freezing. And you're barefoot ...' he says.

'Is it? Am I? I hadn't noticed.' My feet are like blocks of ice.

'Come on back down below. I'll make us another cuppa.'

This morning Monsieur Lange arrives early, ready for another fruitless few hours trying to get the engine's cogs lined up. From his sunken demeanour I can tell that even he knows he isn't going to be able to sort it out but I can't face telling him to stop trying. No matter how unlikely his chances of success, I don't want him to give up.

Meanwhile, I want to explore our other options. A sleepless night has resulted in an interminable list of things we could do. Unlike Shiv, I can't put the engine to the back of my mind. I have to chase solutions relentlessly. I've scribbled the pros and cons of our choices on the inside back cover of the diesel engine manual. It's the only book I'm never far from at the moment.

I carve up responsibilities. I'm going to investigate the cost of the two main options: craning the engine out and getting *Friendship* transported to the UK on a truck. In case we have to wait for a crane, Shiv's going to see if she can find somewhere for us to keep the boat for a few weeks more.

Just a few days ago we were debating the merits of going to Spain versus Italy. Now we're wondering whether we have to go home on a flatbed truck. I feel a great sense of failure.

Failing to get to the Med will probably kill Damian. This dream has kept him going for years through his dark and stressful times in advertising.

I'm determined to find us somewhere to hole up with *Friend-*

ship. Taking up my position in India's bunk, I have my mobile in hand and my legs under a duvet. It feels cosy in here, especially with the kids next to me in Noah's bunk, sharing a duvet as they watch *Postman Pat's ABC*.

On my lap *The Mediterranean Almanac* lies open. I telephone numerous small towns, working westwards from Aigues-Mortes. If we can book into a marina somewhere ... If we use the outboard and giant oar to get us there ... If we spend a fortune and get the engine lifted out ... Then we can stave off certain depression. A lot of ifs, I know. But there is enough of a thread of hope to have me ringing marinas with the urgency of a 999 call. As long as we stick to the canals we know we can travel safely under our 'outboard-oar' system.

Grau-du-Roi, Palavas-les-Flots, Frontignan and eventually Sète – I call them all. They're all full. No visitor berths. 'Rien' – and that is after using every sympathy card, including the 'two small children' one.

There are other harbours too, accessible only from the sea, but without a powerful engine it's too great a risk to take with the kids on board. If I kept the kids ashore, there is no way Damian alone could manage the outboard, giant oar and any manoeuvring over waves.

'Nothing,' I state as Damian tramps back on board and peeps his head into the forepeak.

'Nothing? Nowhere?' queries Damian in disbelief to the cheery sound of Postman Pat's van trundling along to Greendale.

'It seems the south coast of France is one of the most desirable places to stay in the Med. Everyone huddles here over winter, ready to let loose when the weather turns. I have even tried places further back, all the way to Arles. Nothing.'

'You're joking.'

'I wish I was.'

Damian rubs his beard and shakes his head.

'Well I've got even worse news,' I say quietly to Shiv. I almost don't want to say the words out loud.

'Worse?? How?' she asks, clearly bewildered.

'The crane at the marina here is broken and they aren't planning to fix it for a while. Apparently there's no call for it over the winter so they are spending their money on a new pontoon instead. The crane will get repaired in April, ready for the new season.'

'April? But that's months away. Will they let us stay here until then?'

'There's no room. Legally they can't let us stay long term on the visitors' moorings and there are no other spaces free. I even asked the capitaine if we could keep *Friendship* on the bank, out of the water. He said we could, but we aren't allowed to live on board – something to do with insurance.'

'What are we going to do?' asks Shiv.

'I don't know. I spent an hour calling other local mechanics to see if they had any ideas. Half of them have already been here with Monsieur Lange and the other half all said the same thing: if Monsieur Lange can't fix it, no-one can. We are officially up a creek without an engine.'

'Did you find out the cost to trailer her back to England?' Shiv asks without really wanting to know the answer.

'At least five grand,' I reply flatly. '*Friendship*'s width puts her in the "expensive" bracket. Apparently we'd need a special trailer and a police escort for the whole trip.'

'What?!'

That night the silence is strange on board. We are both sombre and depressed, not talking, just going about our jobs in automatic mode. Damian does not even turn on the iPod.

I check on the kids and I rearrange their covers. They're both in deep sleep, snuffling with colds, dressed in pyjamas and fleeces under their bedding. My breath turns swiftly into white vapour in the freezing cold air of the forepeak. There's no way the kids could survive a whole winter here anyway, I think to myself. I would worry about them getting frostbite.

My last job after washing up is to return the milk to the

'fridge', which, for the past two weeks, has moved to a spot just outside the cabin door. It's minus four at night now so this saves our early morning dash across the cockpit.

A fresh, biting wind whistles in when I open the wooden doors. Something is going on. It's too quiet out there. It feels like the whole of Aigues-Mortes is mourning with us.

Looking out into the canvas-covered cockpit, I notice that the back flaps are loose and I nip over to close them.

'Wow! Dame, come and have a look. Quick.'

'What . . .' comes a low growl from the cabin.

'It's worth it. It's something beautiful. Really,' I tempt.

Damian shuffles up slowly into the cockpit and I draw back the canvas.

It's snowing. Great big, irregular, soft flumps of snow drift down, settling on the back deck, sticking to the green canvas awning and melting on our warm faces.

'Wow,' says Damian, and we stand there like kids transfixed by the sight of Father Christmas.

The next morning there's excited talk of making snowmen at breakfast.

'What's a noman, Mummy?'

'A round man made of snow. You remember? We made one once in Queen's Park.'

'Bark,' echoes India. 'MummyDaddy, bark, bark.'

'What's Queen's Park?' says Noah.

It hits me that India has never seen snow before, so we rug up – thermals, hats and gloves – and head out to play. It's 9 am, minus something degrees and the ropes securing *Friendship* to the quay are frozen solid.

Some early risers, including a few seagulls, have already left prints in the snow on the quay. We hold hands and follow their footprints. India slips and slides on the snow, only an inch deep, even though I'm holding her hand.

'No, no, MummyDaddy,' she screeches, scraping at the snow with her mittens and licking it off.

Ice and snow have covered the only ugliness around Aigues-Mortes. The bins, the grey tarmac road separating us from the city walls, the litter collected by winds in corners – all are beautified by a white covering.

Day after day now we wake up to an icy cabin, icy winds and icy walks. The decks are now too slippery to step on. The ropes are frozen coils. Even the once pleasant stroll to the launderette has become a head-down march, hats pulled down low to avoid the biting wind. The inside of the boat is not particularly welcoming any more either. Every morning the windows are wet with condensation. Rivulets of water run down the varnished bulkheads when I cook and there's a constant smell of damp clothing.

I'm beginning to wonder whether this is nature's way of telling us it's time to end our journey. That it's some kind of sign. If only we could work out how to fix that blessed injector. I remember my strategy and push the thoughts of finding a solution from my mind.

It's early, maybe four in the morning. I'm lying rigid and awake, picking over every detail of our situation but always coming to the same conclusion: we're allowed on this mooring for only a few more days and then we have to be gone. It's crunch time and Monsieur Lange is nowhere nearer to fixing the engine. It looks like a truck home is going to be our only option.

My head is so full I fear it's going to burst. This afternoon I rang back one of the boat haulage companies. They said they could pick up *Friendship* next Tuesday. He confirmed there is no room for us in the truck, so we'll have to get a plane home. Probably from Perpignan, which is a long cab ride away.

I run through all the costs, timings and logistics that are flying around my mind and exhale loudly. If the truck turns up on Tuesday, it means we'll never have made it to the Mediterranean. Sure, we got within walking distance, but we'll never actually sail on the sea. We will never be able to say that we crossed the whole of France by water. One day we'll have to explain to Noah and India that we didn't quite

**achieve our dream. We had to give up with the end in sight.
I hate that. I bloody hate it. Of all my dreams, this is one that
I desperately wanted to fulfil. I twist and turn in our bed, safe
in the knowledge that I won't wake up Shiv. She's lying
next to me with her eyes wide open, staring at the cabin
roof.**

I jolt upright. 'That's it. I've got it!' I shout, bashing my head on
a beam.

'What?' says Damian, clearly wide-awake too.

'My digital camera – that's the answer,' I say.

'What *are* you talking about?' Damian is too on edge for
puzzles or roundabout talk.

'What if you used my digital camera to take pictures of the
dial that's inside the inspection hole? The camera is self-focusing
and small enough for you to hold underneath the engine to take
a picture of the dial.'

'But it'll be too dark.'

'No, it won't – the flash comes on automatically so it'll light
up the numbers on the dial.'

'Bloody hell. Bloody hell. Bloody – bloody genius is what it
is. Yes of course. Why didn't I think of that? Christ, Shiv. I think
you've cracked it,' shouts Damian and continues babbling. 'It'll
work. All we have to do is adjust the cogs and keep taking
pictures until the numbers on the dial in the inspection hole are
correct.'

'Yes, exactly,' I say.

'It's a brilliant idea. I think it might just work. What the hell
made you think of it?' asks Damian.

'I was thinking about nothing. That's exactly the point,' I say.

Damian, ever impatient, pulls on his trousers, a fleece and a
beanie hat over his ears.

'You going to do it now?' I ask incredulously, sliding back
under the duvet. It's nearly five o'clock and pitch dark.

'Too right. You make some tea and come join me. Let's see if
we can breathe life back into the old girl,' says Damian on his
way out of the cabin.

'What, me or *Friendship*?' I banter, the old easiness returned between us now there is a glimmer of hope for our journey.

'I'll just have five more minutes in bed,' I say.

I cannot possibly wait till daylight. This idea is so good I have to see if it works – now. Armed with Shiv's compact digital camera, I stretch my hands under the engine and feel for the inspection hole. With my right hand I can just trace its edges, while with my left I angle the camera upwards and press the shutter. I pull the camera back and look at the screen. The flash has illuminated the bottom of the engine beautifully and although I couldn't see what I was doing, in the top right-hand corner of the picture I can just make out the inspection hole. Eighteen photographs later and I've found the right angle to hold the camera and there it is – the dial that will help me line up all the cogs in the engine. I check the manual and see that the dial should be set at 21.5. That's the magic number. Currently it's registering number 4. Monsieur Lange was miles off.

Photograph then turn the engine a fraction. Photograph then turn the engine a fraction. Photograph then turn the engine a fraction. Little by little, I adjust the cogs and check the camera until the dial finally reaches 21.5.

This is the moment of truth. I go to the wheel and turn the key.

***Friendship*'s engine fires into life. On the button. First time. Un-bloody-believable. We've done it. How could the impossible problem have been so easy to solve? I think to myself how much I love Shiv as I ostentatiously rev the engine in glee.**

I roll over under the duvet and listen. Completely familiar, yet strange at the same time. It's definitely the unmistakably joyous sound of *Friendship*'s engine. I hop out of bed and burst through the cabin doors. Damian is grinning ear to ear. He is a Cheshire cat with Botox, revving the engine in neutral, hands covered in grease, bloodshot eyes twinkling with joy.

'Yeehaaaaaaaaaaaaaaaa!!!!!!!!!!!!!!!!!' I scream, for once not worried about waking the kids, and then I do a little on-the-spot jig.

'Now we'll make it. We *can* get to the sea!'

'Where's that tea?' jokes Damian, giving me a huge hug that winds me.

As I finish the last dregs of my tea, Monsieur Lange arrives. He is stunned at the sight of blue/black smoke streaming from our exhaust. He has barely got out of his van before I have explained to him how we lined up the cogs. I show him the photos of the dial and he roars with laughter. It's the first time I have seen him even smile. I think he's just relieved that this job has suddenly gone away.

While he inspects the engine to check all is well, I ask him what he thinks the chances are of something else breaking down. He looks at me, surprised.

'Don't be reediculous. Zis engine 'as ardly ever been used. Ze compression is excellent. Ze oil pressure is excellent. Ze parts are not worn. Eet is very strong. Tres forte. Look 'ow big eet is. Seventy horsepower and four litres. Eet is like a truck engine but so little use – it will last forever.'

'Hardly used . . . but we've just travelled almost a thousand kilometres,' I say in surprise.

'Oui, zat is nothing for an engine like zis. Ze most important thing is *before* zis trip – aw much did you use ze boat?'

'Hardly ever.'

'Exactement. And before you owned ze boat? 'Ow much was eet used?'

The penny finally drops. 'It *wasn't* used. I found it abandoned and from my research into previous owners it looks like the furthest it ever travelled was a little way up the Humber Estuary.'

'Umber est?' asks a confused Monsieur Lange.

'Don't worry. You're right. *Friendship's* hull might have been a wreck when I found her but because she had lain ashore for so many years it meant her engine was never even turned on. She's almost as good as new.'

I could kiss Monsieur Lange but the thought of his and my beards getting tangled together is too much to bear. Instead we shake hands and secretly hope we never need to see each other again.

Monsieur Lange's news does it for me. I want to leave right now – to set off while we are all in our pyjamas. I just want to get *Friendship* on the Med. Having thought we would never achieve our dream, I don't want to waste another moment. Energy, enthusiasm and optimism are coursing through me again. We are invincible now.

My impetuous side wants to leave right here and now, but Damian is shattered. He hasn't slept for over a week, and I know him. Now the problem's solved, he will collapse.

Though I loathe being the sensible one, I insist that Damian gets some sleep, that we spend the rest of the day stocking up on water, fuel and supplies for the next part of the journey, and also saying our goodbyes to our new marina friends Chris and Celia.

Chris is astounded that we have got the engine running again. When I tell him about Shiv's idea with the digital camera, he shakes his head and laughs. 'What a wonderful idea. It's brilliant. You know, no-one of my generation would have thought of that. Digital cameras are still very new to us. I wouldn't be surprised if Monsieur Lange has never even used one. Ha, I bet he'll be rushing out to buy one now. I reckon your little digital camera trick is going to be copied by mechanics all over southern France.'

I smile, proud of Shiv but also secretly disappointed that I didn't come up with the genius idea that mechanics everywhere are going to talk about from now on.

Back on *Friendship* we decide to enter the Mediterranean at Sète, a fishing port a little further down the coast. Sète was created in the 1660s because Paul Riquet, who was constructing the 'Canal du Midi', was looking for a suitable outlet to the Mediterranean Sea and at the same time, Louis XIV wanted a new sea route for his royal galleys. The Cap du Sète was identified as the most suitable site to serve both purposes and so the new town of Sète was born.

This is no Milton Keynes though. Sète is described as the 'Venice of the Languedoc' and is home to some of France's finest seafood cooking. Local specialities include mussels stuffed with sausage meat; monkfish with aïoli and vegetables; octopus pie; cuttlefish stew and of course, bouillabaisse.

It's really the Grau-du-Roi that is the closest entry point to the Mediterranean but the journey to Sète will take us through two great landscapes: one is the wild and romantic countryside of the Camargue and the other is the wide expanse of the Etang de Thau (the Thau Lagoon). This trip is going to be a fitting and spectacular swansong to our time in France.

After a full night's sleep without Damian tossing and turning beside me, we both wake at first light feeling human again, light-hearted and worry-free. There's no wrestling this morning about who should make the tea – on this, possibly our final morning on the canals, I'm happy to put the kettle on.

Let's face it: without PG Tips this voyage may never have happened. Gallons have lubricated the planning, preparing, highs and lows of the journey. French coffee has been the stimulant that kicks me out of the boat and into cafés far and wide in search of that eleven o'clock fix, but tea has been with us through everything. It has been a much more loyal companion.

Standing in the galley I fill our two blue and white, toughened porcelain mugs (detailed with a line drawing of a schooner) with boiling water, pour in the milk and nip outside to twist the gas off. I place Damian's mug in a mug-holder by the steering wheel.

'Tea's ready,' I announce, quietly, so as not to wake the kids.

The next 15 minutes is a burst of activity. First I tackle the cabin down below: wash up last night's meal, check sharp knives are stowed in the knife-block, replace books in shelves, store bedding under the starboard bunk, hang loose clothes on pegs, find sunglasses and put them in the wooden holder on deck.

Next, the cabin ship-shape, I come up on deck to help Damian finish up. I check all ropes are coiled and hung from the stanchions (Damian has just poured the rest of our kettle water on them to unfreeze them), all loose items on deck are stowed and kids' toys put in Tupperware boxes so we don't slip on a loose piece of Lego.

Damian loads the bikes and locks them to the front of the boat. He folds the buggy and squeezes it between the bikes and the inflatable. He has already completed the engine checks, topped up with water, cleaned the Porta Potty, emptied the bilges and prepared the logbook open by the steering wheel.

'Seacock open?' I ask and wink at the same time.

'Aye, aye, seacock open,' says Damian in a Captain Pugwash voice from the bank where he is preparing the lines for our departure, leaving just the one attached to the bank.

Damian starts the engine. I loosen the solitary line from the bank and push us off the quay as the comforting rumble of *Friendship*'s engine growls her way out of Aigues Mortes.

I could do all this in my sleep now. It's a comforting rhythm that sparks our new and final day on the canals.

We're like the Royal Navy, seamlessly and silently gliding about the boat as if we have been doing this forever. It's hard to believe that when we left Calais we didn't even know what a lock looked like and couldn't tie up to a bank without having a shouting match.

Now the canal turns towards the coast, becoming a straight line of grey-brown almost like a road disappearing off into the distance. On both sides are stones and reeds. Beyond is flatness. Rice fields, marshland and lakes provide an eerie landscape that we can barely make out from our low height on *Friendship*.

In the distance, the foothills of the Cevennes rise up, white-covered peaks reminding us of the snow in Aigues Mortes. Behind us the Tour de Constance stands guard and seems to be watching us leave.

I wrap my scarf tighter around my neck. It's bitter this morning. Along the towpath, ice has crusted over the thin grass, heightening the desolation and strangeness of this place. Tiny fishing boats cram along the canal, well placed for exiting to the sea to our left or into the vast Etang on our right.

In the sharp morning sun, it doesn't look like a lake but a slash of bright blue just under the horizon. A heron is wading knee-deep in the water to the side of us, presumably hunting for breakfast. Conical fishing nets are strung row after row along the banks, one end tied to bamboo poles dug into the water.

'This isn't like any of the other canals is it?' I say to Damian, no need for shouting from my position close by him on the side-deck. He is steering, taking pictures, sipping tea and beaming.

'This is incredible,' he gushes. 'Look at those little huts on the banks. Probably for the fishermen.'

As he finishes the sentence a white horse, one of those famous wild horses of the Camargue, rears its head and whinnies. We motor within metres of it as it nibbles grass by the bank, shakes its head and carries on.

'It just gets better. I wonder if there is a cowboy nearby? You know there are real cowboys here called Gardians. Hats, lassoes, the lot,' says Damian taking a photo.

'Noah and India have got to see this. I'll wake them up.'

The Camargue is everything I wanted it to be. The white horse is the icing on the cake. I look out at the horizon, which is composed of three horizontal bands: the water; the thin strip of the towpath and the bright blue winter sky. It's almost graphic in its simplicity. No signs of man destroy its perfection.

I want to capture this beauty with my camera but there's no way I can do justice to the panoramic vista before me. I'm reminded of a photographer whose work I love – Harry Cory Wright in Norfolk. He takes pictures on a massive Victorian wooden camera. The negatives are huge, meaning he can produce prints that are so large you want to fall into them. I wish I had that camera now.

For the next few kilometres we follow the brackish water of the canal, eyes darting left and right from our ringside seats on the foredeck. The wind has died, the winter sun is warming our bodies and we sit in our familiar huddle on a waterproof rug surrounded by chocolate milk and jam croissants.

'Look! A horse,' yells Noah.

'MummyDaddy, MummyDaddy, up, up,' yells India and I lift her high so she can see the strong, white horse that canters past.

'Look, far far away can you see that black thing? That's a bull,' I say.

'Rarrrr,' says India, doing her tiger impression from under layers of thermals.

Soon the Camargue is interrupted by the Etang de Thau (lagoon). It's the largest of a string of lakes that stretch along this coast from the Rhone to the Pyrenees. In fact, at 21 kilometres long and eight kilometres wide, it's the second largest lake in France.

The Etang de Thau is a shock to the system. We haven't seen an expanse of water this large since we were on the English Channel. Our canal runs right along its edge. We are merely a few feet away from the lake, separated by the thin, man-made towpath. If I squint my eyes, it's as if we're on the lake itself.

For as far as we can see, there are the signs of the thriving fishing industry that make this Etang so famous in France. Eighteen different types of shellfish are taken from here, the most important being oysters, 13,000 tonnes of which are gathered annually. The oysters are marketed as Bouzigues Oysters and because the water in the Etang de Thau is so pure (Graded A), the oysters can be consumed within minutes of being caught. The thought of the cuisine in Sète is even more tempting now.

With Noah and India absorbed in the activities of the fishermen, Shiv shuffles closer to me and we start playing our 'List Game', luxuriating in the memories of our journey. I fire the first question: 'Top Three Surreal Memories?'

She thinks for a while and then says quite quickly, 'Number One, Caveman Damian, with two cave-children in tow; you in your pyjamas on the streets of Compiègne. Number Two, Noah refusing to wear any clothes apart from his shoes for two days while we were in Cambrai. Three, you keeling over on your bike outside the hypermarket in Valence because you had overloaded it with eighteen plastic shopping bags.'

I laugh at the memory and then Shiv interrupts. 'Wow – look. Look, over there.'

I'm pointing and laughing. I can hardly believe my eyes. Pink flamingos, necks scooped in wonderful curves, bend into the water beyond.

'What's a flingo?' asks Noah from the front.

'A beautiful, beautiful bird. You're very lucky to see them in the wild.'

With the 'flingos' gone, Shiv returns to our game. 'OK, my turn. When were you most alive? ... Most excited?'

I smile to myself. 'Most excited eh? Hmmm. I'm tempted to say that time when you came out of the shower and danced naked across the cabin to the Bee Gees. It was 'Staying Alive' which was on full blast as I recall – I must make a note to play that more often. But I guess even that vision was topped by seeing the Eiffel Tower for the first time and then finding out we could moor right next to it. And realising that I could actually grow a proper beard was pretty emotional for me too,' I add, laughing.

'But maybe in hindsight the most exciting time for me was when we found ourselves alone on the canals for the first time.' I pause to remember those early days in northern France when everything was so overwhelmingly new, thrilling and frightening.

I ask Shiv what was the 'Best Advice' she was given.

'That's got to be the old Dutch woman we met in Watten. She was watching Noah and India playing in a large puddle and said to me, "Water is the best toy of all. It's free and it's everywhere." Isn't that beautiful? So simple and so true.'

'All right,' continues Shiv. 'No Top Three's this time, just your thoughts. What have you learnt from this trip?'

'Wow, that's a big one,' I reply and start going over the many, many things that I have taken from this adventure. Finally I say, 'I remember not respecting the person I had become in London and desperately but quietly hoping I could change. For me, this journey was never about travelling through France. It wasn't about discovering wines, seeing sunflowers or marvelling at tourist attractions. I wanted this trip to be about finding myself and then hoping I liked what I discovered.

'What I hadn't expected was how much I would learn about you, Noah and India. I guess I thought I already knew you (after all, why else would I have married you?). As for the kids, they're only three and one, what's to learn? Lots as it turned out. You've become more than a mum and a wife. You're more vibrant, strong and confident than I've ever known you. Noah and India are so pure and open that they've highlighted to me just what a miserable, cynical, selfish old bastard I'd become. But I think I've learnt to be a more relaxed, interested and calmer person now. Although I realise that one adventure won't change everything. This isn't the movies; I still have to work at being someone who Noah and India will look up to, rather than the other way round. The good news is that at least I've started trying ...'

We're silent for a while and then I ask, 'What about you?'

'I've learnt that anything is possible. The fact that we survived all that intensity, the rain, the breakdowns, the snow, and we are still here, together, and in a few minutes we're about to sail into the Mediterranean Sea, well, I would never have believed it a few years ago. If we can do this, with Noah and India so young, we can do anything.

'The other thing I have loved is the simple things. That's what

I want us to hang on to, the ability to keep simplicity in a complicated world. You know, picking blackberries, our bankside picnics, you and me talking in our cabin with no television. I don't want us to have to do grand, big things all the time. Just simple ones.

'I have learnt about myself, about you, the kids. I could ramble on for hours, but you won't let me, I know that now.' I laugh and Damian laughs too.

'You know it feels like we have crossed a continent. I feel like one of the great explorers, about to stick a flag in the soil.'

Our musing is dissipated by the emergence of Sète in our line of vision. The tall buildings, cranes and spires are a far cry from the flat expanse of the Etang that surrounds it. In my mind's eye I imagine us cruising majestically into town where we have a celebratory glass of wine and a meal before setting off once again to enter the Med.

I get a shock when I look through the binoculars and all I can see is the sea. The canal doesn't go through the town at all; it skirts its edge and instead heads straight for the Mediterranean. Ahead of us are two sea walls, one on either side with a small lighthouse at the end of each. Beyond is shimmering silver water.

I don't say anything, I simply hand the binoculars to Shiv.

Oh no, oh yes, oh no. There it is. Glinting at us, drawing us in. It's the Mediterranean. Not bright Technicolor blue, but almost silver. I wasn't prepared for it to happen so quickly. Despite the months and months in the canals that sometimes seemed to go on forever, I want to back-pedal, go in reverse, quickly, pretend we haven't seen it.

Sadness and loss well up and big fat tears blot out my view. I don't want to lose the magic we've had in the canals, the closeness between all four of us. The continent I've also crossed in getting back to Damian. And myself. I do not want the sea to burst our bubble or the world to come in.

We're getting close now, the red and green markings on the lighthouses are clear to see and I can hear the waves crashing against the other side of the sea wall.

Shiv is still looking through the binoculars. She hasn't said a word since I gave them to her.

'Left or right?' I ask.

Shiv pauses, puts down the binoculars and looks me in the eye. I'm sure I see tears.

'Right.'

THE END